GARAVI GUJARAT PUBLICATIONS
2020, BEAVER RUIN ROAD,
NORCROSS, GA-30071-3710

The Washington Senators

D1355457

WRITING SPORTS SERIES
Richard "Pete" Peterson, Editor

The Cleveland Indians
Franklin Lewis

The Cincinnati Reds
Lee Allen

The Chicago White Sox
Warren Brown

Dreaming Baseball
James T. Farrell

My Greatest Day in Football
Murray Goodman and Leonard Lewin

The Detroit Tigers
Frederick G. Lieb

The Philadelphia Phillies
Frederick G. Lieb

The Washington Senators
Shirley Povich

The Washington Senators

Shirley Povich

Foreword by
Richard "Pete" Peterson

The Kent State
University Press
Kent, Ohio

© 2010 by The Kent State University Press, Kent, Ohio 44242

ALL RIGHTS RESERVED
Library of Congress Catalog Card Number 2010006385
ISBN 978-1-60635-052-2

Manufactured in the United States of America

Library of Congress Cataloging-in-Publication Data

Povich, Shirley.
  The Washington Senators / Shirley Povich ; foreword by
Richard "Pete" Peterson.
    p. cm.
  Originally published: New York : Putnam, 1954.
  Includes index.
  ISBN 978-1-60635-052-2 (pbk. : alk. paper)∞
  1. Washington Senators (Baseball team : 1886–1960)—History.
I. Title.
  GV875.W3P63 2010
  796.357′6409753—dc22
                                            2010006385

British Library Cataloging-in-Publication

14 13 12 11 10   5 4 3 2 1

To Ethyl

Foreword
Richard "Pete" Peterson

When I became the editor of the Southern Illinois University Press Writing Baseball Series in 1997, I decided to supplement our publication of original writing on baseball with reprints of baseball classics.

I contacted book dealers and collectors around the country and asked them for a list of long-out-of-print baseball classics that needed to be made available again for baseball readers. Their responses ranged from Alfred H. Spink's 1911 publication, *The National Game*, arguably the first baseball history, to Eliot Asinof's brilliant 1950s novel, *Man on Spikes;* but their most consistent recommendation was for reprints of the Putnam team histories.

In 1943, G. P. Putnam's Sons began a series of team histories with the publication of Frank Graham's book on the New York Yankees. From 1943 to 1954, Putnam published histories for fifteen of the sixteen major league teams. The Philadelphia Athletics ball club was the only one not included in the series, though Putnam did publish a biography of Connie Mack in 1945.

Thirteen of the fifteen team histories in the Putnam series were written by four sports writers who were later honored by the Hall of Fame with the J. G. Taylor Spink Award for "their contributions to baseball writing." The famed New York columnist Frank Graham, after launching the series with the Yankees history, added team histories for the Brooklyn Dodgers and the New York Giants. Chicago sports editor and journalist Warren Brown, once dubbed the Mencken of the sports page, wrote both the Cubs and the White Sox team histories, while the eloquent *Washington Post* sportswriter Shirley Povich contributed the Senators history. The legendary and prolific Fred Lieb, who, at the time of his death in 1980 at the age of ninety-two, held the lowest numbered membership card in the Baseball Writers Association, authored six team histories for the Putnam series. He also wrote the Connie Mack biography for Putnam.

Beginning with the Cardinals and the Cubs in 2001, the SIU Press Writing Baseball Series reprinted eight of the Putnam team histories, including the Yankees, Dodgers, Giants, Pirates, Red Sox, and Browns/Orioles. During that period, the Northeastern University Press decided to get in on the fun by publishing a reprint of the Putnam Boston Braves team history.

When I became editor of the Kent State University Press Writing Sports Series in 2005, we continued the tradition of publishing the Putnam classic series with reprints of the Indians and the Reds team histories. Since then, the Kent State University Press has reprinted Putnam's team histories for the White Sox, Tigers, and Phillies. With this reprint of Shirley Povich's Washington Senators team history, the mission to publish reprints of the original fifteen Putnam team histories, begun a little more than a decade ago, is now complete.

In his Preface to the Washington Senators team history, Shirley Povich wrote that in the early years of the twentieth century, the Senators were so terrible that every baseball fan in the country knew the popular vaudeville gag that "Washington was first in peace, first in war, and last in the American League." When I was growing up in the 1950s, the Senators were so awful that the gag was as popular as ever. At the end of the 1959 season, the Senators, perhaps trying to get some distance from being the butt of baseball's most popular joke, left Washington, took a northwest passage, and became the Minnesota Twins.

As bad as the original Senators were at the beginning and the end of their history in Washington, they were certainly blessed by having Shirley Povich write their team history for the Putnam series. In *No Cheering in the Press Box,* Jerome Holtzman, in commenting about Povich's long-running "This Morning" column in the *Washington Post,* wrote, "the column stands as a treasure of literary elegance, and offers textbook examples for all sportswriters." Povich was such a standard bearing for excellence in journalism at the *Washington Post* that its editor, Ben Bradley, once claimed that for many years his columns and reports were "carrying the paper."

Shirley Povich, thanks to his unusual first name, could also claim the distinction of being the only male listed in *Who's Who in American Women.* In the early 1960s, he received an invitation from its editors to fill out some data, which he threw away. Undaunted, the editors took Povich's entry from *Who's Who in America* and reprinted it in their volume. The entry made national headlines, and *Time* actually ran a photograph of Povich smoking a celebratory cigar.

Born in 1905, Shirley Povich began his career with the *Washington Post* as a copy boy when he was seventeen. He was still writing columns for the paper up until the day before his death at the age of ninety-two. He had his first byline as a sportswriter in 1924, and in 1926 he became the youngest sports editor for a major newspaper in the United States.

His first report for the *Washington Post,* published August 5, 1924, was on a Senators team, led by "boy manager" Bucky Harris and the great Walter Johnson, that went on to win the World Series that year. His last column, published on June 5, 1998, the morning after his death, was a cautionary note on the home run heroics of Mark McGwire: "To judge McGwire a better home run hitter than Ruth at a moment when McGwire is exactly 300 home runs short of Ruth's career output is, well, a stretch."

Povich was a master of colorful and elegant prose. In describing Don Larsen's perfect no-hitter in the 1956 World Series, he wrote, "The million-to-one shot came in. Hell froze over. A month of Sundays hit the calendar. Don Larsen pitched a no-hit, no-run, no-man-reach-first-base game in a World Series."

Povich could also capture the drama and significance of a moment of baseball history in a simple and powerful sentence. When Jackie Robinson crossed baseball's color line on April 15, 1947, Povich wrote, "Four hundred years after Columbus discovered America, major league baseball reluctantly discovered the American Negro."

In his team history of the Washington Senators, Povich doesn't avoid writing about "the little men of the early years who made fumbling attempts to produce a winning team and resorted to sharp practices and the unconscionable duping of the patient and loving fans." His best moments, however, come when he writes about the Washington Senators' "big men," like Hall of Famers Walter Johnson, Clark Griffith, Bucky Harris, and Joe Cronin.

For Shirley Povich, the real story of the Washington Senators begins with the acquisition in 1907 of Walter Johnson, "the kid pitcher from Weiser Idaho," after the team received letters from a Washington traveling salesman urging the Senators to sign "this boy . . . the strike-out king of the Snake River Valley League." With his blazing fastball, Johnson would go on to become the most dominant pitcher in baseball.

In 1924, after years of individual greatness and team frustration, he finally pitched in a World Series. After struggling early in the Series, he became the winning pitcher in the seventh and deciding game that gave Washington its World Championship.

While Walter Johnson became the most celebrated player in Washington Senators history, the most important figure in the team's history was "the Old Fox," Clark Griffith. In 1912, Griffith became the manager of the Senators, and, by 1920, he was able to buy out the old and inept Washington ownership.

Often criticized as an owner for being too conservative and tightfisted, he took the bold step of hiring of twenty-seven-year-old Bucky Harris as player manager in 1924. The "boy manager" led the Senators to back-to-back American League pennants in 1924 and 1925 and to the franchise's first and only World Series victory in 1924. In 1933, Griffith appointed another boy manager in twenty-six-year-old Joe Cronin, who led the Senators to the 1933 American League pennant, the last in Washington's team history.

Because of the popular vaudeville line, baseball will always remember the original Senators for being "last in the American League," but the truth is that under Griffith's leadership the Senators were a first division club in nearly half of his more than forty years as a manager and owner. His teams won three American League pennants and a World Series title and had only three last place finishes from the time he became manager in 1912 to his death in 1955, just one year after the publication of Shirley Povich's team history in the Putnam series.

Shirley Povich once said that a confident writer has the independence to write history the way it actually happened and not pander to the public taste: "You say to yourself, 'They're the ball players. Let them play the game. I'm a reporter.'" But he also admitted, "for a reporter, it's more than just a game. It's a great challenge in the sense that there it is—it has happened in front of you and now you must sit down at the typewriter. It's a task."

Happily, for his readers, Shirley Povich was always up to the task of writing stories and columns on our national pastime for the *Washington Post* and certainly up to the task of writing the Putnam team history about his Washington Senators.

Preface

THE most-heard vaudeville gag of the early years of the century coupled baseball's Washington Senators with the illustrious father of the country. The folks in the theater, the man in the street, and the children in school knew that Washington was first in peace, first in war, and last in the American League.

If vaudeville couldn't survive under the incessant impact of that type of humor, the Washington Senators succeeded nevertheless in going on to acclaim. Their early failures produced hardy fans in the nation's capital. They had to be of Spartan stuff or become extinct, the victims of almost continual heartbreak, knowing no triumph until Clark Griffith came along in 1912.

That year manager Griffith strode into the Washington scene with his cowpoke gait and lifted the Senators all the way from seventh place to the heights of a second-place finish. It had taken the Washington team twenty-four years, including twelve seasons in the old twelve-club National League, to get solidly into somebody's first division. In fact, at the turn of the century, the old National League had willingly given up Washington and dropped the city completely. Lopped off with Washington in the cutback to eight teams were Louisville, Cleveland, and Baltimore.

Two years before Griffith took over the team and brought in the new era of baseball to the nation's capital, a four-alarm fire early in the spring of 1910 brought the horse-drawn engines clanging to Washington's American League Park, then being readied for the opening of the new season. Hours later, a huge chunk of the rickety wooden grandstand and the weathered pine bleachers was a charred mess, waiting for a 20,000-dollar insurance adjustment. The District of Columbia's mustached fire chief poked into the smoking wreckage, pulled reflectively at his upper-lip foliage and delivered the opinion that "a plumber's blowtorch must have started this thing."

Out in Chicago, a former manager of the Washington Senators read of the blaze the next day and instantly agreed with the chief's findings. "The chief is probably right," murmured Joe Cantillon, "and the plumber was probably playing third base." It was an understandable reaction by Cantillon, who had joined the long list of Washington managerial alumni, having been fired at the end of the '09 season after piloting the Senators into the cellar twice and seventh place once, in his three-year term. Cantillon was painfully familiar with the incompetents, rejects, and so-called player material given to Washington managers.

The story of the Senators, their struggles, long-delayed triumphs, new frustrations, and more triumphs, is the story of two kinds of baseball men and a city's loyal fans. There were the little men of the early years who made fumbling attempts to produce a winning team and resorted to sharp practices and the unconscionable duping of the patient and long-suffering fans. Then along came the big men: Walter Johnson, with a transcendent skill at playing the game; Clark Griffith, with a low bankroll but a high faith in the capital's baseball future, plus a genius for assembling teams; Stanley (Bucky) Harris, the indomitable boy wonder, a manager who brought two Washington pennant winners; and Joe Cronin, another Cinderella kid, who won another pennant.

It was the modest, beloved Walter Johnson and his pitching feats that set new records in the books, who stood virtually alone against the national scorn for Washington's hapless teams of the early 1900's. The reverence toward Johnson displayed by Washington fans spilled over into the national community, and in 1924 America rose in applause for the man who, after toiling uncomplainingly for seventeen years on Washington teams, found himself pitching in a World Series.

The idolatry in which Johnson was held was best expressed one day by Edward T. Folliard, a native Washingtonian and famed Pulitzer-prize-winning correspondent on national and international affairs. Recounting his more important assignments, he recalled tours with Presidents of the United States, his coverage of visiting royalty, and his experiences as a war correspondent on the European front. He listed, too, the day he covered the Walter Johnson story at Rappahannock, Virginia, when Johnson (the Big Train) emulated George Washington's legendary feat of throwing a silver dollar across the Rappahannock River. "As man and boy, that was my biggest thrill," said Folliard. "You see, I was the fellow who held Walter Johnson's coat."

Griffith prefers to separate himself from the dismal history of the Senators prior to 1912. In that year he gave up the direction of the Cincinnati Reds to move to the capital city as manager. Against the advice of his associates who reminded him that Washington was the graveyard of all baseball operations, Griffith even demanded a stock interest along with the job of manager. He didn't walk into Washington unacquainted with its unfortunate past. In the 1890's Griffith hit Washington regularly as the star pitcher of Pop Anson's Chicago Colts of the old National League. And from 1901 to 1908 as manager of the Chicago White Sox and New York Highlanders, he knew of the lean crowds in Washington. Yet in 1920 his faith in the town was so great he sank his last dollar and pawned his Montana farm holdings to buy forty per cent of the Senator's stock, half of the controlling interest.

Since then, he has controlled by far the tightest family operation in the major leagues. Griffith kin occupy the front office and run the concessions. Griffith has never departed from a custom of naming one of "my boys," meaning his former ball players, to the job whenever a managerial post on the Senators was vacant. If Griffith has had to operate snugly on the fiscal side—and this is necessary because he is trying to run a big-league team in the smallest town in the American League—he has been an eminently successful operator. Today his Washington team is completely debt free, an unusual circumstance in the major leagues.

If Griffith's teams have not exactly terrorized the American League in the forty-one years of his managership-ownership, neither have they been pushovers. They have won three pennants and a World Series, and in twenty of those forty-one years they have finished in the first division. To keep the Senators operating, Griffith was forced to manipulate his limited player talent. Rarely did he make a player deal without cash accruing to the Senators. Washington fans were not always pleased with those deals. "He'd even sell his son," the fans complained on occasion. They were almost right. Griffith did sell his nephew-in-law, Joe Cronin, to the Boston Red Sox in 1934. The compensating factor was 250,000 dollars of Tom Yawkey's money, the highest cash price ever paid for one player.

It was Johnson's pitching feats and his drawing power that sustained Griffith during the lean years and virtually kept big-league baseball in Washington. Griffith made the most of Johnson as a gate attraction. He carefully spaced the Big Train's appearances both at home and on the road to draw the biggest crowds, and was not above calling sports editors on the telephone the night before the game and pleading, "Johnson's pitching tomorrow. Give us a headline."

Baseball in Washington, short on pennants until the happy year of 1924, was long on history, however. The game in the nation's capital was two years old before the Confederates fired on Fort Sumter.

Chapter I

THE threat of a great civil war hung heavy over Washington, D. C., in 1859, and the people of the nation's capital moved with uncertain step, caught up in the restive spirit of the onrushing schism between North and South. Never a gay city, Washington in that year appeared to the visitor even more solemn. Crime was at a new high, uniforms were more numerous than usual in the streets, and the slavery issue was flaring in the taverns, the drawing rooms, and on Capitol Hill.

But with the wishful thinking characteristic of some people in grim times, one segment of Washingtonians was attempting to continue with the usual social activities. They went to dances at the Drover's Rest to whirl in the Virginia Reels or skip in the Boston Fancy, or to Odd Fellows Hall to laugh at the antics of one Wyman, a comedian of the times. During the summer they piled on the steamer *James Guy* for cruises down the Potomac to Piney Point.

It was during this tense period that the Game of Base Ball —thus it was called, with capital letters—first made its appearance in the parks of Washington. In the summer of '59, government clerks, fascinated by newspaper accounts of the Game of Base Ball in other cities, formed a team called the Potomacs.

The government clerk of that era was a considerable force in the social life of the city. He was an upper-bracket, middle-class worker envied for the wages and security of his job. Thus a team of government clerks could give tone to the new game. Historians of the times report that many were "thrilled" by the prospect of deserting the Willard and Ebbitt Hotel bars for the wholesome, invigorating outdoors, and the game

1

caught on to the extent that a second team, the National Club, was organized in November of the same year.

Most of the team members came from the then-fashionable Capitol Hill section. James Morrow and J. L. Wright, both government officials, were elected president and vice president of the National Club. The secretary was Arthur Pue Gorman, scion of a noted Maryland family, who was later to be United States Senator from his state.

It was the Potomacs, though, from the "first ward" area, roughly bounded on the east by Fifteenth Street and on the west by Rock Creek Park, who were the more skilled team. In the spring of 1860 the interloping Nationals were challenged to a series of battles at Base Ball.

On the White Lot, then called the back yard of the White House and now known as the Ellipse, the first game was played. The Potomacs won, but the score is still clouded in doubt created by a lack of common understanding of the rules. It was conceded that the Potomacs scored thirty-five runs, but varied accounts of the game credit the Nationals with as few as fifteen and as many as thirty runs.

It soon developed that the Nationals could not provide the opposition the Potomacs needed, so the latter team looked curiously toward Baltimore, where a club called the Excelsiors was establishing a reputation as one of the finest teams in the East. On June 6, on the White Lot, the Excelsiors satisfied the curiosity of the Potomacs, who gained a better understanding of the game, plus a 40-to-24 defeat. In the polite reportorial language of the day, an account of the game read:

> The friendly match between the Potomac Club of this city and the Excelsior Club of Baltimore came off on the grounds south of the President's Mansion yesterday afternoon. Quite a number of visitors were present and witnessed the sport and were highly pleased with the result throughout, the opposing clubs bearing their defeats with perfect equanimity. The Excelsiors came out winner at the close of the game. At night they partook of rich entertainment prepared for them by Gunther at the order of the Potomac Club. We understand the Baltimore club made 40 runs to 24 by the Washington Club.

2

(The city directory listed Gunther as the bartender at the Ebbitt Hotel, so the type of "rich entertainment" provided may be well imagined.)

The Potomacs disbanded with the outbreak of the Civil War, but the Nationals, despite depletions in manpower when many team members left to join the colors, culled enough players to stay in competition. Baseball didn't ask for a green light from President Abraham Lincoln, but it is assumed any such request would have gained favorable consideration. The President was a fan. One of his biographers, in a pamphlet entitled "Abraham Lincoln in the National Capital," tells of Lincoln's frequent visits to the games.

In fact, Lincoln brought a baseball background to the White House, according to the late Steve Hannegan, the high-powered publicist engaged by Baseball Commissioner Landis in 1939 to help acclaim baseball's Centennial Year. Hannegan either resurrected or invented an episode which supposedly took place in Springfield, Illinois, in 1860 and illustrated President Lincoln's affection for the game. The following appeared in the Centennial Year literature:

"Tell the gentlemen they will have to wait a few minutes until I get my next turn at bat."

The speaker was a tall, gaunt man named Abraham Lincoln. And the gentlemen he was telling to cool their heels were a side-whiskered delegation from the Republican National Committee. . . . If they gasped through their facial foliage, it was quite understandable . . . because to Abe Lincoln, whom they found playing baseball on a Springfield, Illinois, stubble field, they had come bearing momentous tidings. They had come to tell him the Chicago convention had nominated him for the Presidency of the United States.

But Lincoln, engrossed in his ball game, would suffer no interruption. Not even to learn that he might become the nation's sixteenth president. . . . You see, he didn't want to miss his turn at bat.

The close of the Civil War found the Nationals solidly in the esteem of Washington fans, with the club's shortstop, slight, twenty-three-year-old Arthur Pue Gorman, the darling

3

of the spectators. Young Gorman quickly rose to stardom on the not-too-brilliant Nationals. He worked on Capitol Hill, and the fact that he later became a senator from Maryland moved many historians to associate the name of "Senators" with the Washington baseball teams.

By 1865 the nation's capital was so baseball-conscious that clerks of the government agencies were excused early to permit them to watch the Nationals play the Brooklyn Atlantics and the Philadelphia Athletics in an intercity tournament on the White Lot. By game time six thousand fans were assembled, and on that August day a President of the United States, Andrew Johnson, became the first chief executive in history to watch an intercity baseball game.

High officialdom turned out in force with Army and Navy bigwigs flanking President Johnson in chairs that lined the field for the two days of the series. The first game was a sad blow to the Nationals, who lost to the Athletics, 87 to 12. Although no charge of a rabbit ball was raised, it is a fact that the visitors hit eighteen home runs. On the following day the Atlantics added to the misery and disillusionment of the Nationals by winning a 34-to-19 victory, scoring twenty-two runs in the last two innings.

The tournament, if not a competitive success for the Nationals, was a social bonanza for both teams and the game of baseball. With the visiting players, the members of the Nationals called on President Johnson at the White House and later were received by Congress and banqueted at the Willard Hotel.

Not content with their local games, the Nationals bravely struck out on the first western tour in the history of baseball, a staggering undertaking for the time because it was a nine-game trip into six different cities in states as far west as Missouri. The entire journey was three thousand miles.

At whose expense? Their own, of course. They were amateurs and gentlemen, were they not? To accept pay or guarantees would be profaning the social implications of the game, and on July 11, 1867, the team left from Washington under the supervision of the president of the National Club, Colonel Frank Jones.

4

One substitute comprised the team's entire reserve strength, and one pitcher constituted the pitching staff as the ten-man squad entrained for Columbus, Ohio, scene of their first game, against the Capital Club of that city. In fact the Nationals were outnumbered by their loyal fans who also made the trip. Thirteen "sports" entrained with the team and, like the players, paid their own expenses.

Also accompanying the party and lending the dignity and authority of his name to the tour was Henry Chadwick, the first professional writer of baseball, who was a powerful factor in the development of the early rules of the game.

At Columbus, Ohio, the baseball tourists from Washington were hailed as daring adventurers and immediately impressed their western opponents with their skill at the game with a 90-to-10 victory. It was an unprecedented score for western baseball, and the game was called at the end of seven innings with the Columbus team and the spectators conceding the matchless talents of the Washington club.

Victory after victory fell to the touring Nationals in the West. At Cincinnati, on consecutive days, they defeated the Cincinnatis with the famous Harry Wright in their lineup, 53 to 10, and the Buckeye Club of the same city, 88 to 12, in six innings. They won at Louisville, Indianapolis, and St. Louis, and took a six-game winning streak to the scene of their next game, Chicago. And then came disillusionment. Against the Forest City Club of Rockford, Illinois, a team of schoolboys that was playing in Chicago, the Nationals were beaten 29 to 23, on July 26. Fresh-faced, seventeen-year-old A. G. Spalding, a Rockford grocery clerk, who was later to become a giant figure in the sport, was the winning pitcher.

The defeat of the Nationals was as sensational as their string of victories had been. Unfeelingly, the Chicago newspapers taunted the Nationals for that defeat by the Rockford schoolboys and predicted a victory the next day for their own "Champions of the West," the Chicago Excelsiors, who were to be the Nationals' final opponents on the tour. The Excelsiors earlier in the month had twice defeated the Forest City conquerors of the Nationals, and in anticipation of further humiliation of the Washington club, the largest crowd ever to witness a baseball game in the West paid the admission fee of half a dollar.

Humiliation was the word for what took place that day, but it was the Excelsiors, not the Nationals, who were humbled. The Nationals took an early 7-to-0 lead to demoralize the Excelsiors completely and give them a sound beating by a score of 49 to 4. It was a glorious finish of the tour of the Nationals.

And then scandal broke briefly. The *Chicago Tribune* flatly accused the Washington club of "throwing" the Rockford game for betting purposes before taking on the Excelsiors. In high outrage, president Jones of the Nationals, accompanied by Arthur Pue Gorman, stomped into the *Tribune* office and compelled a retraction of the charge.

There followed a distinct departure from the game as it was originally conceived and played in Washington. At the outset it was accepted as the sport of quality folks, with the city caught up in a frenzy over the success of the well-born young Nationals on their 1867 tour of the West. But within a decade, so-called roughnecks were also playing the game and playing it better. The hub of baseball in Washington for a twenty-year span that carried into the late eighties was Mike Scanlon's Ninth Street poolroom, and Scanlon was the organizing force behind Washington teams.

Scanlon was an adventurer with an honest affection for the game that he first played as a Union soldier after joining the Army at fifteen, as a commissary clerk. He drifted to Washington in 1866 with only his Army pay in his pocket and bought on credit the poolroom at the corner of Ninth and S Streets, N.W., that was to bear his name until his death, sixty-five years later.

The sporting blood of the city gravitated to Scanlon's pool hall and in an atmosphere where it was possible to get down a bet on the ponies or the eight-ball in the side, or a wager on a ball game, baseball talk was foremost. Scanlon preached the desirability of getting Washington into an organized league, and to his side he drew many of the social elite who shared his ideas and interest in the game.

To this man who talked baseball so ambitiously came

6

Colonel Frank Jones, president of the Nationals Club; Arthur Pue Gordon, the senator-to-be from Maryland; Nicholas Young, head of the Olympic Club, who was to become a president of the National League; and Robert Hewitt, a wealthy Washington businessman who was an avid fan of the game.

With Arthur Gorman as his partner in their baseball enterprises, Scanlon had entree to the White House during the administrations of Presidents Andrew Johnson and Ulysses Grant. On taking office, President Grant commissioned Scanlon to outfit the White House with a billiard room. In later years, Scanlon proudly displayed a gold-tipped cue stick that was the gift of Grant.

Scanlon was an authority on baseball rules, with which most players of the day had only a vague familiarity. He trained them, arranged games, and soon was rewarded with popular fan support. As early as 1868, crowds averaged four thousand at the Saturday afternoon games on the White Lot behind the White House. President Johnson, an eager fan, ordered the Marine Band to play at every Saturday game. After President Grant was elected, he watched the games faithfully from the vantage point of the White House's south lawn.

Scanlon built the first baseball park in Washington with a fence around it. In 1870 he obtained a lot near the corner of Seventeenth and S Streets, N.W., constructed five hundred seats, and charged an admission fee of twenty-five cents. Twenty-one years later he not only selected the present site of Griffith Stadium but was instrumental in having a park built there.

Scanlon's dream of a Washington club in an organized professional league was realized in 1871 when, with the backing of Nick Young, the Olympic Club was given a franchise in the National Association of Professional Baseball Players, known then merely as the National Association. Young, president of the Olympic Club, had helped to organize the league.

Young, like Scanlon, was weary of the chaos of intercity competition without organization, with teams failing to respect scheduled games if more gate receipts were promised in other cities. Players were being induced to jump teams for a financial consideration, and the whole business of schedule making was unstable.

And so the Olympics found themselves in a league with the Athletics of Philadelphia, Red Stockings of Boston, White Stockings of Chicago, Forest Citys of Cleveland, Forest Citys of Rockford, Illinois, the Haymakers of Troy, New York, the Kekiongas of Fort Wayne, Indiana, and the Mutuals of New York.

Playing a thirty-one-game schedule in 1871 the Olympics did well enough, winning sixteen games and losing fifteen, finishing fourth among the nine clubs, with the Athletics winning the pennant with twenty-two wins and seven defeats.

But the club owners had many difficulties following this first attempt at an organized league. Player raids continued with the same regularity as before, and the Olympics lost their star pitcher, Bob Leech, to the Nationals despite the fact that the latter club was playing an independent schedule and was technically classed as an amateur team while the Olympics were playing as professionals. In the case of the Olympics and other league teams, there was no regular salary arrangement for the players, whose earnings were based on the generosity of the club owners. Few players made a living wage from the gate receipts.

Overshadowed in 1871 by the league-member Olympics, the Nationals sought and gained entry to the National Association in 1872, an eleven-club league that season. The result was a fearful blow to Washington's pride in its baseball teams. The Olympics and the Nationals both failed to finish the season after being far down in the standings. Boston beat out Philadelphia for the flag.

The Olympics quit the Association in 1873 with no great sense of loss, since the circuit was beset by financial troubles that caused four clubs to abandon league play shortly after the season started. The Nationals were one of the latter, after winning only eight of thirty-nine games.

Baseball in Washington during the next decade was decadent. At least the town had no big league pretensions. The fans were overfed with the futility of Washington teams trying to compete in the National Association, and the city lapsed into a bush town of baseball.

The National Association, renamed the National League in 1876, was in disrepute anyway. Four Louisville players, Al Nichols, Jim Devlin, G. W. Hall, and W. Craver, were expelled on charges of throwing games. Washington began to take a new pride in its amateur teams comprised of government clerks playing in a departmental league. It was not fast baseball, but it was at least above suspicion.

And then, in 1885, a Washington team suddenly won a pennant. The Nationals found a franchise open in the Eastern League, a shaky organization comprising teams from small cities in New Jersey and Virginia, and finished on top. But it was a hollow triumph. They were in second place, being outdistanced for the pennant in September when the league-leading Richmond Club suddenly dropped out of the league for lack of funds. Nobody exulted over Washington's first pennant, no parades were held. The baseball I. Q. of the Washington fan was sufficiently advanced in 1885 to permit him to distinguish between major-league and bush-league baseball.

The team, for the second straight year, made money, and during the winter Hewitt and his other backers made overtures to Nick Young, by now president of the National League, for the next franchise. When Providence and Buffalo quit the league, Washington and Kansas City were awarded new berths. Almost immediately the stock of the club was boosted from 5,000 dollars to 20,000 dollars. In an attempt to provide the best of playing conditions, the club management leased from W. M. Gait and Thomas W. Smith an entire square of ground bounded by F and G Streets and Delaware Avenue and North Capitol Street. This playing ground was named Capitol Park. The ground was leased for five years at an annual rental of 500 dollars for the first year, 1,000 dollars the second year, and 1,250 dollars during the last three years. Compared to parks in other cities, the playing grounds were not sumptuous. Nevertheless, the property provided an area 800 feet by 400 feet, one of the largest playing fields in the East.

9

The financial success of the club was not matched, however, by the performance of the team. The Nationals, managed once again by Mike Scanlon, and now calling themselves the "Statesmen," soon found the competition in the big leagues was more than slightly tougher than that afforded by the Eastern League. Shortly after the opening of the season they found themselves lodged in the cellar, the first of many Washington teams to sink to that unenviable position in the major leagues.

During the summer the fans and sports writers clamored for the scalp of Manager Scanlon, and he was finally released on August 20. Umpire John Gaffney then resigned from his position to replace Scanlon. Fan support dwindled as the season drew to a close and the backers, who started the season with high hopes, were desperately seeking new talent to bolster the team for the following season since it was already too late to help the cause in 1886. Their search turned to Hartford, Connecticut, where a battery combination of pitcher Frank Gilmore and catcher Cornelius McGillicuddy was burning up the New England League.

Hewitt's primary interest was Gilmore. He was regarded as a welcome addition to the pitching staff, which then was headed by fiery Hank O'Day, a recent purchase from Philadelphia. Gilmore asked Hewitt if it would be all right to take along young McGillicuddy, since they had operated as a team for so long. Three other players, enthusiastic at the prospect of entering the big leagues, also persuaded Hewitt to buy their contracts. The result was an addition of five players to the Washington fold at a cost of 3,500 dollars.

On his arrival in Washington, Gilmore failed to justify his promise at Hartford, but young McGillicuddy, whose name promptly was shortened to Connie Mack by the sports writers, caught on immediately. Although warned that Mack's batting was weak, manager Gaffney inserted him in the lineup, and Mack proceeded to make liars out of his critics by batting .361 for the ten games in which he appeared. But it was his brilliant defensive play behind the plate which won him the recognition of the fans and sports writers alike. He turned out to be the most popular player on the team, and the season ended on a note of optimism. The new acquisitions, especially Mack, were sure to bring better baseball days to Washington in 1887.

The high note of optimism was retained throughout the winter and flowed over to the opening day of the 1887 season, which was marked by a long parade down Pennsylvania Avenue. Enthusiasm wasn't dulled when the Boston Beaneaters won a 14-to-9 decision in the opening game. But as the season progressed, it developed that even the new players from Hartford couldn't make up the difference between a good minor-league team and a bad major-league team. Manager Gaffney also had his difficulties with the players who refused to keep training rules. The upshot was a poor season, but still better than 1886. The Washingtons finished seventh in an eight-club league. Their record: forty-six victories, seventy-six defeats for a percentage of .377. At the season's end, only one of the five players purchased from Hartford was still around. He was the skinny catcher nobody thought would be successful—Connie Mack.

Here is what the Washington *Evening Star* of April 7, 1888, said of Connie Mack:

Connie Mack is a Washington favorite. He is always willing to play and plays hard to win. The public would rather see any other man on the ball field make an error than Catcher Mack. His success in his difficult position is due largely to the fact that he always keeps in good condition. His manager doesn't have to keep his eye on him for fear he will sneak off and get drunk. Whatever else may happen, he knows that Mack will play the same game week in and week out.

... He is a steady catcher, an accurate thrower and a first-class hitter. He has little or nothing to say during a game but keeps his jaws going quietly all the time. He is six feet and weighs 160 pounds. It is a common saying while the players are practicing that Connie won't chase the ball because he is afraid he will lose a pound.

The Statesmen of 1887 became the Senators of 1888, but the change of nickname didn't change the baseball fortunes of the team. In fact, they were worse in 1888, when they once again descended to the cellar of the National League. Connie

Mack was used chiefly in utility roles during the 1888 season as the Senators underwent numerous personnel changes, due not only to the losing baseball of the players but also to some of the extracurricular gambling and drinking activities of the stars. Ted Sullivan, a former player, was named manager of the team in midseason, but the fans were staying away from the Capitol Park, and the management, fearing another baseball eclipse, took an unprecedented step in the winter of 1888 to improve the team. On November 24, President Walter Hewitt bought the release of the famous John Ward from New York for 12,000 dollars, the highest price ever paid for a baseball player up to that time. Ward, a wealthy socialite, was then in Europe and balked at the deal. Hewitt immediately crossed the Atlantic and tried to talk Ward into accepting his terms, but Ward was adamant and the deal fell through.

Faced with the collapse of his team, Hewitt tried to get the best available talent from other teams, but was unsuccessful. Few players wanted to associate themselves with a club which gave no promise whatever of emerging from the cellar in the foreseeable future. Connie Mack was still behind the plate for the Senators in 1889, but Hank O'Day, his favorite pitcher, was sold to New York in midseason—a deal which clinched the pennant for the New Yorkers. Meanwhile, the team was going from bad to worse. A man named "Honest John" Morrill was installed as manager, then fired within two weeks for incompetence. Hewitt placed himself in charge of the team and finished the season in last place with a group of discontented ball players on his hands. Threats of players jumping to the newly-formed Brotherhood League were rife as the season drew to a close. Hewitt was summoned to Nick Young's office at National League headquarters. He expected the worst and got it. The Washington franchise was turned over to Cincinnati. Connie Mack jumped to Buffalo, of the rival Brotherhood League. Washington again had flopped as a major-league city.

Chapter II

ALL of a sudden in December, 1891, the Wagner brothers from Philadelphia, George and J. Earl, popped into Washington to announce themselves proprietors of a Washington franchise in the newly-expanded, twelve-club National League. For the next eight years the city's fans found themselves in the cold clutch of a pair of baseball brokers who talked big, spent little, pocketed nice profits, and pulled out before they were kicked out.

Washington was back in the major leagues, and what a whirl the Wagner brothers gave the town. It may have been the Gay Nineties for baseball fans elsewhere, but for Washington fans the era of the Wagners was frustration piled on frustration. The two Philadelphians piously professed to be rabid baseball fans, do-gooders for the great national game, but they revealed themselves as promoters who were trying to collect a huge return, and did.

During the eight years of Wagner control, from 1892 to 1899, no Washington team finished better than a tie for sixth place. But so eager were the fans that Earl Wagner left Washington with a neat profit of 230,000 dollars for his ventures in baseball, much of it reaped in Washington. In fact, the National League owed him 35,000 dollars when he left town.

The Senators were not the first baseball operation of the Wagners. When the National League bought them out at the end of the 1899 season, it marked the third time a league had been forced to pay off the Wagners to get rid of them. In 1890, as owners of the Philadelphia Brotherhood team of the American Association, their first venture at organized baseball, they were floundering financially. But they talked the league into reimbursing them with 60,000 dollars, provided they would quit at the end of the 1891 season. They were paid off in 1890, and a year later when the entire American Association quit and merged with the National League, the Wagners cleaned up 56,000 dollars more in another settlement.

When the National League, to kill off any more competition by other leagues, voted to expand to twelve teams for 1892, it found no local backers enthusiastic about sinking more capital into organized baseball. The Wagners, still in the market for new killings, fast-talked the Washington stockholders into selling them the franchise at fifty cents on the dollar, and for an investment of less than 16,000 dollars moved in as members of the new National League. They bought the franchise, of course, with their recently acquired National League money, of which they expended only a fraction. They bossed Washington baseball until the Spring of 1900 when they cashed in their holdings for 46,500 dollars, representing another payment by the National League to get 'em out of the game.

Earl Wagner was the more active partner, with George making only rare visits to Washington on leave from his Philadelphia meat business. But there was no discord between them in baseball matters. Earl hired Bill Barnie, veteran manager of the Baltimore Orioles, as manager of the 1892 Washington team and two days after the season started he fired Barnie "for talking back to George Wagner." All that George Wagner had done, it seems, was to ask Barnie to resign, and Earl construed Barnie's "No" as talking back, according to the baseball historians of the times.

The Wagners demonstrated that they never did consider managers as indispensable or hard to replace. Even before the 1892 season started, it was currently rumored that Manager Barnie wouldn't last long on the job and that Arthur Irwin would succeed him any day.

The team Irwin took over from Barnie had a pair of former National League stalwarts in the infield in Danny Richardson, the second baseman who had been with New York, and Henry Larkin, formerly with the Athletics. The aging Hardy Richardson, previously with Boston, was at third base and at shortstop the Wagners produced Paul Radford, once with Cleveland. W. F. (Dummy) Hoy, who was deaf but not completely *mute*, was the only established outfielder on the club, having played with Washington clubs in previous years. Catching was Jim McGuire, another veteran of Washington.

A. A. clubs. Frank Killen, a rookie, was the top pitcher on a four-man staff.

The Senators trained in Savannah, and manager Barnie found himself with twenty-three seasick athletes when they finally disembarked at camp after the ocean trip from Washington. The first act of center fielder Hoy in the training camp was to post a prepared statement to his new colleagues on the Senators. It read:

> Being totally deaf as you know, and some of my clubmates being unacquainted with my play, I think it is timely to bring about an understanding between myself, the left fielder, the shortstop and the second baseman and right fielder.
>
> The main point is to avoid possible collisions with any of these four who surround me when in the field going for a fly ball. Now whenever I take a fly ball I always yell 'I'll take it!'—the same as I have been doing for many seasons, and of course the other fielders will let me take it. Whenever you don't hear me yell it is understood I am not after the ball and they govern themselves accordingly and take it.
>
> If a player hears the patter of my feet, pay no attention as I am only backing up. I watch both the player and the ball, and never have I had a collision.

Greeted by an overflow crowd of 6,400, the Senators lost their opening game of the season to Boston, 6 to 4, but the fans were tolerant with the exception of those who made their way to the park on bicycles. The cyclists squawked not only at the twenty-five-cent charge for bringing their wheels into the park, but also against the Wagner policy of providing no special gate which forced them to lift their wheels over the turnstiles.

It was the only year of the split season in the National League, and the Senators finished sixth in the first half, with catcher Johnny Milligan batting .277 to lead the club in hitting. But Dummy Hoy, who was batting .279 and making the most hits on the team, apparently wasn't making good in the eyes of the Wagners. They asked him to take a salary cut on July 1, under pain of being released. Hoy, with no other job in sight, took the pay cut.

Irwin didn't last out August as manager. On the night the

Senators lost their ninth in a row at Cincinnati, the Wagners got a new manager. Their choice was playing-manager Danny Richardson. Of Irwin, George Wagner told reporters, "Irwin was unpopular. It was against the wishes of the fans that he was hired originally."

Under Richardson, the no-hit, no-field, no-pitch Senators plummeted into tenth place where they finished the season. At St. Louis they completed one losing streak of eleven games. That was the day George Wagner went on the field and commanded manager Richardson to take his team off in the seventh inning and forfeit the game.

Wagner at the time was feuding with Chris Von Der Ahe, St. Louis owner. He was furious when Von Der Ahe withheld 300 dollars from the day's gate receipts, a sum he claimed was due him from the Wagners for some earlier transaction. Richardson refused to take his team off, and not until he pointed out to Wagner that the Washington Club would incur a $1,000-dollar fine if it forfeited, did Wagner go into some quick arithmetic and decide to forget the 300 dollars.

In preparation for the 1893 season, one of J. Earl Wagner's first moves was, in effect, to fire his manager. In February he traded playing-manager Danny Richardson to the Brooklyn Bridegrooms in what was announced as a straight swap for third baseman Billy Joyce, but later Wagner admitted he also got 2,000 dollars cash in the deal. He made that trade in preference to a deal suggested by Pittsburgh who sought Richardson in a swap for catcher Connie Mack, who was now on the Pittsburgh team.

Three local directors of the Washington club, Charles E. White, Mike Scanlon, and Edward Sutherland, resigned from the board in protest over the Richardson deal, but Wagner was not perturbed by that inasmuch as they had only been placed on the board as local windowdressing.

Barely a month before the season, the Wagners announced their new 1893 manager, James (Orator Jim) O'Rourke, the veteran member of the Boston Red Stockings who was famed chiefly for his handle-bar mustache and his run-ins with the umpires. In July, at Pittsburgh, while the Senators were losing a tough one, Orator Jim lost his temper and was fined 50

16

dollars by umpire McLoughlin. In the next inning after catching Stenzel's fly ball, O'Rourke taunted McLoughlin with "safe or out?" and was informed by the umpire, "He's out but it just cost you 5 dollars for the information."

After making the deal for Joyce, the Wagners refused to meet his salary terms, and he stayed out of baseball in 1893. They had salary trouble too with young Frank Killen, their top pitcher who balked at an 1,800-dollar stipend for the season and was traded to Pittsburgh for catcher Duke Farrell.

The '93 Senators got off to a commendable start with nine wins in their first fourteen games, and then they headed for last place with eight losses in a row. They went west in eighth place and dropped to eleventh. Young Killen shut them out with five hits in Pittsburgh and himself hit a triple and homer. By early August, Killen had licked them three straight times. Criticism of the Killen deal mounted, and the only reply of George Wagner was the announcement he was taking a wife.

Brother Willie Wagner was holding a post as secretary of the club, and in June he announced the release of pitcher Cy Duryea. J. Earl Wagner immediately cancelled it on the grounds that Willie had no authority to release anybody or even release a statement about anybody's release. League president Nicholas Young ruled that Duryea was still the property of the club, and in his next start the pitcher beat Brooklyn with a seven-hitter.

The unpopularity of the Wagners in Washington attained a new high in late July when, after playing to a crowd of 15,000 in Philadelphia, they announced that three games scheduled between the Athletics and Senators in Washington later in the season, would be transferred to Philadelphia. Three other home games were also transferred to Cleveland, and after the fifth of August Washington fans discovered the Senators were down for only nine home games. The Wagners got away with the transfers, but the league in its Winter meeting hurriedly wrote in a 1,000-dollar penalty for the same kind of trick in future seasons.

As usual, the Wagners fired their manager before another season opened. O'Rourke's '93 club had hit twelfth place in August and held its own in that spot to the end of the season.

17

Their new choice was Gus Schmelz, who had moved in as a sort of advisory manager in the late days of '93. He had managed Columbus, Atlanta, and Cincinnati in previous seasons and now was moving up from Chattanooga of the now disbanded Southern League.

Schmelz was more famed for his flowing mustache and heavy beard than for any managerial successes. Like his predecessors he had no voice in the signing or disposal of players, and the Wagners did him no favor when they traded their best outfielder, Dummy Hoy, for pitcher Mike Sullivan. They also made some extra cash by selling the good battery of pitcher Jouett Meekin and catcher Charley Farrell for 7,500 dollars.

The club did get a couple of good breaks. Out of the New England League the Wagners bought a strikingly handsome young pitcher named Win Mercer who was to become a sensation one year later, and they prevailed on third baseman Billy Joyce to return to the game after his one-year salary holdout.

But the Senators were never a factor in the race. Manager Schmelz couldn't think any runs across the plate for his weak-hitting lineup. Hoy's batting was sadly missed. In May, the Senators lost seventeen in a row before young Mercer halted the streak with a two-hit victory over Louisville.

With the Senators in eleventh place in July, Schmelz in the fashion of the day with losing ball clubs, gave out an interview in Cincinnati that was a bitter attack on the league's staff of umpires. He attributed the Senators' poor showing to the miserable work he had received from the umpires and added:

> Simply because we are tail-enders the umpires think they have license to rob us. If we had anything like a square deal we would be up alongside the third-place Brooklyns instead of our present place in the race. We have been sand-bagged, skinned and robbed on every hand. Umps have taken games away from us with every team except the Baltimores. There they had no chance to rob us for the Baltimores played so much better ball they won in hollow style.
>
> Here are the Philadelphias going around whining about being badly crippled up. We have more men on the hospital

list than they have. John McMahan, our catcher and one of the best hitters in the league hasn't been able to play a game with us all season. Petty, our pitcher, is also laid up with a lame hand. 'Scrappy' Joyce has a sprained ankle and Pitcher Otis Stocksdale has a bad arm. We have had nothing but hard luck and the usual run of villainously bad umpiring that always falls to the lot of the tail-ender.

Washington did cause something of a stir in the major league in 1894, but it was nothing that Schmelz or the Senators contributed. It was on August 24, when the 550-foot shaft of the Washington monument was the locale of the first attempt to catch a ball thrown from such a height.

Pop Anson's Chicago Colts were in town with their good catcher, Bill Schriver, and Anson had long maintained that if it were possible for a ball dropped from the monument top to be caught, Schriver could do it. And so a party of the Colts repaired to the monument for what is recorded as the first attempt at the feat.

Colt pitcher Clark Griffith was selected to toss the ball, and it was a case of poor reporting when the Washington newspapers announced the next day that Schriver had caught the second of Griffith's two tosses. Griffith in later years nailed that legend.

> I had time to make two throws to Schriver before the monument police hustled up the elevator and demanded to know what nonsense was going on in the monument. We beat a hasty retreat before we were all locked up,

relates Griffith.

> Schriver had no chance to catch the first throw, but that was my fault. I tossed it out too far and he couldn't reach it. The second toss, I merely dropped out of the monument and the ball carried directly into his mitt, but he couldn't hold it and it plopped out. It wasn't a catch, no matter what the papers say. Schriver was too nervous to hold the ball, and I don't blame him. He'd have caught one I'm sure if the cops had left us alone.

Schmelz was a notable Washington manager in one respect. He wasn't fired at the end of his first season. Although the

Wagners retained him as manager of their 1895 club, they had more important duties for him than managing the Senators. He managed for the Wagners, but what he was managing was another Wagner interest—a wild west production called "The Texas Steer Show," which they were backing. He didn't show up as manager of the team until May 27, when the "Texas Steer" failed somewhere in the Midwest.

In those early weeks, the Washington club was handled by "Scrappy" Joyce, third baseman, field captain, and one of the few good ball players on the team. On paper, the Senators looked like a better ball club. The Wagners drafted Gene DeMontreville, the good shortstop out of the Eastern League, and they came up with a smart first baseman in Ed Cartwright as well as with one of the league's better outfielders, young Al Selbach.

It was the year that young Mercer became something of a sensation with eight wins in his first eight starts, going the route in all of them. Despite skepticism of the Wagners, a record crowd of 9,255 greeted the club in its season's opener and watched Mercer beat the Giants, 6 to 3.

In succession, Mercer went on to seven more wins before he met defeat. He reeled off his second, third, fourth, and fifth victories against Brooklyn by scores of 12 to 10, 8 to 5, 6 to 4, and 4 to 3, doing well with his batting as well as his pitching.

Going into the West, the Senators showed seven wins in their first twelve games, and five of those were out of the pitching fist of Mercer. He got his sixth in a row by beating Cleveland, 5 to 3, and his seventh was a 14-to-9 win over Pittsburgh. To that point, the Senators had won only nine games, and seven belonged to Mercer. He got his eighth straight by beating Cincinnati on seven hits, 6 to 4.

For Mercer, the irony was that his streak was stopped on the day he pitched his best ball game. He held St. Louis to four hits but was the loser in a 5-to-1 duel.

A crowd of more than 9,000 welcomed the Senators on their return to Washington in eighth place on May 27, and a special song was written in honor of pitcher Mercer called "The Win Mercer Caprice." It was no help as Mercer faced the Reds and surrendered nineteen hits in an 18-to-5 defeat. The Reds made three runs in the first inning and three more in the second, and that Mercer played the entire game under the circumstances was a tribute to his hitting.

A home run by Gene DeMontreville that beat Cleveland, 5 to 3, on June 1, lifted the Senators to seventh place in the standings, and in mid-June they attained fifth place with Mercer and "Silver" King giving the club good pitching. They finished in sixth place.

The team's slow start in 1896 prompted the Washington *Post* to ask:

> What's the matter with the Washington Baseball Club? This is the question that is agitating loyal fans of Washington. It has been rumored that one pitcher and several outfielders have not taken care of themselves. The Post has information from reliable sources that certain members are indulging in the flowing bowl. In justice to the fans, The Post appeals to the management to take certain measures to correct this fault.

The Wagners met the crisis in typically Wagner style. They sold their good third baseman, "Scrappy" Joyce, to the New York Giants for third baseman Charley Farrell and catcher Carney Flynn. The day after the trade, Joyce made four hits in four times up for the Giants, and the Washington papers were calling Farrell "a back number" and pitcher Flynn "an exploded phenom."

Joyce had actually been managing the team until his sale, with the red-bearded Schmelz in the role of observer. J. Earl Wagner met criticism of the Joyce deal calmly enough and revealed himself as the master of the second guess in a notable statement he issued after the deal:

> I have always liked Joyce personally and we are the best of friends, but friendship leaves off where business begins. The downfall of the team on the Western trip convinced me that Joyce wasn't the man for the job . . .
>
> We failed to play the game properly on the bases, in the field and at bat. The players on a team naturally look to their leader for instruction and advice but they received none from Joyce. I hinted to him when I joined the team in Chicago that great benefits could be derived from sacrifice hit-

ting, but he failed to act on my advice. He could never be depended on to sacrifice, so how could he expect his men to accomplish any teamwork at bat ...

I found it utterly impossible to advise or correct Joyce. He won't stand for advice or suggestions. He is of rather a suspicious nature and is constantly under the impression that somebody is "knocking" him. Then how could he succeed as captain? Something had to be done, yet Joyce failed to make the improvements ...

It was impossible to retain Joyce with Schmelz as bench manager. One or the other must go and Schmelz was too valuable an employe for me to sacrifice in order to satisfy the patrons of the game who favored Joyce. Of course Joyce had a large following in Washington but I could not allow that to stand in the way of my judgment and my interests.

Mr. Schmelz, I will admit, is not as popular as I would like to have him and this I attribute to the fact that he is of a quiet and retiring disposition, and not inclined to jollying and hand-shaking.

One of Wagner's pet tacks in the low periods of the Senators was to make grandiose announcements of the high-priced players he was trying to buy for the Washington club. For two years he took bows by offering 2,500 dollars for the great pitcher Amos Rusie whom he knew was unavailable at any such figure, and with the Senators skidding in midseason of 1896 he announced, "I have just offered the large sum of 5,000 dollars to Baltimore for third baseman John McGraw."

Wagner wasn't kidding the sports editor of the Washington *Post,* though. He wrote:

That $5,000 offer of J. Earl Wagner for Muggsy McGraw recalls the first part of the old minstrel gag: "Mr. Interlocutor," says Bones, "Ah almost got a hoss give ter me today. Ah asked Mr. Brown if he would gib me dat hoss and he say 'no.' If he said 'yes' Ah would 'er had dat hoss."

The *Post* went on to comment:

These alleged offers for players by the Washington management are intended as a sop to the baseball fans. But such moves are as transparent as window glass. Wagner promised a successor to Joyce to plug the void at third base. His $5,000 offer for McGraw is no fulfillment of that promise. Ed Hanlon says $10,000 wouldn't buy McGraw from the Orioles.

After Schmelz succeeded Joyce in charge, and despite J. Earl Wagner's insistence on the use of the sacrifice hit, the Senators went into a new nose dive and lost sixteen of their next eighteen games. Outfielder Selbach, catcher Jim McGuire, and shortstop Gene DeMontreville were hitting far above .300 at that point, but the club was weak in the field and only Mercer was a consistent pitcher. They did stage something of a comeback in September, and on the final day of the season climbed into a ninth-place tie with Brooklyn with a record of fifty-eight wins and seventy-three losses.

Schmelz wasn't around in 1897 when the Senators achieved a Washington ball club's greatest fame since the old Nationals of 1859 swept triumphantly through the West on their own expense tour of the amateur days. The '97 Senators were the darlings of the capital, zooming into a sixth-place tie on the last day of the season. They had a powerful voice in the winning of the pennant by Boston by beating the second-place Orioles in the game that clinched it for the Red Sox.

At last the Senators got good pitching. Mercer was a consistent winner, and also Jimmy McJames. The veteran Charles Koenig, known to fans as "Silver" King, chipped in with timely victories and so did Albert Maul, the flash-dressing right-hander who was a walking advertisement for his off-season jewelry business.

During one of his preseason salary debates with J. Earl Wagner, Maul showed up "wearing a diamond of the circumference of a sewer top on a checkerboard shirt bosom and dangling a gold-tipped stick as big as a crow-bar. The incendiary tints of Maul's makeup were augmented by a fawn topcoat, and the waistcoat contributed to the clamor of the resounding regalia."

By June 7, all Schmelz had to show for his managerial efforts was an eleventh place team that had a record of nine wins and twenty-five losses, a dismissal by Wagner as manager, and an elks watch charm given him by the players as a token of something or other.

Tommy Brown, center fielder, moved into the managerial job. He was a veteran of the Boston Brotherhood and American Association teams in 1890-91, and under Brown the Senators moved magically to five wins in a row. Brown himself led the club in hitting, and they captured twelve of their first fourteen games under his management.

The hitting of DeMontreville who on August 7 was the league's seventh leading batter with an average of .349, the slugging of catcher Farrell who led the league in runs batted in, plus Jim McGuire's .338 average, couldn't keep the Senators up there. They sagged into eleventh place, but suddenly Mercer, McJames, and Hillary Swaim reeled off eight wins in succession, and there were new visions of a first-division finish.

The Wagners purchased a young pitcher on August 12. Getting bare mention in the papers, however, was the addition of a Lima, Ohio, eighteen-year-old named Roger Bresnahan.

Young Bresnahan contributed three victories in a row. In his big league debut, he shut out St. Louis with six hits 3 to 0, issuing only one walk. The *Post* headlined: "Kid Pitcher a Wizard." But Bresnahan was no wizard at talking salary terms with the Wagners. They had their own ideas how much an eighteen-year-old boy should be earning, and at the end of the season Bresnahan quit in a huff to join the Toledo club closer to home, before returning to the major leagues with the Giants as probably the greatest catcher of his era after switching positions.

Toward the end of the season, the Wagners also bought Jake Gettman, a young outfielder from Fort Worth, Texas, who was credited at the time with holding the record for circling the bases, which he was able to do in fourteen seconds flat. Gettman made good immediately in the Senators' outfield.

It was the Red Sox who ended the Senators' September winning streak of eight in a row with a three-hit shutout at Boston, and if J. Earl Wagner was unhappy at that spectacle he was unhappier still as he started to make his way out of the park. The Boston sheriff grabbed the Washington owner. He was being seized for an unpaid 800-dollar printing bill—a relic of the Wagners' "Texas Steer Show" venture, J. Earl was told. He spent the night in jail before bail could be arranged in the morning. As a concession he was not lodged in a cell, but occupied a corridor chair with the turnkey. Complicating his situation was the fact that Wagner had in his pocket the train tickets of the Washington club that was due in New York the next morning. Manager Brown barely raised enough money among the players to get them to New York via the cheaper Fall River Line boat.

In their September drive the Senators won eight of nine games in one week. Rookie Gettman, already impressive with his fielding, made ten hits in a row against the Cleveland and Cincinnati clubs. It was a duel with Brooklyn for sixth place, and the Senators wound up with four games at Baltimore. After losing the first game with the Orioles, Win Mercer pitched his team to a 9-to-3 victory in the game that knocked the Orioles out of the pennant race and put Boston in first place.

That night Brown received a telegram from manager Frank Selee of the Red Sox which read:

> Congratulations on your timely boost that sends us to the top of the flagpole, and the best wishes for the success of you and your players. Our boys send remembrances. In the language of Johnny Ward, let the nectar go round.

On the last day of the season it was still a deadlock with Brooklyn for sixth place, with both teams showing records of 60 to 71. Bresnahan started the finale against Baltimore but retired with the Orioles leading, 3 to 1. Swaim took over and pulled out a 6-to-3 victory for the Senators. This assured them the sixth-place tie which Brooklyn maintained by beating the coasting Red Sox, 15 to 6.

That night in the rotunda of Baltimore's Carrollton Hotel, J. Earl Wagner expressed his pleasure at Brown's managerial job with a bonus check of several hundred dollars and a new contract for 1898. But less than two months after the new season opened, the Wagners became disenchanted with manager Brown and on June 6 fired him. In the opening weeks of the season it had been rumored that first basemen Jack

Doyle and Brown were leading fighting factions within the club. Wagner heatedly denied those reports, but unblushingly appointed Doyle as manager after disposing of Brown.

Doyle joined the Washington club only in April in a six-player swap with the Orioles for which Wagner was roundly cussed by Washington fans. In the swap the Senators gave up Jim McJames, their good right-hander, Gene De Montreville, one of the league's better shortstops, and first baseman Danny McGann. They received the veteran Doyle, second baseman Heinie Reitz, and pitcher Doc Amole with Wagner maintaining, amid high skepticism, that no cash was involved.

The Senators had started off badly under Brown, and on May 29 had won only seven of their first thirty-one games, with Mercer a four-time winner. They lost eleven out of fourteen on their first road trip. The war with Spain was reducing attendance and a June 15 game at Baltimore saw only 70 dollars in the house.

Doyle's span as manager lasted exactly twenty days, and actually he was at the head of the club only a week when J. Earl Wagner announced, "Mr. Doyle is taking a two-week vacation because of ill health." It was later revealed that Wagner had secretly invited bids for Doyle within ten days after appointing him manager.

Doyle was still Washington club property when Wagner announced on June 30 that his veteran catcher, Jim McGuire, would be permanent manager. Ten days later he had a new announcement. He personally would help McGuire manage the team. "I will suggest certain ideas and exchange views with McGuire as to points of play," Wagner stated, "such as the selection of certain pitchers to work against certain clubs and other details involved in the conduct of a team." The Washington *Post* immediately titled Wagner "Director of the Scene."

Wagner peddled Doyle to the Giants for 2,000 dollars and berated himself for making the six-player deal with Baltimore earlier in the year. He declared Doyle had actually cost him 15,000 dollars because "I could have obtained 7,500 dollars each for DeMontreville and McJames, the players I sent to Baltimore in the Doyle swap."

26

Under the comanager system, the Senators lost fifteen of their next eighteen games, and comanager McGuire announced in early August that he wanted to get out. There was dissension all around, and Win Mercer declared frankly he wanted to pitch for Cincinnati, not Washington. Wagner called Mercer "ingrate" and declared he paid Mercer "more salary than any pitcher in the league gets except Charles Nichols of Boston."

The Senators passed through Washington en route to Boston on their way back from a western trip in which they won only one game in eleven, and the temper of the fans was interpreted by the *Post*'s reference to the trip: "The Senators passed through their home town unmolested on their way to Boston." The Senators finished eleventh with their dissension-ridden club. Injuries to Selbach and Gettman crippled the outfield and pitchers Mercer and Bill Donovan were drafted for service there. John Anderson was added to the outfield but never reached the hitting fame he was to attain with Brooklyn.

Before the season was over, the Senators had their fourth manager of 1898. He was Arthur Irwin who was back for a second fling after replacing Bill Barnie in 1892 and getting fired at the end of that season. There was a Wagner-Irwin tie-up before the new announcement on September 7 that Irwin would manage the club. Irwin was managing Toronto which the Wagners had been operating as a Washington farm team. The announcement of Irwin's appointment was accompanied by a new mouthful of Wagner double-talk. J. Earl stated: "Arthur Irwin and his friends have purchased an interest in the Washington club and will take charge on September 13. We retire on and after that date and will not actively be connected with the club."

But the Wagners didn't retire from the Washington club, actively or otherwise. And there was no other evidence that Irwin had purchased any interest in the team. The Wagners made all announcements of player deals and continued in as active a role as before.

One of the late September announcements of the Wagners was the acquisition of six players from Irwin's Toronto Club.

Among the six was outfielder Buck Freeman, the man who was to go on the next year to set a new home run record for the major leagues with his fabulous production of twenty-five homers for the Senators in 1899. Notices of Freeman's hitting power had preceded him to Washington. Among his clippings was one reference to "The left-handed hitting Freeman whose wicked bat has made the hearts of Eastern league pitchers quake with craven fear." He hit two homers against Cleveland the first day he broke into the Senators' line-up.

If the Wagners went into retirement from the affairs of the Washington club, they came out of it suddenly in 1899 to "retire" Arthur Irwin as manager. He lasted only until August, with the team well on its way to its ninth-place finish, and second baseman Dick Padden got the managerial job.

The Wagners added to their income the season before, saving the salary of a bench manager by firing Irwin. They sold shortstop Sailor Wrigley, first baseman Charley Carr, and pitcher Bill Donovan to Richmond of the Atlantic League for 500 dollars each and then swung a deal that sent third baseman Doc Casey and catcher Duke Farrell to Brooklyn for shortstop Cassidy, catcher Heydon, and pitcher McFarlan. Wagner said no cash accrued to Washington in the deal. The Brooklyns said they gave him 2,500 dollars.

Selbach and Gettman, two outfield fixtures, had been traded to Cincinnati and Kansas City during the winter, and pitcher Mercer was playing first base and the outfield throughout May. The club won only four of its first twenty-four games and was in last place in mid-May. Of the club's mere thirteen wins on June 4, the veteran Gus Weyhing had won eight.

The lone bright spot was Buck Freeman's hitting. He and Mercer were the only .300 hitters on the club. Freeman wound up with a .318 average and the new record for homers. He hit his twelfth homer on July 30, five ahead of the pace of Ed Delahanty of Philadelphia, on that date. He swatted his seventeenth on September 11, and his twenty-fourth on October 5, finally getting his twenty-fifth. The Senators finished eleventh with a record of 53 to 95, and were never in danger of going into the cellar since Cleveland won only twenty of its one hundred and fifty-four games that season.

28

Even before the 1899 season closed, there were rumblings that the National League was taking a dim view of Washington as a major-league town and of the Wagners as major-league club owners. There was rampant talk of a reduction of the league from twelve clubs to eight.

J. Earl Wagner met this talk by big talk of his own. He said, "Washington will be in the major leagues when Baltimore and Brooklyn are in the minors," but he was already asking offers for the Washington franchise. That Washington wouldn't last long in the majors was indicated at the winter meeting of the National League in December, 1899. George Wagner was voted off the board of directors of the league in the session held in Room 51, at the Batholdi Hotel.

James A. Hart, the Chicago owner, reported frankly that the Wagners were asking 50,000 dollars for their Washington franchise and declared: "they must take $25,000." J. Earl Wagner ridiculed that latter figure by declaring he could get 20,000 dollars for only five of his players—Mercer, Freeman, Dineen, McGann, and Weyhing.

The National League's new directors held a secret meeting at Cleveland on January 25, 1900, and it leaked out from that session that Washington was being dropped along with Cleveland, Louisville, and Baltimore. The next day J. Earl Wagner denied that report with a telegram to the *Post* which read: "All statements made concerning our transfer to the American Association are fakes and pipe dreams. We will be doing business this summer at the old stand at National Park just the same." But Wagner two weeks later sold off enough players to wreck the Washington club. The sales leaked out when Wagner went to Wilkes-Barre, Pennsylvania, to sign Buck Freeman to a 1900 contract that showed the Boston club, not Washington, to be the "party of the first part." Then it was revealed that Wagner had sold both Freeman and pitcher Bill Dineen to Boston for first baseman Barry and 7,500 dollars. President Soden of Boston had made the buy with the provision that the Wagners first get the players signed to next season's contracts. Freeman, after his twenty-five homers of 1899, signed to play for 2,000 dollars.

There were reports also that Wagner had disposed of Win

Mercer, Dick Padden, Jimmy Slagle, and John O'Brien, and the Washington *Post* wrote of "wholesale traffic in human thew and brawn," but the Wagners denied the sale of those four.

J. Earl Wagner admitted the 7,500-dollar deal with Boston but declared the Senators would still be part of a ten-club National League and hinted that his new manager would be Win Mercer, but on March 9, 1900, the whole story was out—and so were the Senators.

The Wagners sold out to the National League for a compromise price of 46,500 dollars from which the 7,500-dollar payment by the Red Sox was deducted. The cost of the whole funeral in the League's reduction to eight clubs was 104,000 dollars. The National League paid Louisville 10,000 dollars, bought out Baltimore for 30,000 dollars, but gave the Orioles the rights to their players, and paid off Cleveland 25,000 dollars.

The twentieth century dawned blackly for baseball in Washington. With the Wagners out, local backers had no stomach for a return to the minor leagues after an eight-year stay in the majors, but succor was not too far distant.

Chapter III

ON a late September evening in 1900, Washington was unaware that it had a stake in a clandestine meeting of three men who were plotting a new major league over beer mugs in an unfashionable Polk Street cafe on Chicago's West Side. But on that day the American League, as a major league, was conceived in the pioneering minds of the trio: an ex-newspaperman, a retired ball player, and a pitcher who was enjoying stardom in the National League. Out of their efforts came a place for Washington once again in the majors, after the city's 1899 expulsion by the National League.

The ex-newspaperman was Byron Bancroft Johnson, then holding office as president of the American League which in former seasons had submissively accepted minor-league status. Charles Comiskey was the retired ball player, now owner of the Chicago team of the minor American League. Final member of the trio was star pitcher Clark Calvin Griffith, thirty-one-year old hero of the Chicago Cubs, whose thoughts now were running toward a higher place for himself in the national game.

Big-league baseball had fallen off in the closing months of 1900. The year had been a lean one for the National League. Only the pennant-winning Brooklyn team and a few other clubs had been able to show a profit, and there was grave doubt that several of the league franchises could support baseball the following year.

The energetic Ban Johnson and the shrewd Comiskey, now discontented with their lot as minor leaguers and aching for the day when they could organize a new big league, found a kindred spirit in Griffith. It was in stealth that Griffith joined the plotters. They had no National League allegiances, but he was an established star still under contract to the Cubs of the National League.

In September, 1900, Ban Johnson was quarreling with the National League. He balked at signing his minor American League to a new agreement patterned after the expired contract which gave the National League the right to draft American League players without restriction, on payment of 500 dollars for each player. Kansas City, the previous year, had lost five of its pennant-winning ball players through the National League grab, and Johnson was in a fighting mood for his league. Johnson wanted the new agreement to limit the draft of two players from each club, and he also wanted permission for the American League to put teams in territory vacated by the National League, particularly Louisville, Cleveland, and Washington.

A few days before the fateful Johnson-Comiskey-Griffith conclave in Chicago, Johnson had waited in a Philadelphia hotel for the National League to act on his requests. Johnson expected to be summoned by the National League committee which was meeting in that city. He wasn't. They sent him word that he could "wait until hell freezes over," and they would not even consider his demands.

Only then did Johnson plan openly to flout the National League. He conferred with Comiskey, his early-day benefactor in the baseball business, and Comiskey suggested that Griffith be called into the consultation. Comiskey knew of Griffith's leanings toward a second major league. Johnson made it plain to Comiskey and Griffith that he courted war with the National League. If the National had granted his demands, Johnson said, then the American would have been content to go along as a minor league. But it was only on the basis of major-league status that Griffith consented to go along.

They outlined an eight-city league, but Johnson admitted doubt of the new league's ability to lure enough star players from the National League to give the new league a semblance of big-league caliber. Griffith was confident on that score and pointed out that he was gambling his own baseball future as an established star to join the new league.

Griffith had a plan. He advised Johnson and Comiskey to withhold their next move until December when he would be in a better position to tell them where they stood with respect to big-league playing talent. Griffith at the time was vice president of the Ball Players' Protective Association, at one time a loosely-knit and weak organization that professed to represent the major-league players. But in recent months it had become militant for improved conditions and better salaries for the players. Griffith pointed out to his coplotters that the Ball Players' Protective Association was nearing a showdown with the National League, and that a meeting to be held in New York in December might prove the perfect opening for the formation of a second big league, if the new league could deal with disgruntled National League players. Johnson and Comiskey agreed to await the outcome of the showdown.

Charles Zimmer, Cleveland catcher, was president of the Ball Players' Association, and Hughey Jennings its secretary. But Griffith and Jennings habitually swayed Zimmer.

Under the National League rules, 2,400 dollars was the maximum salary for players in the league, no matter what their skill, and they were forced to pay for their own uniforms. At the meeting at the old Fifth Avenue Hotel in New York, the Association presented to the National League, in petition form, the request that the salary limit be raised to 3,000 dollars and that the clubs provide the player uniforms.

But unknown to the National League club owners, Griffith and Jennings had strengthened their position. At a secret meeting of the players at Griffith's urging, when all clubs were in the East at one point late in the season, the three officers exacted a unanimous pledge from the players. They promised not to sign contracts with their teams in 1901 unless advised to sign by the Association officers following the New York showdown.

The Association officers, carrying their petition to New York, proceeded to the sumptuous headquarters of the National League and there awaited word that the league club owners would receive them. Word came and Griffith, Zimmer, and Jennings went in to meet the owners.

At first glance, Griffith knew the ball players' demands would not be met by the club owners. He saw in the presiding chair, not the familiar figure of Nicholas E. Young, president of the National League, but A. H. Soden, vice president. Griffith was familiar with the tricks of the National League bosses. He knew that when the club owners wished to sidestep or stampede an issue, it was their custom to retire the staunch, honest Young from the chair and install vice president Soden.

Scarcely had Griffith entered the room when he felt a tugging at his coat. Turning, he noted that League president Young, seated on a small steamer trunk near the door, was trying to attract his attention. Griffith looked inquiringly at Young who whispered: "Son, they ain't gonna give you anything in this meeting. I just wanted to tell you." It was no less than Griffith expected, but with a look, he thanked the aging league president warmly and then managed a smile.

Vice president Soden was coldly businesslike as he asked the players' committee if they were ready to present their requests, and he was handed the players' petition. When Soden asked Zimmer if he had a statement to make, Zimmer declined, but Griffith asked for a hearing and plunged immediately into a detailed list of the players' grievances. Jennings also spoke.

Soden heard them out with obvious impatience and then advised the delegation that the owners would give the petition full consideration. With that Soden seemingly terminated the hearing and, after looking inquiringly at each other, the ball players' committee left the room.

Griffith, Jennings, and Zimmer repaired to the hotel bar and over their beers managed to laugh at the treatment they had been given. Less than five minutes later, Griffith noted with some amazement that the figure descending the staircase into the bar was none other than Soden. The league's vice president apparently had thought to elude the players' committee by avoiding the lobby and making his way to the street via the bar.

In good humor, despite his frustration, Griffith called to Soden and invited him to a beer. Soden, flustered, accepted and then attempted to explain his early departure from the meeting upstairs by telling Griffith he was forced to hurry to another appointment. "I've left your petition with the club owners," he explained. But as Soden leaned forward to reach for his beer mug on the bar, Griffith noticed protruding from his coat pocket the same bulky manuscript which he recognized as the petition Soden said he had left with the owners. He accused Soden openly of lying to the ball players' committee, and the vice president, after protesting feebly that the petition would get serious consideration, fled the place.

Convinced that the league would never give in to the players' demands, and realizing that big-league ball players throughout the country were awaiting the outcome of the hearing, Griffith, Jennings, and Zimmer determined to take action at once, even in the absence of the league's decision. The three officers of the Association made an announcement to the Associated Press. They claimed to have learned their demands would not be granted by the National League, and were advising all ball players to respect their pledges and refuse to sign contracts with their teams for the 1901 season.

Griffith telephoned Ban Johnson and Charles Comiskey

who were impatiently awaiting word on the hearing, and into the phone he literally shouted to them: "There's going to be a new major league, if you can get the backing. Because I can get the ball players!" Johnson and Comiskey found a financial angel in Charles Somers, Cleveland coal magnate, and immediately announced that the American League was to become a major league, with Cleveland, Chicago, Milwaukee, and Louisville as its western cities, and Boston, Baltimore, Philadelphia, and Washington as its franchise holders in the East.

For Washington's long-suffering and hope-spent baseball fans December 7, 1900, was a great day. On that morning they awakened to read that American League president Ban Johnson had kept faith and was awarding Washington a franchise in his new major league that had now declared total war on the National League.

This time Johnson was specific. For Washington, this was a new opportunity. The city was to have an American League team headed by a solid baseball man, Jimmy Manning, owner and manager of the Kansas City Club of the old Western and American Leagues. He would bring experienced players to the nation's capital from Kansas City.

The Washington *Post* on December 9, exuberantly introduced Manning as "The fortunate gentleman who was Mr. Johnson's personal selection to carry the American League banner into Washington." With blithe disregard for Washington's wretched record as a major-league town under the old National League banner, the *Post* continued:

> Mr. Manning was president of the Kansas City Club for seven years until the Eastward Ho! campaign of the new league forced that Missouri town into an undesirable corner geographically, and Manning was offered the Pearl of the American League's new Eastern possessions—Washington.

Manning, however, wasn't named president of the Washington club, only manager. From Chicago, Johnson announced that Fred Postal, owner of the Griswold House, a Detroit hotel, had bought an interest in the Washington club

35

and would be president. It was assumed that Postal would own a controlling interest, but Johnson didn't reveal the real arrangement to Washington fans, and he didn't discourage the assumption.

During the winter of 1900-01, however, Manning let it be known that the Washington franchise actually was under the control of League president Johnson. He revealed that all of the clubs in the new league had agreed to permit Johnson to hold fifty-one per cent of their stock. Individual ownership was a myth, and it was syndicate baseball of the type that in later years was to be detested, but Washington fans in their happiness to be back in a major league apparently didn't care about such items as stock control.

The National League still held rights to the stadium at "The Boundary" of Seventh Street and Florida Avenue, later to be the site of Griffith Stadium, but Manning, Johnson, and John McGraw of the Baltimore American League club toured the city and selected a new park site near Fourteenth Street and Bladensburg, N.E. Construction of the grandstands was under way within two weeks and Washington fans were jubilant.

The Washington team of 1901 looked suspiciously like the Kansas City team of 1900, and with reason enough. Manning brought to the capital nine of the regulars who had been with him in Kansas City. Outfielder Sam Dungan was touted as the star with a .337 average in 1900. Shortstop Bill Coughlin had hit .309 and outfielder Charlie Hemphill brought a .300 average. Bill Carrick, one of the National Leaguers who had left the Giants and was the fifth leading hurler in that league in 1900, was the prize of Manning's pitching staff.

The Senators reeled off four victories in a row to open the season. Bill Carrick and Win Mercer pitched them to 5-to-1 and 11-to-5 victories over Connie Mack's Athletics at Philadelphia to glamorize the long awaited opening in Washington against the Baltimore Orioles. The players rode to the park in a Pennsylvania Avenue parade behind a tallyho drawn by a team of four to the accompaniment of the oom-pahing of Haley's Band. For the first time in history, a Washington team was playing to a turn-away crowd. Hundreds of fans were denied admission as the park was jammed to capacity with Admiral Dewey among the 9,772 fans present. When the Senators whipped McGraw's Orioles, 5 to 2, that afternoon and repeated with a 12-to-6 victory the next day, baseball madness reigned in the nation's capital.

It didn't last. Early in May, the Senators dropped into sixth place and stayed there. The club's hitting faded to a whisper. Over one stretch of six games in July, the Senators totaled only six runs. The nadir of their futility was achieved in Cleveland on May 23. The Senators went into the ninth inning leading, 13 to 5, and didn't win. Staging a rally with two out and nobody on in the ninth, Cleveland came up with the nine winning runs. But the Senators did win sixty-one of their one hundred thirty-three games and beat out the Cleveland and Milwaukee clubs for sixth place.

Manning quit at the season's end. His first statement announcing his retirement was polite enough. "I have been offered a good business venture of another nature than baseball and have decided to accept." But the next day, under questioning, he told a different story. He couldn't get along with his onetime friend, Ban Johnson. "Mr. Johnson's nature is such that he brooks no opposition whatsoever," said Manning. "I wasn't even invited to confer when Mr. Johnson called in representatives of other league clubs. I asked for funds from the league's reserve fund, to which I had contributed, in order to buy new players and he refused me."

Manning sold out his interest in the club to Postal for 15,000 dollars, and again Washington fans were assuming that Postal was the controlling stockholder.

The next to accept the managership of the Senators was Tom Loftus, who had managed Columbus in the old Western Association and like Manning was installed in Washington by Johnson, with club president Postal having little voice in the matter. The club showed a profit for its 1901 operation after drawing 358,692 home attendance, and in the annual meeting of directors rewarded Washington fans by raising the grandstand prices to seventy-five cents.

Baseball hit the front pages in Washington during the winter of 1901-02. The Senators staged a sensational raid on the Phillies of the National League, inducing four of the Phillies' established stars to jump to the Washington team. Prize of the quartet was Big Ed Delahanty, the slugging outfielder who was lured to the Senators after eleven years with the Phillies and whose extra-base hitting had brought him fame. Back in 1888, the Phillies originally paid the Wheeling, West Virginia, club of the old Ohio League 1,900 dollars for Delahanty, then the record purchase price of baseball. On July 13, 1896, against the Cubs at Chicago, Big Ed had established a record of four home runs in a single game.

Third baseman Harry Wolverton and pitchers Al Orth and Jack Townsend were the other players induced to jump to the Senators from the Phillies, and it was all very simply done. Loftus simply offered to pay them more salary than the Phillies were paying them. Delahanty broke his 3,000-dollar contract with the Phils to accept 4,000 dollars from the Senators. Wolverton, whose wage with the Phillies had been 2,100 dollars, signed with the Senators for 3,250 dollars. Orth was raised from 2,400 dollars to 3,250 dollars, and Townsend's Philadelphia salary of 1,200 dollars was doubled.

The anguished screams of the raided Phillies' owners after their player loss fell only on deaf ears in the American League, but shortly before the 1902 season opened the Philadelphia club gained a decision in the Pennsylvania Supreme Court enjoining Nap Lajoie from joining the Cleveland Indians of the American League, the team to which he had jumped. Cleveland later circumvented that court order by rerouting Lajoie on the team's trips into Pennsylvania, but the Phillies now threatened court action against the four who had jumped to Washington.

Manager Shettsline of the Phillies dispatched a telegram to players Delahanty, Orth, Wolverton, and Townsend that read:

Supreme Court upholds us in Lajoie case. Decides our contract absolutely binding on you. You are hereby ordered to report forthwith to me at the Philadelphia ball park for performance of your duties under your contract. Refusal to obey this will be at your peril.

But Wilton J. Lambert, attorney for the Washington club was unimpressed by any peril to the four jumping players and told them succinctly to "Forget it. The ruling applies only to Pennsylvania and Lajoie."

The Senators couldn't improve on their sixth-place finish of the year before. Delahanty justified his 4,000-dollar salary by leading the league in hitting with .376, but the club was incompetent afield, and only the work-horse pitching of Case Patten, Al Orth, and Bill Carrick, who totaled fifty victories, kept them out of the cellar. The Senators' home attendance of 188,158 was scarcely half of their drawing power in their maiden year in the league, and so strong were the rumors that the Washington franchise would be shifted to Pittsburgh that president Postal was constrained to issue a formal denial in December.

The club's miseries were piled high in 1903. The Senators settled into eighth place early in the season and stayed there—last in the American League. Whatever hopes the team had of climbing out of the cellar were doomed in July of that season when Delahanty, then batting .338 and second only to Lajoie in the league hitting race, met tragic death.

The big slugger, who had a well-known weakness for the bottle, was mysteriously missing from the team's Detroit Hotel Oriental. The only clew his teammates could offer was that they had seen him walk out of the hotel the day before, hatless. It was not his first disappearance. Manager Loftus was not unduly disturbed until, on July 7, he received a letter from the Buffalo Pullman Company superintendent informing him:

A passenger was in altercation with the conductor of the Michigan Central Railroad and at Fort Erie, Ontario, he was forcibly ejected. Later a bridge tender found a man on the International Bridge who had successfully evaded the guard. The bridge tender put a lantern to the man's face, started to ask him questions and then heard a splash, and the man apparently had plunged into the Niagara River. On the train was found a suitcase and clothes containing complimentary pass No. 26 of your baseball club.

Delahanty's body was found a few days later.

By August, club president Postal was ready to resign. Manager Loftus was unhappy because Postal wouldn't put up more cash for talent. Ban Johnson dashed to Washington to smooth the troubled situation. At the Oxford Hotel, Johnson met with Postal and vice president Charles Jacobson, a prominent banker of the city. Jacobson offered to buy Postal out, but balked over the item of the club's 12,000 dollars worth of bad debts. Then Johnson stepped in, paid Postal 15,000 dollars for his stock, assumed the club's debts, and thus admitted for the first time that the Senators were league-controlled, as they had been from the outset.

Before the month was out, Johnson broke with Loftus, placing the club manager in an untenable position with the blunt statement, "Mr. Loftus won't return as manager next season. . . . He failed to please the Washington people."

With no desire to retain the skimpily financed Washington franchise, League president Ban Johnson finally succeeded in March of 1904 in unloading the controlling interest to a half-dozen Washington men. The man who rounded up the buyers was William Dwyer, former Associated Press baseball writer turned promoter, and his chief angel was Thomas C. Noyes, of the publishing family that owned the highly profitable Washington *Evening Star*. Wilton J. Lambert, the team's attorney since 1901, was installed as president with Dwyer as vice president and business manager, but not until a month before the season opened did Washington fans know for certain who would be manager of the club.

All of Tom Loftus' holdings supposedly went into the sale to the new owners who now claimed to control seventy-five per cent of the stock, but as late as March of 1904 Loftus was still a part of the Washington scene and discounting reports that he would be replaced as manager. He was hearing reports that the new owners were dickering with P. J. (Patsy) Donovan, star of the St. Louis Cardinals to move into Washington as manager, but Loftus declared that Donovan would be signed only as a player.

Dwyer had other ideas, however. He was waiting only for Donovan to get his release from the Cardinals before ousting Loftus. A week before the season opened, with Donovan's status still uncertain, Dwyer acted anyway. He fired Loftus and installed the veteran catcher, Malachi Kittredge as manager until Donovan could report.

The St. Louis club was attempting to hang on to Donovan, and awaiting a decision from Garry Hermann, Cincinnati owner who headed the arbitration board. Donovan claimed he was entitled to his release because the Cardinals owed him 3,600 dollars on a contract they had failed to fulfill, and on April 28 he was awarded to the Washington club.

By the time Donovan reported to take over the managerial duties from Kittredge, the Senators were already in bad shape even with the season only a week old. Against the Red Sox and the Yankees, they were shut out in three of their first four games. Only 3,000 saw the opener in Washington. They didn't win a game until their thirteenth start of the season. Dwyer quit town on May 11 and left the vice presidency open. The club won only ten of its first fifty-five games. They finished eighth and drew only 132,344 customers at home, despite the fact that the American League attendance in 1904 showed a 700,000 increase.

The only balm for the stockholders was the club's showing in the final weeks of the season when there was vast improvement, including the sensational development of Jake Stahl as a first baseman. Stahl led the team in batting with .261, and already was being talked of as the Washington manager for 1905.

On January 31, 1905, stability came to the Washington franchise for the first time. Thomas C. Noyes accepted the presidency of the club, and was to retain it for the next fifteen years. In the reorganization, Washington businessmen acquired fifty-five per cent of the club's stock, with the American League holding forty-five per cent. Newspaper support was assured when Scott C. Bone, managing editor of the Washington *Post,* joined Noyes of the *Evening Star* in the club's official family as a heavy stockholder. William Rapley, manager of the National Theater, was named treasurer, with Benjamin F. Minor, prominent attorney as business manager. The capital stock was increased to 45,000 dollars. Other stockholders included Henry Litchfield West, Commissioner of the District of Columbia, banker Corcoran Thom, and realtor Edward J. Walsh.

Stahl was the toast of Washington in mid-May of 1905. The Senators returned from an eastern trip in the league lead on May 3, and red fire burned in the streets to welcome them. Indeed, freshman manager Stahl appeared to have a team of destiny. On April 18, at Boston they had only one hit from pitcher Winters but won the game, 1 to 0, with Wolf allowing the Red Sox only four hits. The Senators scored their run on a fumble, a walk, a second fumble, and a force play.

The Senators were in the first division until midseason, then drooped. Injuries and the illness of Stahl were factors. But two veteran outfielders, John Anderson and Charley Hickman bolstered the team. The new owners of the club had paid 5,000 dollars for the pair, and for the first time in history Washington fans could agree that there was no stinginess in the front office. Tom Hughes, a big right-hander obtained from the Highlanders in a trade for pitcher Al Orth, won seventeen games. Another addition to the club was a strapping young outfielder from Notre Dame, Frank Shaughnessy, now president of the International League.

The report to the club's stockholders in December of 1905 showed that the team had bought players worth 12,910 dollars during the year, and sold players only to the value of 3,125 dollars, a radical change from past policy. President Noyes was accepting only a salary of 600 dollars per year. At the end of the season, the Washington players cut up a bonus of 1,000 dollars promised them back in April by president Noyes if they finished out of eighth place.

Before the 1905 season opened, the club's owners invited the city's fans to submit a new name for the "Senators," hopeful of getting away from the misfortunes that had afflicted the team under that nickname. From thousands of suggestions they selected the name of "the Nationals" as the most acceptable, but it was in vain. Newspapers and fans in other cities and even in Washington persisted in labeling them as the Senators.

Jake Stahl was deprived of one of his best men in 1906, even before the season opened. Late in March word was

42

received of the death, in Chester, Pennsylvania, of Joe Cassidy, victim of typhoid fever. Cassidy had been signed from the Pennsylvania sandlots a couple of seasons before and was developing into one of the top shortstops of the league. Despite the tragic loss of Cassidy, the Senators were leading the league on May 4, and among Washington fans Stahl was presidential timber. But a week later the Senators were fourth, and after June they were anchored in seventh place, where they finished.

Lave Cross, the backsliding veteran of the Athletics, had been picked up to play third base, but the infield missed Cassidy's smart play. A bright spot was the base running of John Anderson who stole thirty-nine bases to tie Elmer Flick of Cleveland for the league lead. Catching was Howard Wakefield who batted .280 in his first season in the majors. Wakefield did not live to see his son, Dick, accept a 52,000-dollar bonus for joining the Detroit Tigers in 1940. Dick Wakefield later led that club in hitting.

The dreary 1906 season did see the Senators gain one distinction. It was not their feat of losing three double-headers in three days to Clark Griffith's New York Highlanders. They achieved some fame on August 25, when they stopped the White Sox's winning streak of nineteen in a row by beating (Big) Ed Walsh in both games of a double-header and ruining Walsh's private winning streak of eight in a row.

Astonishingly, Stahl was let out at the end of the season, and the announcement was made that Joe Cantillon would be the 1907 manager. Cantillon had umpired the first American League game ever played in Washington. As a manager, his fee was high. President Noyes had to offer him a 7,000-dollar-a-year contract for three years and ten per cent of the profits. The Senators found in Cantillon a new kind of manager.

Chapter IV

IT was a more exciting if not more abundant life for the Senators with the arrival of Joe Cantillon on the managerial scene. Pongo Joe, onetime Chicago saloon owner and graduate of San Francisco's boisterous Barbary Coast, was not an even-tempered soul. The Washington club lured him from Milwaukee where he had some success as a manager in the American Association, but the terrible-tempered Mr. Cantillon was no stranger to Washington fans when he took the job. They knew him as the brawling umpire of earlier days of the American League.

Back in 1901, before John McGraw left the American League to join the New York Giants, he had one disagreement with Cantillon that is memorable. It involved also Clark Griffith, then pitcher-manager of the Chicago White Sox who long had been feuding with McGraw. McGraw was violently disputing Cantillon's decisions on balls and strikes all afternoon, but Pongo Joe, with an astonishing display of reserve, made no move to run McGraw out of the game. McGraw finally singled from one of Griffith's pitches, and from first base McGraw cupped his hands and yelled insults at Cantillon.

In the custom of the times, the game's lone umpire was working behind the pitcher, and now Griffith heard Cantillon whisper to him, "Pick him off first base!" Griffith needed no more authority than that. Tricking McGraw off first with an obvious balk motion, Griffith wheeled and fired to the first baseman who tagged McGraw six feet off the bag. "Yer Out!" screamed Cantillon.

"Balk! Balk! It was a balk!" McGraw screamed in a fury. He raved, ranted, and raked Cantillon with abuse, but the decision stood and McGraw was out.

The next hitter made a single, but Griffith didn't register much concern. Going into the same balk motion with which he had picked McGraw off, he fired the ball to John Ganzel, his first baseman, and the base runner was tagged four feet off the bag, whereupon Cantillon screamed "Balk!" and waved the runner to second base. Now Griffith ranted, but to no avail.

"Listen young man," said Cantillon sternly. "You picked McGraw off the first time as a personal favor to me. If you wanna pick anybody off for yourself, you gotta obey the pitching rules."

As manager, Cantillon ruled firmly if not wisely. His method of punishing his drunken ball players was to make them play nine innings. He didn't allow any rebellion against his authority. Back in Milwaukee, he had a fuss with George Stone, then the leading hitter in the American Association. Stone was benched and a pinch hitter put in his place. When Germany Schaefer, then hitting .380 for Milwaukee, complained about Stone being benched, Cantillon blithely put in a pinch hitter for him too.

In 1909, his third year as Washington manager, Cantillon ended a long and close friendship with Charles Comiskey, owner of the White Sox. With the White Sox fighting Detroit and Cleveland for the pennant in the closing days of the season, Cantillon had his Senators one run in front at Chicago. The White Sox put in Mike Welday, a left-handed pinch hitter to bat against Bob Groom, the Senators' right-hander. Then Cantillon pulled out Groom as a pitcher and sent him into right field, moving the left-handed Dolly Gray in to pitch to Welday. Gray retired Welday, and Groom went back to the mound to pitch against the next hitter, a right-hander, with Gray now playing right field. They alternated that way for the rest of the game, depending on what type of hitter was at the plate, and beat the White Sox. Comiskey wanted to murder Cantillon.

Joe Cantillon's three-year term as manager of the Senators, 1907-09, was not a complete blight on baseball in Washington. Cantillon's crew stumbled into eighth place his first year, floundered into seventh the next season, and relapsed into the cellar again in 1909.

Yet Washington fans had something to cheer about, and if Cantillon never contributed anything else to baseball in the nation's capital, he could take a deep bow for the inspiration that moved him to inquire into the ability of a young pitcher, then a native of Weiser, Idaho.

The young pitcher was, of course, Walter Johnson, and the story of Johnson in the big leagues began with what Cantillon at first regarded suspiciously as a traveling salesman's joke. In letters to Cantillon, a Washington traveling man covering a far western area, was urging that the Senators sign "this boy, Walter Johnson, the strike-out king of the Snake River Valley League." The self-appointed talent scout, obviously an incorrigible baseball fan and professing deep devotion to the Senators, attributed to young Johnson a pitch that was faster than Amos Rusie's and control that was better than Christy Mathewson's.

At first Cantillon ignored the correspondence, putting it down as the naive appraisal of an overexuberant fan, but the letters continued from points in Idaho and California. Each one was a more glowing description of "this young pitcher, Walter Johnson," with the fervent hope that the Washington club "look him over." At what point Cantillon came to a decision to give some credence to Johnson's admirer is not known, but it could well have been when he read in a mid-June letter: "This boy throws so fast you can't see 'em . . . and he knows where he is throwing the ball because if he didn't there would be dead bodies strewn all over Idaho."

Cantillon gave to Cliff Blankenship, a convalescent catcher who was out of the Senators' line-up with a broken finger at the time, the scouting mission that was to wind up with the signing of Johnson. But Johnson wasn't the primary target of that trip. Cantillon's chief instruction to Blakenship was to sign Clyde Milan, young outfielder in the Western Association. Cantillon had been impressed by him when the Senators played an exhibition game at Wichita that spring on their way home from training in Galveston, Texas.

No scout ever had a more productive scouting trip. Milan was duly signed and was Washington's best outfielder for the next fourteen years. Johnson was signed and was the American League's best pitcher for most of the next twenty seasons.

Milan later recalled that Blankenship, after buying him from Wichita for fall delivery for 1,250 dollars, was bemoaning "this wild goose chase Cantillon's sending me on to look over some palooka who is striking out everybody in Weiser, Idaho, in a semi-pro league. All that distance to see some punk who probably isn't worth a dime."

Blankenship's first look at young Johnson was an eye-filler. He happened into Weiser on the day that Weiser was playing the Caldwell club, and he recognized the figure of Johnson even before the game started. The townspeople had already described to him those long arms and the behind-the-plow gait of their young phenomenon, and he was easy for Blankenship to identify.

One look at Johnson was enough for Blankenship, although it was a twelve-inning look. It would be nice to say that he saw Johnson win, but he didn't. What he saw was fair enough, though. Johnson lost on an error in the twelfth, 1 to 0, after two were out.

On a piece of wrapping paper, Blankenship wrote out a quick contract, flashed 100 dollars in cash as a bonus, and said he would guarantee Johnson 350 dollars a month for the rest of the season if he joined the Washington club. The young giant agreed it was a lot of money, but wanted to know about traveling expenses to Washington. Blankenship consented to pay those too. Johnson said he'd have to ask his dad.

The next day Blankenship had his man signed. But he had to make one more concession. The youth who was to become the greatest pitcher in the American League cautiously held out for his return fare to Idaho in case he was released.

Blankenship didn't know that he had acted none too soon. En route to Weiser on that day was a scout from the Seattle club, owned by D. E. Dugdale, with emphatic instructions to sign young Johnson and bring him back to Seattle "if it costs a thousand-dollar bonus."

Pittsburgh, not Washington, might have been the locale of Walter Johnson's pitching feats for the next twenty-one years, had manager Fred Clarke of the Pirates heeded a Pittsburgh well-wisher. The late George Moreland, the baseball historian, relates that an umpire named McGuire who had been

47

working in the Idaho League, tipped him off to the striking promise of young Johnson.

Moreland relayed McGuire's tributes to Clarke whose Pirates were training at Hot Springs, Arkansas, in that spring of 1907 and suggested that Johnson be called to Hot Springs for a tryout. Clarke demurred and pointed out that the Pirates were to break camp in a couple of days, and there would be no time to look Johnson over. At that time, the Pirates could have signed Johnson for an outlay of nine dollars, the railroad fare from Weiser to Hot Springs.

The Washington team was in New York when Cantillon received from Blankenship a telegram that read: "Signed Johnson today. Fastest pitcher since Amos Rusie." Cantillon jubilantly announced the news to Washington baseball writers traveling with the team and the Washington *Post* correspondent wrote with great excitement:

> New York, June 29—Manager Joe Cantillon has added a great baseball phenom to his pitching staff. The young man's name is Walter Johnson. This premier pitcher of the Idaho State League was secured by Cliff Blankenship. Cantillon received word from Blankenship today, telling of the capture! Johnson pitched seventy-five innings in the Idaho State League without allowing a run, and had the wonderful strikeout record of one hundred sixty-six in eleven games, or more than fifteen strikeouts per game.
>
> Blankenship is very enthusiastic, but fails to state whether the great phenom is left-handed or right-handed.

Johnson wasn't rushed into action by Cantillon. He didn't make an appearance on the mound for the Senators until August 2, but by that time the city was buzzing about the fast ball the Idaho farm boy was supposed to have. When Cantillon did unveil him it was in the opening game of a double-header with Detroit, the strongest hitting team in the league with Cobb and Crawford in the Tigers' line-up, and more than 10,000 fans stormed American League Park to see his first test.

Their first sight of Walter Perry Johnson was enough to make them gasp. This couldn't be the fast-baller they had

48

heard about. He was pitching sidearm, almost underhand, with a long sweeping delivery, and no great snap of the wrists. That's not what fast-ballers were made of.

But there he was out there, whipping the ball past the Tigers. Now it was the Detroit players who were amazed at this big boy from the country who didn't look as if he were throwing a fast ball, yet was unleashing a pitch that hissed with danger. Early in the game, the Tigers were impressed with the futility of taking their regular cut against Johnson. Sam Crawford did get hold of one pitch for a home run, but Ty Cobb twice found it expedient to try laying down bunts.

On one bunt, Cobb reached first safely. On a bunt that followed, Cobb scrambled all the way from first to third, and later scored. Two of the six hits Johnson allowed were bunts. A third was an infield scratch. Johnson went out of the game in the eighth inning for a pinch hitter when he was trailing, 2 to 1. The game wound up with the Tigers in front, 3 to 2, but Johnson was on his way to fame.

Wild Bill Donovan, manager of the Tigers, was babbling about Johnson after the game. "In two years he'll be greater than Mathewson," Donovan said.

For the later-day baseball historian who identifies Walter Johnson as the symbol of fast-ball pitching and grace on the mound, there is something of a shock in the yellowed newspaper files of 1907 which tell of Detroit manager Donovan seeking out Manager Cantillon two days after Johnson's debut, and saying:

> If I were you, Joe, I'd tell that young big kid of yours to quit fooling around with that spit-ball he was trying to throw against us. He doesn't need it. He's got too much speed to need anything else. All spit-ballers except Ed Walsh are in-and-outers.

Success came to Walter Johnson in his second start for the Senators. Five days after his losing effort against the Tigers, he faced Cleveland and won, 7 to 2. He allowed four hits, two in the first inning, two in the ninth, and the four walks he issued were all to left-handed batters. The next day it was written: "Johnson's speed was so terrific several Cleveland players acted as though they took no particular delight in being at the plate."

That was the first reference, perhaps, to the reluctance with which American League batters stood up to the plate against Johnson in succeeding years, and their admitted confessions of fright are numerous. It was in 1908 that a New York player declared that there was only one way to time Johnson's fast ball. "When you see the arm go up, swing."

Twelve years later, in the same season in which he was killed by a fast ball thrown by Carl Mays of the Yankees, Ray Chapman of Cleveland expressed his own esteem for Johnson's fast ball. After taking two strikes with his bat on his shoulder, Chapman started to walk away from the plate. When umpire Billy Evans yelled, "You got another strike coming," Chapman didn't break stride, but over his shoulder he told Evans,

"You can have it. It wouldn't do me any good."

Walter Johnson's third start for the Senators, on August 11, 1907, was a defeat. He held the Browns to six hits, but lost the ball game when second baseman George Nill failed to cover the bag, and Johnson's throw went into center field. It was a 1-to-0 defeat. Johnson, before he hung up his glove twenty seasons later, was to pitch fifty-nine more 1-to-0 games, win forty of them, and lose most of the others in heartbreaking fashion while working for weak teams.

Although Johnson was welcomed as stout help to the Washington pitching staff, there was no tip-off to the capital's fans in that first year, when he won only five games and lost nine, that they had in their midst the man destined to win more games than any other pitcher in American League history.

The Senators were never better than a seventh-place ball club in the seven seasons that ended in 1911, but by that time Washington fans were reveling in the pitching feats of the gangling country boy with the long arms and the fast ball that was setting records.

Johnson's fame was solidly launched in his second season with the Senators, on that historic week end in early September, 1908, when he suddenly vaulted from the status of local idol to national hero of the pitching mound. He pitched three shutouts against the Yankees in four days!

Time hasn't dimmed the brilliance of that feat by Johnson, unlike the calendar's treatment of other record-breaking performances that, stacked against later standards of excellence, often lose their importance. Johnson's three shutouts in four days becomes the more incredible in the light of modern pitching routine which labels a pitcher overworked if he averages as many as two starts a week. Of all Johnson's records, that one promises to withstand challenge. They don't play the game that way any more.

The New York Yankees, then the Highlanders, had no early clew that they were to be the victims of Johnson's amazing shutout feat when on September 4, he held them to five hits and won his game, 3 to 0, in the old wooden park at 168th and Broadway.

The Highlanders probably gasped a bit, though, on the next afternoon when they saw young Johnson warming up again before the game, with no other Washington pitcher making any motions toward taking the mound. Sure enough, it was Johnson pitching for the second straight day, and the incredible twenty-year-old youngster demonstrated that his five-hit shutout of the afternoon before was something of a slump for him. In this second start, Johnson didn't allow the Highlanders any kind of a hit until Wid Conroy beat an infield bounder in the second inning, and Johnson shut out the Highlanders this time, 6 to 0, with a three-hitter.

New York's sabbath laws precluded any idea Johnson might pitch the following day, but Manager Joe Cantillon hinted, "Maybe he'll go again Monday." The Washington *Post* correspondent reported frankly that Cantillon was kidding.

Meanwhile, following his Friday and Saturday shutouts, the Washington sports pages were choked with stories on Johnson. The *Post* reported that "Johnson is pitching these games at his own request," and even speculated that Johnson might try to make it three in a row.

51

It seems that some of the players talking of pitching feats said no pitcher could win three shutouts in a row, and others said Walter Johnson could do it. They asked Johnson, and he said in the quiet way characteristic of him, "I think I can do it."

On Monday, the Senators were to play a double-header in New York. Johnson went out merely to play catch with Gabby Street before the first game when he noted that he was the only Washington pitcher warming up. He looked over at Cantillon on the bench in wonderment, and in return got a vigorous nod from the Washington manager. Nothing more was said. Johnson let out a few notches in his warm-up pitches, came back to the bench and said to Cantillon, "It's all right with me if it's all right with you."

And then it happened—Johnson's third shutout of the Highlanders in three starts within the space of four days. If he was weary, there was no evidence of it during the nine innings he mowed the New Yorkers down. He won, 4 to 0. And his pitching had become progressively better. A five-hit shutout on Friday, a three-hit shutout on Saturday, and on this Monday, September 7, he shut out the Highlanders with only two hits.

Actually, from Monday to Monday, Johnson had made four appearances on the mound for the Senators, having pitched four and two-thirds innings earlier in the week against the Red Sox.

What a milestone that was in pitching history! Four days after his three straight shutouts of the Highlanders, he was on the mound again beating the Athletics, 2 to 1, on eight hits. The next day he started again and beat the A's, 5 to 4. Three days later he pitched three innings of shutout ball against the White Sox as a reliever, and two days after that he lost a 2-to-1 duel to Rube Waddell in St. Louis in ten innings when a pop fly bunt beat him, although Waddell struck out seventeen of the seventh-place Senators.

Four days after that Johnson held Cleveland to three hits and beat them, 2 to 1, allowing nobody to reach base after the second inning, and two days later he pitched four and two-thirds innings of relief. Three days after that, the pace told.

On September 29, the Tigers batted him out in two innings. For that kind of pitching, the Washington club was paying him a salary of 2,700 dollars a year.

Already there was general recognition of the modesty of the amiable young giant who was giving the fans of the nation's capital their first chance to acclaim a baseball idol. Washington *Post* sports editor J. Ed Grillo wrote of Johnson, following a 2-to-1 victory over the Athletics in September of 1908:

> It is not often that a baseball player admits that luck favored him in anything. It was therefore quite out of the ordinary to hear Walter Johnson say after his victory of yesterday that he did not think he deserved the victory. He considered himself lucky to win because he did not have his usual stuff.
>
> There is something about this boy aside from his ability that makes him popular with the patrons of the game. He is absolutely honest in everything he does. He never complains about umpires' decisions and he is modest to a fault, believing his teammates more than himself entitled to credit for what the team does when he is pitching. Manager Cantillon took Johnson's word for it that he did not show enough stuff in his 2-1 victory in the first game to warrant being pitched in the second game of the double header, and Tom Hughes was given the job. He lost, 7 to 0.

Johnson was all that Washington had to boast about during Cantillon's sad three-year turn at managing the Senators, 1907-09. They won only forty-nine of one hundred fifty-one games in finishing eighth in '07, and were never higher than sixth. Young Clyde Milan, the rookie outfielder from Wichita, was an exciting addition to the club late in '07, however, and catcher Charles (Gabby) Street was bought for 1908 delivery. The Washington owners angered the fans late in '07 by selling outfielder John Anderson, whose .288 had led the club in hitting, to the White Sox.

If Walter Johnson's fame in 1908 was monumental, then so was that of his batterymate, Charles (Gabby) Street, and in Street's case it was literally monumental. At what was supposed to be risk of life and limb, Street caught a ball tossed

53

from the top of the Washington monument, the five-hundred-fifty-foot obelisk that stands in the nation's capital a short distance from the White House.

In Washington the ability to catch a ball thrown from the monument was a favorite topic of debate, intensified by the failure of all previous attempts at the feat. There was speculation that any misjudgment of the ball would surely produce a broken arm or even fatal injury. As far back as 1894, it had been risked when William Schriver, the catcher of the old Chicago Colts, tried and failed. In subsequent attempts the old catchers, Charlie Snyder and Buck Ewing, were unequal to the task, failing to get close to the ball on its descent out of the skies. An outfielder, Paul Hines, similarly admitted defeat.

Street's attempt stemmed from a 500-dollar bet made by two well-known Washington clubmen and fans, Preston Gibson and John Biddle, with Gibson putting his money on Street. In contrast to the stealth with which Schriver's attempt was made fourteen years before, when the principals were chased from the monument grounds by the authorities, formal permission for Street's test was obtained from the superintendent of parks. Police, photographers, and fans were on the scene at eleven o'clock on the morning of August 21 as Gibson and Biddle ascended the monument with a basketful of balls and a wooden chute designed to carry the ball beyond the wide tapering base of the monument.

Wearing his street clothes but taking off his coat, Street took up a position several feet from the monument's base, and donned the catcher's mitt which had contained the smoke of Johnson's fast balls. He waited for prearranged signals from the pair at the monument top.

On the first ten balls that descended, Street had no chance for a catch. The chute failed to carry the balls beyond the monument's base, and they caromed off the sides of the big pillar. Discarding the chute, Gibson pitched the balls out. Now they were clearing the monument, and on the thirteenth toss, Street made his historic catch.

He took the ball in his mitt with both arms high above his head, in no manner different than catching a routine high pop foul. But the impact was scarcely the same. Street staggered and the force drove his mitt nearly to the ground, but he held the ball. Mathematicians estimated that he had caught three hundred pounds of energy at the end of the ball's five-hundred-fifty-foot drop.

"I didn't see the ball until it was half way down," Street said. "It was slanting in the wind, and I knew it would be a hard catch. The twelfth ball they dropped hit the end of my mitt, but I wasn't set for the catch. I could tell then that I was risking a broken arm if I didn't make a clean catch." Five days later Street did break a finger on a foul tip from one of Johnson's pitches.

Johnson pitched two two-hitters in 1908 and a pair of three-hitters. One of his three-hitters in which he fanned nine men, stopped a Cleveland winning streak of ten in a row. But despite Walter's tremendous effectiveness, he could win only fourteen games while losing fourteen, so hopeless was his support. Long Tom Hughes was the club's leading pitcher with eighteen wins and fifteen losses. Second baseman Jim Delahanty was the only regular to hit more than .300, but the club had come up with a young shortstop named George McBride, whom Washington fans were to know as manager of the club a dozen years later. The Senators barely stayed out of eighth place, but they had a loud voice in the winning of the pennant by Detroit. The Cleveland club, beaten out by only a half game by the Tigers, was licked fourteen times in twenty-two contests with Washington.

Financially, the Senators didn't do badly for their owners. Cantillon, with his bonus arrangement of ten per cent of the profits, drew a year-end check of more than 2,000 dollars, and the club declared a fifteen per cent dividend to stockholders that amounted to 23,900 dollars.

It was a sad picture in 1909, though. Johnson came down with a persistent cold in Galveston, Texas, where the club trained, and was a liability until late June, with Washington fans and the league in general now wondering if he were finished, so consistently was he being battered.

It was the worst year of Johnson's career. He won thirteen games but was charged with twenty-five defeats. The only record he set was one of dubious worth. He made four wild pitches in St. Louis, the city that often jinxed him. Johnson didn't have much to pitch for, though Jim Delahanty who had batted .317 in 1908, slumped to .232, before he was traded to Detroit for second baseman Germany Schaefer. Bob Groom and Dolly Gray who, with Johnson, were the work-horse pitchers, had dismal records. Groom won six games and lost twenty-six. Gray won five and lost nineteen. Wid Conroy was bought from New York to play third base in an infield that saw Bob Unglaub at first, Delahanty and Schaefer at second, and McBride at short. Nick Altrock was signed as a free agent to bolster the pitching staff, and didn't.

The 1909 Senators won only forty-two of one hundred fifty-two games, went into eighth place in June, and stayed there. President Noyes, in despair, offered his resignation to the club's directors who rejected it.

The club directors took action in another direction, however, at the season's close. They fired Joe Cantillon as manager, his three-year contract having expired. The Senators had finished eighth twice and seventh once during his term. Where to find a new manager? Of Cantillon it was said, "Yep, he was fired but he didn't leave any vacancy."

American League president Ban Johnson stepped into the picture with the recommendation that the Senators hire Jimmy McAleer, Johnson's pal of former days, who was then managing the Browns. McAleer's success with the Browns was hardly a recommendation since the only club they had beaten out in 1909 was Washington, but the Senators' owners couldn't be choosy. Washington was coming to be known as the graveyard of managers, and only brave men would take the job. McAleer did.

For the first time in his twenty-one-year career with the Senators, Walter Johnson was unveiled as an opening-game pitcher on April 14, 1910, and it was an historic afternoon for baseball. The season was being launched with White House blessings. President Taft threw out the opening ball, setting the precedent that every Chief Executive after him has followed.

The game, however, was nearly marked by tragedy. Secre-

56

tary of State Charles Bennett, sitting in the White House box with the President and Vice President Sherman, was struck on the head by a foul drive from the bat of Home Run Baker of the Athletics, and the park was in panic until Bennett waved off first aid and demonstrated he had not been hurt.

After Taft made the ceremonial throw, Walter Johnson took over the pitching and shut the Athletics out, 3 to 0, with one hit, before the crowd of 12,000. It was the first of fourteen opening games he was to pitch for the Senators. Eight of them he won, and seven of those victories were indisputable because seven times he shut out the opposition.

As usual, Johnson was the only item Washington fans had to boast about in 1910. But now he was something super. With a seventh-place club behind him, he won twenty-five games, and most of his seventeen losses were chargeable to incompetent castoffs he was pitching for. Johnson pitched a pair of one-hitters and two two-hitters. He led the league in strike-outs, in innings pitched, and in complete games.

Now he was being hailed as the strike-out king. Briefly he was credited with a new mark of 313 strike-outs for a single season, until it was discovered that he had merely surpassed Rube Waddell's 1903 record of 301 strike-outs. A later check revealed that Waddell in 1904 had fanned 343 batters.

To what heights Johnson might have climbed if he had a catcher capable of holding his speed in 1910 dazzles the imagination. Gabby Street, who had been riding to fame as Johnson's batterymate, was injured and out of the game for long periods, and Johnson admitted that he was forced to ease up in pitching to Street's substitutes.

The Senators of 1910 were a dismal batting club, with a team average of .236. Kid Elberfeld, like so many other over-the-hill ball players, found a refuge in Washington that season as a third baseman after being released by the Yankees. Bob Unglaub was at first base, Bill Cunningham at second, and the reliable but weak-hitting George McBride at short. Clyde Milan was notable in the outfield with a .279 batting average and forty-four stolen bases.

Johnson's teammates in later years admitted that the Big Train never was aiming for shutout or strike-out records,

57

and in fact declared that he was an artistic loafer, content to win by any satisfactory margin. There was evidence Johnson fit that description when he pitched and won against the Browns at St. Louis on July 8. The Big Train fanned seven men in the first two and one-third innings, struck out an eighth man before the third inning was over, and after getting a big lead apparently didn't bother to strike out anybody else for the rest of the game.

There was no great criticism of McAleer at the year's end, at least not by the front office. Despite the fact that attendance was down generally in the American League, the Senators' home attendance increased to 269,881, and only on the last day of the season were they forced into seventh place. Johnson pitched them into sixth place in the first game of a doubleheader that day, but they lost the second game to fall behind the sixth-place White Sox. McAleer was given a new two-year contract extending through 1912.

Before he pitched a ball for the Senators in 1911, Walter Johnson made front-page news. At the club's spring training camp at Atlanta, Johnson and his roommate, Clyde Milan, were holdouts. Johnson, after his twenty-five victories of 1910 for a seventh-place club, was demanding the fabulous salary of 9,000 dollars a year, "just as much as Ty Cobb," he said. His figure was double the 4,500-dollar salary he drew the year before. Young Milan, who had become one of the better outfielders in the league and Ty Cobb's chief challenger for the stolen base title, wanted 4,000 dollars.

McAleer, in panic, asked President Noyes to come to Atlanta and negotiate with Milan and Johnson. Noyes capitulated to Milan and signed him for 4,000 dollars. He offered Johnson a contract for 6,500 dollars for three years. Johnson said "nothing doing," which in point of length was a typical Johnson speech, and walked out of the camp, catching the next train to Coffeyville, Kansas, where he threatened to stay as a worker on his dad's poultry farm.

Washington fans were in an uproar at the dispatches from Atlanta and accused Noyes of stingy tactics against Johnson. There were published reports that the Senators would trade Johnson to Philadelphia or Detroit. Noyes defended himself by declaring, "No other American League pitcher is paid as much as the 6,500-dollar offer Johnson is turning down." He might have added that no other American League pitcher was capable of winning twenty-five games with a seventh-place club.

The Johnson holdout collapsed suddenly later in the week. He was at his Coffeyville home only thirty hours when he took a train to Washington to sign a three-year contract for 7,000 dollars a season, two days before the opening game.

Johnson didn't pitch the opener. It wasn't until April 15 that he made his 1911 debut. He beat the Red Sox and contributed another chapter to Walter Johnson pitching lore. That was the day he fanned four men in the same inning, yet was scored on.

Big Walter opened the inning by striking out Eddie Collins and Gardner. But his third strike to Gardner got away from Eddie Ainsmith and the batter reached first. Johnson then fanned Harry Hooper for his third strike-out of the inning. Meanwhile, Gardner stole second, and scored a bit later on a double by Tris Speaker. Johnson bent to his task again and fanned Duffy Lewis for his fourth strike-out of the inning.

They called it a poor season for Johnson in 1911. He won only twenty-three games and lost fifteen. On May 17, the Senators found their niche—seventh place—and stayed there for the rest of the season. The aging Germany Schaefer, who was now playing first base, hit .334, but young Clyde Milan was establishing himself as a star with a .315 batting average and fifty-four stolen bases. The stolen base record was second only to Cobb's. Milan was the pet protege of McAleer, who had been a great outfielder himself, and he chastised the rookie for the fancy one-hand catches he was making in the outfield.

"Cut out that fancy stuff," said McAleer. "If you can catch a ball with one hand, you can catch it with two. I never made a one-handed catch in my life. If you have to catch a ball with one hand, it shows either that you misjudged it, or loafed, or made some other mistake."

By the end of 1911, Eddie Ainsmith had replaced Gabby

59

Street as Johnson's regular catcher. The Senators paid the Lawrence, Massachusetts, club 3,500 dollars for Ainsmith the preceding fall, and had also signed an Amherst College catcher named John Henry by giving the Amherst baseball coach 600 dollars and the player nothing, which was the standard operating procedure of big-league clubs in that era.

Johnson recognized the rough job his catchers faced when he cut loose with his fast one. "I know when I have control I'm easy to catch, but if I'm pitching high or low, it's murder on the catcher. Ainsmith does the best job," said the Big Train.

Suddenly on September 15, 1911, McAleer announced that he was leaving the Washington club, despite the fact his contract had another year to run. He thereby could claim a certain distinction. He was the first manager in the Senators' history who wasn't fired, but was leaving of his own volition.

McAleer announced he was moving to Boston as half owner of the Red Sox which he had bought in partnership with Robert McElroy, until then the secretary to American League president Ban Johnson.

The *Reach Baseball Guide* of 1911, commenting on the new shuffle in the ownership of the Red Sox, noted: "A young railroad man of Chicago named William Harridge, succeeds Mr. McElroy as secretary to League President Ban Johnson."

The Senators were a club without a manager until October 27 of 1911, when Clark C. Griffith applied for the job, and then took root in the nation's capital.

Chapter V

FORTY-TWO-YEAR-OLD Clark Griffith was eyeing the vacant managerial job in Washington in October, 1911, for various reasons. He was already employed as manager of the Cincinnati Reds and was being offered a new contract by owner Garry Hermann, but at heart he was an American Leaguer. As manager of the White Sox, in 1901 he had won the league's first pennant, and for the next several years had given the National League staunch battle in the latter's war to withhold recognition from the American League.

Griffith had long been friendly with Thomas Noyes, co-publisher of the Washington *Star* and chief stockholder in the Senators. During the world series of 1911, Griffith was approached by Edward Walsh, Washington insurance broker and a director of the team, with the suggestion he give thought to taking over the management of the Senators. At a meeting of the club's stockholders at the Commercial Club, just off Lafayette Square and near the White House, Griffith talked with the directors of the Senators. They pointed out that the stockholders had voted to reorganize the financial setup of the club and to increase its capital stock from 100,000 dollars to 200,000 dollars. There would be more working capital for the new manager to work with, they told him.

Certain stockholders at the same time politely suggested to Griffith that he risk some of his own money in the venture, pointing out that stock would be available. They needn't have been so timorous about it. Griffith himself was already thinking of the job in terms of stockholder in addition to manager. Griffith was becoming more investment-minded. He was a middle-aged man now, with a sixteen-year pitching career and eleven years as a manager in the majors behind him. Sprays of gray were beginning to show about the temples, and now he was given to reflecting that he alone, of the three men who founded the American League, had not made a financial success of the venture. Ban Johnson, as president of the league, had an ironclad contract that called for 40,000 dollars yearly. Charles Comiskey, who with Johnson and Griffith had plotted the launching of the new league eleven years before, was becoming wealthy as the owner of the White Sox, a perennial first division club. And now Jimmy McAleer, with whom Griffith had played at Milwaukee in the old days of 1888, was also becoming a club owner at Boston.

Buy stock? Sure, he would buy stock, agreed Griffith. All the shares they'd let him buy, at a reasonable price. It was a bit of a bluff by Griffith, because he possessed no large amount of cash. But he thought he knew where he could borrow the necessary money.

But Griffith's little speech suddenly produced a seller's market. Impressed by his eagerness to buy into the Washington club, certain greedy stockholders hiked the price. They asked $15 a share on stock for which they had paid $12.50, and Griffith was indignant. The deal apparently was falling through.

Then President Noyes called Griffith aside. He said: "Griff, you can have my 800 shares for what it cost me. I can say the same thing for my friends Ben Minor and Ed Walsh. In all, that figures around 1,200 shares at $12.50. Buy 800 more from those pirates at $15, and that' ll give you 2,000 shares—a tenth interest in the club. It will make you the biggest single stockholder."

That proposition, Griffith accepted with gratitude to Noyes. Now where to get enough money to swing the deal? He entrained for Philadelphia to visit his old friend, League president Ban Johnson. On first hearing that the Washington job was open, Griffith had talked to Johnson who had promised him a 10,000-dollar loan if he wished to buy into the Senators. Enthusiastically, Griffith told Johnson of the deal he had made and now asked the loan of the money. And now Ban Johnson's answer was, "Sorry."

Griffith was incredulous at the new turn of affairs, and reminded Johnson of his promise. "I can't do it," said Johnson with finality, whereupon Griffith, in short temper, said "Well, I know what you can do," and walked brusquely out of the hotel room.

It was useless for Griffith to turn to his other friend of early American League days, Charley Comiskey. He already knew of Comiskey's attitude toward his proposed Washington venture. Weeks before, when Griffith had mentioned the possibility of buying into the Senators, Comiskey had told him, "You're crazy to sink your money into that baseball graveyard."

Eight thousand dollars represented Griffith's available cash assets, and that amount he dispatched to president Noyes as a down payment on the 27,000 dollars worth of stock he had contracted for. Noyes agreed to wait two weeks for the remainder of the cash.

During the eleven years he had been a major-league manager, Griffith had not been prodigal with his earnings. He was the owner of a six-thousand-acre ranch at Craig, Montana, where for a dozen years his elder brother Earl had been operating the land and getting sheep, cattle, and alfalfa to market.

In his desperation, Griffith hastened to Montana and persuaded the First National Bank of Helena to take a 20,000-dollar mortgage on his ranch. With those funds he dashed back to Washington to claim his ten per cent interest in the Senators and a three-year contract as manager at 7,500 dollars a year.

The Clark Griffith story began on the morning of November 20, 1869, when the pastoral peace of Clear Creek, Missouri, was disturbed by the infant cries of a newborn child of the frontier. Down from its accustomed place came the family Bible and into its flyleaf a pioneer father wrote the name: "Clark Calvin Griffith."

Humble indeed were the early beginnings of Clark C. Griffith. Home, to the Isaiah Griffiths in 1869, was a rough-hewn log cabin pitched in a clearing in southwestern Missouri near the Kansas border. At every hand were reminders that these were the frontier days of the early West. Across the oaken door that led into the wilderness beyond was the conventional dropbar. Pine logs ribbed the four walls and roof of the home. Stacked in its appointed corner, and always handy, was the one great guarantee that the Griffiths would eat—a muzzle-loading gun, complete with powder bag and ramrod.

Two years before, that same old muzzle-loader had swung from the back of Isaiah Griffith on the long covered wagon trek from Illinois. Theirs had been one of a long train of prairie schooners bound for the fertile Oklahoma panhandle. Only the foolhardy would travel alone in those unsettled days following the Civil War, with bad men on the trails. In Vernon County, Missouri, Isaiah Griffith abandoned the Oklahoma trek, staked out forty acres, and turned to the soil.

The occupants of that Missouri cabin, frontier folk now, were in truth lineal aristocrats of America. Clark Calvin Griffith, the fifth child born to Isaiah and Sarah Wright Griffith, was of proud stock. Isaiah Griffith was of the landed gentry of Colonial Virginia. In the late seventeenth century, the Griffiths had emigrated to America from Wales, in a semblance of a tribal movement. Paternal grandparent of Isaiah was the General John Ward Griffith who had fought with General Washington in the Revolution. Clark Griffith's father was born in Virginia, the son of a wealthy planter.

On the distaff side, Clark Griffith's ancestry was equally eminent. His mother was the daughter of Abigail Starbuck, descendant of Edward Starbuck. It is recorded in various works on early New England history that Edward Starbuck was one of the ten purchasers of Nantucket, Massachusetts, in 1659. The first English child born on Nantucket was a Starbuck. The family had emigrated with the Pilgrims, and numerous are the heavy brass nameplates and door knockers on Nantucket that still bear the name.

The thirty-one-year-old Isaiah Griffith set out to wrest a livelihood for his family from his forty Missouri acres. But disillusioned by the leanness of his crops, Isaiah Griffith turned his back on farming and reached for his gun. He turned hunter and trapper and, in the parlance of frontier days, "hunted for the market." Jay Gould's Missouri Pacific Railroad was still uncompleted, and in Missouri section hands by the hundreds were still laboring. The task of feeding the workers was a vexing problem for the engineers. The commissary chiefs would eagerly pay cash for victuals.

Deer and wild turkey abounded near Clear Creek, and Isaiah Griffith used the muzzle-loader around the countryside with good results. Venison and fowl fell by his marksmanship, and the railroad people at Fort Scott paid him in gold for his work.

On a February night in 1872, as Isaiah Griffith, gun in hand, leaped a fence on the trail of deer, a shot rang out. A youthful hunter in a nearby field had mistaken him for game.

Lem Batts, seventeen-year-old son of a neighbor, killed the father of two-year-old Clark Griffith, whose saddened mother was again with child.

In the best tradition of frontier women, the newly widowed mother of Clark Griffith laid hold of the situation. Isaiah Griffith's tangible bequests to his six children were scanty: forty acres of lean farming land, a two-story log house, and his gun. But the children were rich in their legacy of a grimly brave mother. She took to the fields in ploughing season, often with little Clark Calvin astride the plough steed. Earl Griffith, four years older, struggled into the fields as a lad of ten with his father's gun. Too small to reload the heavy weapon, he set forth each day with one double load in the old gun and a crotched stick to steady his aim. Like the Indians, the Griffiths pounded their own corn into meal with a mallet striking a grooved rock. Money was an unknown exchange to the little homesteaders of Clear Creek. Corn meal, apple butter, venison, and pigs were regarded as legal tender.

Kindly neighbors visited the Griffiths periodically to offer help. From the backwoods towns of Dog Walk, Buzzard's Glory, Possum Trot, and Stringtown, they came to plough the Griffith fields, put in the Griffith crops, and stack the Griffith firewood. And then at the end of the day's labors, the grateful Griffiths would play host. The log house resounded to the fiddler's tunes and the shuffling feet as farmers, young and old, danced the square dances of the country folk.

Those were the postwar days of the '70s, and that was the country that had been terrorized by the plundering outlaw bands of Quantrill and the James boys. Missouri justice was early engraved on the mind of young Clark Griffith. Near the Griffith cabin was the community "hanging tree," last rendezvous of the horse thieves and robbers. The women of southwestern Missouri had been unprotected during the war because their men were in service, and guerrilla bands had pillaged the country, stealing, burning, and violating.

The Army sent soldiers to clean out the remnants of the organized groups following the war, but angry settlers, mustered out of uniform, were back to exact their own vengeance.

Woe to the outlaw who ventured back five or ten years later. The women identified him, and the men repaired to the hanging tree, first to string up the culprit, then to pump the lifeless body full of buckshot.

At the age of ten, Clark Griffith was contributing heavily to the family larder. With his homemade figure-four traps he snared the salable skunk and coon and possum. At Nevada, Missouri, twelve miles away, the skunk with the white V-mark on its neck would bring the equivalent of $1.25, and the coon hides would fetch $1.00. Possum was sold at the low price of twenty-five cents for each catch, and the red fox that happened into the lad's traps was worthless in the Missouri market. His first pair of store boots he bought after hiring out to a neighbor at the age of eleven. After a summer of chopping corn stalks and general chores around the neighbor's farm, he was paid off in full—with two small pigs.

Clark Griffith's proudest possession in those days was neither his boots nor the traps he had built for himself but an undersized coon dog named Major—half bulldog, half hound. The lad had learned that a purebred hound was too lazy to be used as a coon dog. He had bred Major himself and had taught the dog to bark sharply twice and no more after a scent had been struck.

Griffith grew up to know and be received by Presidents, to become a pitching star in the two major leagues, to manage and own pennant-winning teams and to be elected to baseball's Hall of Fame, but of one incident in his boyhood he is inordinately proud. To this biographer, he told the story a dozen years ago:

> All the boys in Vernon County used to set out trap lines. They helped to cut down the overhead. We'd get possum and coon and sometimes a polecat—skunks we used to call 'em then. But after skinning a skunk, we'd leave our clothes to soak in a bucket of kerosene—or they'd never let us in the house.
>
> My dog, Major, would fight anything from a prairie rat to a grizzly. He was a mongrel, but he had more courage than a pure-bred. When he'd tree a coon, or possum, I'd climb up and shake the tree limb until the thing lost its grip and fell.

66

Down on the ground, Major would handle it until I could climb down and finish it off with my club.

One night Major treed what looked to me like an uncommonly big coon. Up I went with my club. I shook the limb for dear life, but that coon hung on like no other coon I ever saw. Then he skipped to the top of the tree and and looked down at me, snarling and spitting. That coon was different all right.

Anyway I started up after him, and that coon was asking for trouble by jumping at me. I let him have it over the head with my club, and he fell out of the tree.

Major could usually finish off a coon in half a minute, but he was having an awful time with this one. I scrambled out of the tree and they were battling all over the ground. I couldn't use my club right away, afraid I'd hit Major. Finally I conked that coon on the head and that just about settled him. But just to make sure, I swung again. Major jumped in the way of my swing and I knocked him cold. But I brought him around, got that coon over my back, and started home.

Half way home I met a farmer who stopped and looked curiously at my load. "Lad, what you got there?" he asked me.

"A great big coon," I said, "the biggest coon I ever did see."

"Coon, hell, son. That ain't no coon. You got a wildcat," said the farmer.

I looked at the thing again, this time, under a light. Sure enough it wasn't a coon. It was a wildcat all right. Must have weighed sixty pounds. That's about what I weighed. No fooling, I licked my weight in wildcats that night.

At thirteen years old, Clark Griffith was a sickly lad, subject to long spells of chills and fever, and a shut-in for long periods. A kindly neighbor, John Batts, father of the boy who had killed young Griffith's father eleven years before, diagnosed the illness as malaria, dread disease of the lowland country. "Widow Griffith," he warned, "unless you move that boy out of this part of Missouri, he's a-going to die."

The Griffiths went back to Bloomington, Illinois, to find shelter with relatives. It was in Bloomington where Clark Griffith was to launch his baseball career, but back in Missouri the game had already entered his life. At the age of ten, he was the mascot of the Stringtown team that had begun to play the new game the soldiers had brought back from the war. Baseball had been invented some four decades before, but it was still a crude kind of game as the Missouri teams were playing it in 1879, with homespun balls and vague rules. Rivalry was tense among the teams of nearby settlements, and it was to be a great day in the life of young Griffith when Stringtown met the roundly hated team from Possum Trot.

For on that day, they were to play with a "store ball," a genuine horsehide baseball that was to cost a dollar and a quarter. A collection among the members of the team was taken to raise the sum for the store ball. No mere yarn ball would suffice for this important game. As Griffith related the story:

> We gave the dollar and a quarter to one of our boys and sent him on horseback to Nevada, Missouri, twelve miles away, to buy the storeball. Everybody was on edge. Possum Trot was first at bat and their second hitter whacked the ball solidly. It burst completely open; yarn flew in all directions. We couldn't believe our eyes until we investigated. Then we discovered the fellow had bought a twenty-five-cent ball and pocketed the extra dollar. The game broke up, but the embezzler took it on the run and never showed his face in Stringtown again.

The Illinois climate wrought a beneficial change in the health of young Griffith. The malaria spells vanished and, though still a bit undersized, the lad was tolerably strong. Prospering from a boarding house she conducted at Normal, Illinois, Mrs. Griffith reinstalled her young children in school.

In company with the town kids, Clark Griffith often sneaked into the Normal College grounds, and there it was that he first glimpsed baseball under the up-to-date rules of 1883. In that year, the "new" rules stated that seven—not eight—called balls entitled the batter to take his base; the catcher was required to move behind the plate for the third strike instead of catching the ball on the bounce; foul balls that were caught on the bounce were no longer outs; and only for the catcher was a glove considered necessary. Two years later a rule was passed permitting one side of the bat to have a flat surface.

68

Young Griffith, at sixteen, had a local reputation as a pitcher. Control was his forte, inasmuch as his small frame permitted no great speed on the ball, and his fame spread. Bitter rivals of the section were the Danville and Hoopeston town teams. From Hoopeston came an offer of ten dollars to Griffith if he would take the mound against Danville. That ten dollars represented more money than young Griffith knew existed in available cash. His friends declared Griffith accepted the offer so quickly that the Hoopeston folks regretted the generosity of their proposition. In Hoopeston, Griffith won his first game as a professional pitcher.

Bloomington was already baseball conscious. It was the home town of Charles (Hoss) Radbourne, big league pitching ace of the era, and held a franchise in the Inter-State League. In 1888, the seventeen-year-old Clark Griffith was signed as a pitcher. He was beaten in his first game, 5 to 3, by Decatur, but the records show he outpitched his foe, allowing only five hits. Ten errors by Bloomington beat him. Young Griffith's pitching that day was commendable, but his fielding was something else again. Five of his team's ten errors were committed by Griffith himself.

Evidently Griffith learned how to field his position with great suddenness, because it is recorded that in that same season of 1888 with the Bloomington team, the seventeen-year-old lad won thirteen games and lost only two, and was the top pitcher in the league. Bloomington folks, excited by the feats of their home-grown pitcher, in the summer of 1888 arranged an exhibition game with Milwaukee of the Western State League to be played in Bloomington. This was to be the test for Griffith. That game was the springboard for Clark Griffith's big leap toward the majors. He hurled Bloomington to victory, and Manager James A. Hart hired him at a salary of 225 dollars per month to pitch for Milwaukee.

On July 23, 1888, Griffith made his first start from Milwaukee. He was sent to the mound against St. Paul and won his game 8 to 1, allowing six hits. The Milwaukee *Sentinel* documented his triumph with the report: "Young Griffith pitched a magnificent game for the Milwaukees, and although St. Paul had men on base in almost every inning, they succeeded in getting only one man across the plate against the rookie right-hander."

The center fielder for Milwaukee that day was Jimmy McAleer who, twenty-three years later, was to create the managerial vacancy in Washington that brought Griffith to the nation's capital.

By the end of the next season, Griffith had become Milwaukee's best pitcher, and in 1890 he had a record of twenty-five victories and only eleven defeats. Word of the skill of the little Western Association right-hander was spreading, and in the winter of 1890-91, Manager Charles Comiskey of the St. Louis Browns induced Griffith to jump to the St. Louis club, then owned by the colorful Chris Von Der Ahe, who reached the playing field simply by walking out of the back door of his saloon.

It was the beginning of a gypsy tour of baseball for Griffith. In midseason, after he had won eleven games for the St. Louis American Association club, he was traded to Boston of the same league in exchange for one Easton, a pitcher. Finishing the season with Boston, he won three games and lost one.

Boston, boasting such stars as Hugh Duffy, Mike Kelly, and Dan Brouthers, won the American Association pennant in 1891, but Griffith's life with a pennant winner was short. Before the 1892 season opened, the AA disbanded, and the National League occupied the major-league field alone.

In 1892 Griffith trekked to Tacoma, Washington, in the Northern Pacific League—back to the minors. A sore arm he developed at Boston at the end of the previous season made National League owners skeptical of the little right-hander, and he had failed to make a connection with a big league club. With Tacoma, Griffith was penalized for his consistent successes on the mound. The Tacoma club got so far out in front that the league broke up in August, and Griffith found himself without a job.

Then Griffith left the league together with a group of other Tacoma players who had been unpaid for weeks. When they received a telegram from Missoula, Montana, offering to hire the entire Tacoma team to represent Missoula in the outlaw Montana State League, at the same salaries their Tacoma contracts called for, they wanted to accept. But they were skeptical that a small Montana town could live up to its word to pay. The Tacoma manager ignored the telegram, but Griffith announced he was going to Montana and urged the others to go, suggesting himself as team manager. Moving into Montana with ten players who accepted the risk with him, Griffith discovered that his team had contracted to play for a wild mining town in the flush of a boom. Missoula was full of gambling joints, saloons, and honky-tonks crowding each other along the town's one main street. The town received its new ball players with gusto, and saloonkeepers vied with each other in heaping hospitality on the athletes. They learned with satisfaction that the Missoula team was operated by Lou Higgins, president of the Missoula bank and lieutenant governor of the state.

Griffith's opening pitching performance, a 6-to-0 victory for Missoula, caused great excitement in the little town. A Saturday night collection in the saloons netted 700 dollars for manager Griffith and lesser amounts for the other players.

The following week end, Missoula was to play its bitter rival, Helena, and lieutenant governor Higgins deposited 200 dollars with the clerk of Griffith's hotel, to be turned over to Griffith as a gift if the pitcher won his game. Betting on the ball game was wild, with Missoula and Helena miners meeting on a common ground.

Griffith took the mound for Missoula with a second-string catcher, Kid Spears, in the absence of Mike Cody, his regular catcher, who was in the stands after a night of excessive drinking. Going into the ninth inning, he held a 4-to-3 lead over Helena.

Then catcher Spears, the second-stringer, let one of Griffith's pitches skip through his mitt for a passed ball, and Helena's runner on third base scored a tying run.

As Spears dashed to the backstop to retrieve the ball, he found himself in the midst of rabid Missoula fans, and discovered he was looking into the barrels of a pair of hastily produced six-shooters. Those miners were in no mood to trifle. "Son, never let that happen again," Spears was told.

That little gunplay affected Spears to the extent he refused to risk another passed ball. At the end of the inning, he quit the game, vanishing and leaving Griffith and the Missoula team catcherless.

But the incident apparently had a sobering effect on Mike Cody. He came down from the stands to volunteer to catch the rest of the game. A bit unsteady on his feet and strong of breath, Cody donned the catcher's trappings and fearlessly took the vacant position. Missoula won, 5 to 4, and in that year of 1892 Clark Griffith was a hero in Missoula, Montana.

The role of a hero in Missoula did not exactly satisfy Griffith, who had tasted of big-league life in his brief experience with St. Louis and Boston the year before. But when no major league offers came his way, he signed with Oakland of the Pacific Coast League in the spring of 1893.

At Oakland, Griffith met another man who was to precede him as manager of the Washington Senators—Joe Cantillon, then Oakland's star second baseman. The two became fast friends. But the minor leagues of the nineties were unstable. Despite the fact that Oakland, with the help of Griffith's pitching victories, was far out in front in August, owner Robinson was unable to meet the payroll.

The denouement occurred on an afternoon in San Francisco. Unpaid for weeks, the Oakland players revolted with Griffith taking the lead, and they refused to go on the field unless their back pay was forthcoming. Five thousand fans were in the park awaiting the game, but the players in their dressing room were adamant. The Oakland players had the sympathy of the San Francisco press which was hostile to the Oakland ownership, and Charley Dryden, sports editor of the San Francisco *Chronicle,* offered to address the crowd from home plate to explain reasons for the strike. He did and the Frisco fans broke into a cheer as Griffith and his teammates walked from the park to their carriages.

The league broke up with that turn of events, and Griffith found himself out of a job and dead broke.

Those were hard times for young Griffith. He and Joe Cantillon, similarly out of a job, were not averse to "hitting the

72

road." It was natural in those times that they would drift to California's Barbary Coast.

In a honky-tonk music hall, Griffith and Cantillon finally found work. The wild Indian yells he had learned in his native Missouri served Griffith in good stead. He gained a job as a "bad Indian" in a Barbary Coast "mellerdrammer," and Cantillon, as an Indian in the same skit, emptied a six-shooter at Griffith twice a night. Griffith bore up well under the blank-cartridge attack and submitted readily to being "slain" with great frequency, that virtue might triumph and he and Cantillon might eat.

Griffith found himself back in the major leagues suddenly in late August. His old friend, James A. Hart, had remembered him. Hart, manager of the Milwaukee team back in 1888, was now the president of the Chicago National League club, and did not forget the little pitcher who had served him so well at Milwaukee. He telegraphed Griffith to report.

Griffith pitched three games for manager Pop Anson's Chicago Colts before the 1893 season ended. He lost his first start to Philadelphia, 7 to 3, but beat the same club, 12 to 5, in his second. In late September he pitched a relief game against Washington in Washington, quite unaware he was making his first appearance in the city where he was to settle and grow wealthy.

It was during an exhibition tour in California at the end of the season, that Griffith declares he became the first pitcher to throw what is known as the screwball. Like many another discovery, he says, it came about because of an accident to his pitching arm. Overworked, he developed a sore arm, and was being pounded everywhere he pitched. The following story of his efforts gained wide popularity.

His slow ball refused to work, and the batters of the Coast team were hammering his pitches to all corners for extra-base hits. Griffith perspired and fumed, and the more effort he put into his pitching the more vicious were the hits that bounced off the enemy bats.

The Coast hitters were peppering the ball particularly against the left field fence where an enterprising clothing firm of the town had posted a forty-foot canvas sign which offered 50 dollars to every home town batter who could hit the sign. But with no other pitchers available, Griffith's club had to leave him in the box. In the fifth inning, after a half-dozen Coast hits had bounced off the sign, a great yell went up from the stands.

Griffith turned to see what was happening in left field. What did he see? The panic-stricken clothier, envisioning bankruptcy, was feverishly tearing down the sign!

Griffith rejoined the Colts the next spring and started experimenting with new pitches. He was startled to discover that a curve ball released outside his middle finger, instead of between his index finger and his thumb, took an eccentric break away from left-handed hitters that was effective. He could break his pitches away from the right-handed hitters with his conventional curve ball. Further experimentation bore him out, and as the season opened he felt he had added a screwball to his repertoire.

Griffith rocketed to stardom with Anson's team. In 1894 he won twenty-one games and lost only fourteen. Griffith's screwball, he later asserted, was the forerunner of Christy Mathewson's famed "fadeaway." He conceded that Mathewson was actually the first man to perfect the pitch and impart to it an emphatic break, but he was content with the effectiveness of his own mild break on the ball.

A comment on Griffith's development in his eight years as a star pitcher with the Colts was made by the famed baseball writer, Hugh Fullerton, who wrote:

> Clark Griffith is the greatest pitcher I have ever seen, superior even to his instructor Charley (Hoss) Radbourne. Rusie was faster. Dad Clarke had a better slow one . . . in fact, almost any pitcher could beat Griff at some style of twirling . . . but for brains, cunning and ability to mix them all up, Griff was the best. And besides, he lasted longer because he took care of himself.

By 1895, they were already calling the twenty-five-year-old Griffith "The Old Fox." The nickname was a tribute to his canny pitching, his awareness of the batters' weaknesses, his calmness under pressure, his sly tampering with the ball, and

74

all the other tricks which in those days were permissible. He became a positive sensation in 1895, winning twenty-five victories against fourteen defeats.

Baseball writer Fullerton told the story of one of Griffith's triumphs before the turn of the century that was typical of the strategy of the little right-hander:

> One day, Griffith was pitching for Anson's team against the Washington club in Washington. In the ninth, Chicago was one run ahead but Washington had two men on base with Kip Selbach, one of the most feared sluggers in the league, at bat and two out.
>
> Griffith wasted his first pitch, then sneaked a slow ball across for a strike. He finally worked the count to two balls and two strikes. Then he began kidding Selbach. Griff's pitching system was to worry the batter, especially in a crisis. He, himself, was always cool. This day he dallied with his wind-up, took time, inspected the ball, and altogether succeeded in making Selbach over-anxious.
>
> "Throw it up here, Foxy, and I'll knock the cover off it!" Selbach yelled.
>
> "Why, you big bow-legged Dutchman, you couldn't hit this pitch with a shovel," shouted Griffith.
>
> The repartee between pitcher and batter continued for half a minute. Selbach was waving his bat wildly, itching to swing for the fences. Finally Griffith started to wind up and pitch.
>
> "Here, you big stiff, hit this," yelled Griff.
>
> And Griff deliberately pitched the ball up to the plate with an underhand motion that lacked speed enough to break a windowpane. Selbach drew back for a mighty swing, and a mighty swing he took. But the ball had not yet reached the plate and Selbach was out on strikes. Realizing he had been duped Kip threatened to whip Griff on the spot. But Griffith and the Chicago players were already on their way to the clubhouse.

Griffith's reputation as a firebrand was already known in Washington from his old National League days. The Chicago *Record-Herald* on May 20, 1898, said of him: "Clark Griffith bids fair to be the first man held up to the public as a rowdy under the new Brush law. Umpire Thomas Lynch has promised to make charges against Griffith, including use of profane language on the ball field."

Years later, after Griffith jumped to the American League, the baseball writer of the Boston *Post* wrote of him:

> We have seen Griffith pitching for the old Chicago club and what a pesky individual he was to opponents, hostile crowds and umpires. All he seemed to have was a slow ball, a prayer and control, yet he makes monkeys of the men who faced him ... he would stand in the box and procrastinate while the fans yelled for his gore and the batter became fidgety. Then, up would come the ball, tantalizingly slow, and never where the batter wanted it ... Griffith won more games with his head than his arm. And if things did go wrong, Griff used to get after the umpires. He was a star baiter, a graduate of the old school, and probably holds the record for being chased out of ball games, eclipsing that of John McGraw, who was a genius in that line himself.

It was one pitcher-batter tiff between Griffith and McGraw that is credited with one of the most far-reaching changes in the rules—that concerning the foul strike. In 1894, the foul tip was not counted as a strike, but after a game in which McGraw deliberately fouled off Griffith's slow stuff for fifteen minutes in one turn at bat, the rule was changed to count all fouls as strikes until the third strike.

With his decision to cast his lot with the new American League during the winter of 1900-01, Griffith went speedily to work to round up the players he promised to deliver to cofounders Ban Johnson and Charles Comiskey. He left on an historic raid of National League clubs who were still underrating the threat of the new American League and laughing off the idea of two major leagues.

Griffith traveled into New England, along the East Coast, through the South, and as far west as Kansas City on his forays for talent, and he delivered thirty-nine of the forty players he had promised his coplotters. Honus Wagner alone resisted Griffith's blandishments. To reach the home of fielder Jones, at Shinglehousen, New York, Griffith trudged three miles through knee-deep snow and turned his oratory on that star outfielder to convince him that his future lay with the new league. He virtually emptied a number of National League clubs with his raids. For his own Chicago team he took pitcher Jimmy Callahan and infielder Sammy Mertes from the Cubs. He acquired catcher Billy Sullivan from Boston, and fielder Jones from Brooklyn.

He arrived in Philadelphia one day, intent on signing Ed McFarland, star catcher of the Phillies, then owned chiefly by Tom Shibe. Griffith cornered McFarland in a hotel room and turned on the persuasion, but McFarland insisted on a 500-dollar cash bonus before he would sign. "Or maybe there ain't 500 dollars in your whole new league," McFarland taunted him.

Griffith couldn't produce 500 dollars at that moment, but he told McFarland, "Wait here. I'll have it for you in an hour. Don't move."

Inside of an hour, Griffith returned, laid 500 dollars on the table, and got McFarland's signature on a contract. Where did Griffith get the money? He borrowed it from Tom Shibe!

Griffith, as player-manager of the White Sox, led his team to the first American League pennant in 1901. He gave his club a lift with twenty-four victories out of his own pitching fist, losing only eight times. He was the top pitcher in the league that year. The next season, with Rube Waddell making his debut and Eddie Plank also on Connie Mack's staff, the Athletics won the pennant, with Griffith's club taking fourth place.

When the American League, in 1902, recognized the need of a club in New York, Ban Johnson asked Griffith to become manager there. It was now open warfare between the two leagues, with the American invading the territory of the New York Giants, but Griffith and Johnson rounded up a strong club that included five jumpers from the Pirates—pitchers Jack Chesbro and Jess Tannehill, catcher Jack O'Connor, outfielder Lefty Davis, and third baseman Wid Conroy. George Davis, captain and star shortstop of the Giants, jumped that club after a salary argument, and also joined with Griffith.

Griffith superintended construction of the Highlanders'

park at 168th and Broadway and learned that it was a historic site. He watched workmen unearth ancient bullets, gun stocks, grapeshot, and bayonets, and then discovered that the park had once been a battleground of Washington's forces in the Revolutionary War.

Even with a fourth-place club, the Highlanders made inroads into the popularity of the Giants who finished second in 1903, but the next season Griffith solidly established the American League in New York. With Jack Chesbro throwing his new-found spitball and winning fourteen straight games with it, the Highlanders met Boston in a double-header on the last day of the season. If they could take both games, they would beat the Red Sox and win the pennant.

Griffith gave Jack Chesbro the opening-game job. There couldn't be much quarrel with that choice. Chesbro had won forty-one games for Griffith that season, losing only eleven. The Highlanders and Red Sox moved into the ninth inning tied at 2 to 2, with Lou Criger on third base for Boston, Freddy Parent at bat, and two out.

Chesbro had two strikes and one ball on Parent, and then came a wild pitch! It was a spitter that didn't break. Catcher Kleinow never got his mitt on the neck-high pitch that never broke down. Criger scored from third, and the pitch had cost the Highlanders a pennant.

Griffith had four first-division Highlander teams in six years at New York, but he wearied of the Highlanders and vice versa. The club, by then called the Yankees, was in last place on June 24, 1908. They had taken the worst nose dive of any New York club in history, losing all their games on a western swing. There was friction between Griffith and the owners, and following a game in Philadelphia in which he was banished by the umpires, Griffith resigned as manager. His resignation was speedily and gratefully accepted.

Garry Hermann, owner of the Cincinnati Reds, was the first to offer Griffith a new job. He finished the rest of the 1908 season as a scout for the Reds, but was intrigued by reports that Joe Cantillon would retire as manager in Washington. He asked his old friend, Ban Johnson, to get him the

78

Washington management if Cantillon resigned, but Johnson told him the reports were unfounded.

For the next three years, Griffith was at Cincinnati as a National League manager, and unhappy at working in the league he had fought so stubbornly in the infant years of the American. But Hermann was a generous boss, and payed him a 7,500-dollar salary in contrast to the 5,000 dollars he had drawn as manager of the Yankees. He finished fourth with the Reds in 1909, fifth in 1910, and sixth in 1911, at which point sports editor Jack Ryder of the Cincinnati *Enquirer* politely suggested a new manager. Then the Washington job opened up for Griffith.

Chapter VI

THE talent Jimmy McAleer had bequeathed to Griffith was little to arouse enthusiasm. Washington was known as the dumping ground for worn-out ball players, and after surveying the roster of the team that had finished seventh in the last two years and eighth the year before that, Griffith proposed a new deal. Club President Noyes was sympathetic. When Griffith said "I want a young team," Noyes said simply, "Go ahead." Immediately Griffith startled Washingtonians by trading veteran catcher Gabby Street to the Yankees for a young second baseman named Jack Knight. Even Noyes questioned that deal. "Who'll catch Walter Johnson?" he asked Griffith. Griffith told Noyes he thought both of his rookie catchers, Eddie Ainsmith and John Henry, were capable of catching Johnson. "If not I'll handle him myself," he added. Noyes was convinced at least of the hardiness of his new manager.

Griffith also cut loose infielders Kid Elberfeld and Wid Conroy, two of his cronies of the New York Yankees, who were too old by Griffith's standards. Anyway, he didn't want them around. The club's accent was to be on youth. He made Elberfeld a free agent, and he released Conroy to Rochester, inasmuch as the Senators owed that club a player.

The veteran outfielders Jack Lelivelt and Doc Gessler were next to go. Griffith sold Gessler cheaply to Kansas City, and he gave an outright release to Lelivelt. The venerable pitcher, Dixie Walker, whose two sons Dixie and Harry were to become National League stars, was also given his outright release. In all, he let go ten players.

Griffith was planning to build his 1912 team around three pitchers: the sensational Walter Johnson, Tom Hughes, and Bob Groom. The rest of the team was to include: Eddie Foster, the young third baseman; Ray Morgan, a promising second baseman; George McBride, the veteran shortstop; and four young outfielders, Clyde Milan, Danny Moeller, Howard Shanks, and Clarence Walker.

Before the team went into spring training in 1912, Griffith acquired a pair of home-grown rookie pitchers. At Engel's famous E Street bar, where Griffith often drank a few beers, he was introduced to the strapping son of the portly saloon keeper. "He's a ball player, my boy Choe," said the elder Engel, and Griffith invited the young pitcher to the Washington training camp. Thus did Joe Engel begin a thirty-six-year career with Washington as pitcher, scout, and farm system manager.

Griffith was also eager to re-sign a young Washington pitcher who had quit the club a year before, and set out in search of him. He found Buck Becker tending bar on Eleventh Street and took him south too.

But south wasn't far for the Washington club. They set up headquarters in Charlottesville, Virginia, and the players were quartered in a fraternity house. Griffith was manager, cook, porter, and general factotum. His only aide was trainer Mike Martin who had first joined forces with Griffith in New York in 1903. The Senators might as well have trained in New England. They spent the first two weeks shoveling snow off the ball field.

The 1912 training season was notable for one incident. A full complement of Washington baseball writers accompanied the Senators to Charlottesville, and one enterprising newspaper sent a cartoonist as well as its sports editor to the camp. The cartoonist was a young man then nursing the ambition to draw his way to journalistic fame—Arthur (Bugs) Baer.

Young Baer found himself not only drawing daily cartoons in the training camp, but also writing the stories for his sports editor who was busily engaged on another mission—a bit of research to discover if the Virginia moonshiners could produce their famed "corn likker" as fast as he could drink it.

Young Baer's boss was holding his own, too, in the big test and was no bad bet to win the decision. Faithfully Baer protected the fellow with daily stories as well as cartoons. Apparently Baer did his boss's work well. At the end of the first fortnight, the sports editor received the following congratulatory letter from the managing editor in Washington: "Your stories during the first two weeks in training have been the best to appear in any Washington newspaper. You are to be commended and I have already increased your salary. But tell that damn cartoonist if his work doesn't improve, we're calling him home."

The club Griffith brought back from Charlottesville wasn't much, at least for six weeks it wasn't. The Senators were in eighth place when they moved into Boston for a Decoration Day double-header, and the papers were bluntly calling Griffith a flop. Griffith had envisioned no pennant, but he did believe he had a first-division club. He was heartsick, and there were dark looks from the directors as Griffith passed in their presence. They had no disposition to entrust the new manager with any money to purchase players.

The chief lack of the club was a first baseman. Griffith knew that. Jack Flynn, who was holding down the job, was no big leaguer. What Griffith wanted was a young first baseman at Montreal whom the Old Fox had admired during a previous big-league tryout with Chicago.

He found a friend in Noyes who agreed to invest 12,000 dollars in Griffith's hunch. Griffith personally went to Canada to complete the deal and gave Montreal infielder Jack Knight and outfielder Gus Cunningham and the 12,000 dollars for Chick Gandil.

The effect of Gandil's presence with the Senators was magical. Griffith inserted him in the line-up on the morning of

Decoration Day in Boston, and Washington won a game. In the afternoon Gandil again was on first base and Walter Johnson on the mound. Johnson shut out the Red Sox, 5 to 0. It was the beginning of the most sensational winning streak in American League history to that year. The amazing Senators for the next three weeks were the scourge of the league. Moving to St. Louis, they swept a four-game series with the Browns. In Chicago they took four straight from the White Sox. At Detroit the Tigers were licked in four straight. Moving into Cleveland, Washington swept a series with the Indians.

In every western city Johnson pitched and won. In his four starts he permitted only four runs. Long Tom Hughes checked in with five pitching victories on the tour. Carl Cashion won three, and rookie Joe Engel contributed a 7-to-3 victory over the Tigers.

In 1912, Griffith was rating third baseman Dale Foster even a greater hit-and-run man than was Willie Keeler, the "hit-'em-where-they-ain't" genius, who had played for Griffith with the old New York Highlanders. So effective was Foster that Griffith gave him a blank check to swing whenever runners were on base, and out of it evolved what Griffith called "our run-and-hit play."

Griffith made distinction between the traditional hit-and-run and Foster's run-and-hit. With Foster up, base runners were always running under Griffith's strategy. They knew Foster, with his skill at placing hits, would cover their advance with some kind of a batted ball, and with sensational frequency it was with a clean hit between the infielders. In contrast with the usual hit-and-run, with the batter flashing signs and the base runners acknowledging them, Foster's run-and-hit technique involved no signs. It was always presumed the man on base would run with Foster up. The play was definite unless Foster himself cancelled it by a sign.

It was a sixteen-game winning streak that the Senators boasted when manager Griffith chaperoned his team back to Washington for a game with the Athletics on June 18. Washington fans were wildly acclaiming the new manager and his miracle club that had gone west in eighth place and returned as a second-place pennant contender. Thousands greeted the squad at Union Station, and Pennsylvania Avenue was a bedlam as the Senators were serenaded all the way to the ball park. President William Howard Taft was out to see the town's heroes win their seventeenth straight. They did.

But the next day, in Philadelphia, the streak was ended. In a double-header against the Athletics, the Washington winning streak suffered a compound fracture. The Senators lost both games.

The snapping of the Senators seventeen-game streak was heartbreaking. Tom Hughes had Philadelphia beaten 1 to 0, in the Senators bid for eighteen straight, and two were out in the ninth with nobody on. There were two strikes on Frank (Home Run) Baker. Baker fouled the next pitch, and catcher John Henry muffed it. Baker hit the next for a home run that tied it up, and two innings later the A's won the ball game on a Texas League single by Eddie Collins.

But the 1912 Senators stayed in the first division. From May 30 until the finish they were up in the race, usually in second place. Johnson, Groom, and Hughes were work horses on the mound. Clyde Milan was topping Ty Cobb's base record with eighty-eight stolen bases. Young Gandil was a sensation at first base with his fielding as well as his hitting. Young Eddie Foster was established as a dangerous hit-and-run man as well as a defensive star at third base. But it was the Big Train, Walter Johnson, who was the Senators' greatest guarantee of winning a ball game. Thirty-two victories he notched that season, with only twelve defeats. He set a new major-league record of sixteen pitching wins in a row. He led the league in strike-outs and in complete games pitched. "You can't hit what you can't see," was the lament of the batters.

On that July 3 afternoon when Johnson started against the Yankees and was lifted by Griffith at the end of six innings because he had a 10-to-1 lead after allowing only five hits, it was scarcely suspected that he was starting the longest winning streak by a pitcher in major-league history.

Two days later he was facing the Yankees again and winning the second game in his streak. Actually, he was called in to do a relief pitching job after young Joe Engel with his wildness had allowed five runs in three and one-third innings. Johnson took over a 5-to-2 deficit at that point, and for twelve and one-third innings he pitched shutout ball and allowed the Yankees only four hits. Singles by Ray Morgan, Danny Moeller, and Eddie Foster, got him the winning run in the sixteenth inning.

From that point, Johnson settled down to seven-hit quotas for his victims in each of his next four victorious starts.

In making it sixteen straight and his third over the Tigers during his streak, Johnson turned in an 8-to-1 victory over the Tigers on August 23. Those sixteen in a row spanned only fifty-one days' toil for Johnson, with scarcely more than two days rest between assignments. His streak ended on August 23 in St. Louis, his jinx town, where he later was to end a record streak of fifty-six consecutive scoreless innings. Under the modern rules, Johnson would not have been charged with the defeat that finally brought his sixteen straight to an end.

He went in to relieve Tom Hughes in the seventh inning of that game with the Browns, with the score tied at 2 to 2, one out, and men on first and second. He fanned Burt Shotton, but a wild pitch moved the runners up a base. With two strikes against him, Compton reached Johnson for a bounding single through short that scored both runs, and the Browns won the game, 4 to 2.

League president Ban Johnson himself made the ruling that Johnson was the losing pitcher when official scorers were in doubt. The Senators cited an opinion by president John Heydler of the National League to the effect that in his league the defeat would not be charged to Johnson but to the pitcher who put the runners on base. Ban Johnson, however, was adamant, although years later he countenanced a rule that would have reversed him.

At one point the Senators narrowed the margin of the pennant-winning Red Sox to four games, but never were they able to catch up. In the final week of the season they found themselves battling with the Athletics to save second place. In two epic battles, Johnson's pitching prevailed.

The Senators started Tom Hughes against Jack Coombs

of the A's in the first game, and with the score tied at 3 to 3 in the seventh, Griffith rushed Johnson into the fray. It was still 3 to 3 in the seventeenth when catcher Eddie Ainsmith broke his finger, and the Senators were forced to send in a third-string backstop, Rippy Williams, as Johnson's battery-mate.

Umpire Billy Evans tells the rest of the story:

Johnson was still throwing cannon balls in the seventeenth. Williams was having a horrible time boxing his pitches. One Johnson fast ball got away from him and nicked me on the ear. I didn't like it. The next thing I did was to announce "Game called on account of darkness!" There was still some sunlight but my life was worth more than a couple of more innings.

After those ten scoreless innings of the relief shift, Johnson was back at the A's the next day. Again it was as relief pitcher. He started in the seventh against Eddie Plank, pitched twelve shutout innings of relief, and won his game, 5 to 4, in the nineteenth to clinch second place for the Senators.

For the first time in American League history, Washington had finished better than sixth place. The club showed a 96,000-dollar profit for the season. The directors had only one complaint. Griffith had used eighty-nine dozen balls during the season at a cost of 1,400 dollars.

The club officers, in gratitude to Griffith, elected him to the board of directors at the end of the season. The 1912 gate receipts had totaled 308,000 dollars against 1911 receipts of 197,000 dollars, and now the directors, because of the improvement, made the magnanimous gesture, according to the secretary's report of the annual meeting which read: "Upon motion made and passed, the board resolved to give each stockholder the privilege of buying two reserved seats to the next opening game if bought before March 28, at 10 a.m."

President Noyes didn't live to see a Washington American League club finish in the first division, however. After eight years as club president, he died following a four-day illness on August 21, 1912, at the age of forty-four. President William

Howard Taft, Washington officialdom, and the presidents of the two major leagues attended the rites.

Ben F. Minor, the club's attorney and long time friend of Griffith, was elected president of the Senators.

Griffith called his 1912-13 teams "my little ball club." It was indeed an undersized collection of athletes, particularly in the infield, composed of Chick Gandil, Ray Morgan, George McBride, and Eddie Foster. There wasn't a power hitter on the team.

Early in 1913, the Senators began to prove that their second-place finish of the season before was no accident. They were a potent factor in the 1913 pennant race all season and finished second again, this time to the Athletics. Connie Mack of the Athletics was operating that year perhaps the best pitching staff known to the game. Eddie Plank, Chief Bender, and Jack Coombs were taking regular turns, and a couple of rookies named Herb Pennock and Bullet Joe Bush were beginning to show form. Griffith's "little club" was also trying to beat a team that boasted the famed "$100,000 infield" of Stuffy McInnis, Eddie Collins, Jack Barry, and Home Run Baker.

But Griffith wasn't conceding the pennant, even to Connie Mack's collection of super-stars. With one more slugging out-fielder he thought the Senators still might win. Where to get him?

Griffith tried. In one bold stroke he offered to buy Ty Cobb from the Detroit Tigers for 100,000 dollars.

It was no publicity stunt. Griffith was in earnest. To Frank Navin, owner of the Tigers, he tendered his personal check for 100,000 dollars as evidence of good faith. Navin said he would consider the deal, after expressing surprise that Griffith could produce 100,000 dollars.

The fact was that Griffith couldn't. "You'll have to give me a little time to work on that check, Frank, "he told Navin, "but I'll make it good if it buys Cobb. Say two weeks."

The offer for Cobb at the unheard-of price of 100,000 dollars by the supposedly poor Washington club was front-page news. And nine separate and distinct shocks were dealt the

86

nine directors of the Washington team as they pored over their morning newspapers and discovered, with a gasp, that Griffith was attempting to spend 100,000 dollars of their money.

Griffith, in Detroit at the time, soon learned what a hornet's nest he had stirred up in Washington. Nine telegrams from the nine directors of the team scorched the wires. They inquired if Griffith was crazy. Where was he going to get the 100,000 dollars? Who authorized him to spend it?

But Griffith had a plan, and he went back to Washington to explain it. If the Tigers would sell him Cobb, he would raise the money without assault on the club's treasury. He would place on sale 100,000 tickets at one dollar entitling the purchasers to attend any Washington game. Griffith was confident Washington fans would subscribe the cash to enable him to buy Cobb. Skeptical directors were still shaking their heads when Navin eased the situation by returning Griffith's check and calling off the deal.

Those 1913 Senators who couldn't beat the Athletics did slap down unmercifully the Cleveland club that was challenging them for second place, and the Washington club clinched the position by a three-game margin over the Indians. They beat Cleveland in fifteen of the twenty-two games between the two clubs to finish with a record of ninety wins and sixty-four defeats, six and one-half games behind the pennant-winning A's.

Walter Johnson was superb. He had three winning streaks of ten, eleven, and fourteen games. Joe Boehling, a freshman pitcher originally bought from Richmond and brought up later from Chattanooga, won eleven in a row above one span. Milan and Moeller were first and second in stolen bases with seventy-four and sixty-four, in a year when Cobb was fourth with forty-two. Gandil led the club in hitting with .318.

It was the first season in which the league scorers recorded earned-run averages, and the Johnson figures were startling. In winning thirty-six games, including twelve shutouts, and losing only seven, he held the opposition to an average of 1.14 earned runs per game. He pitched five one-hitters.

From April 10 to May 16, big Walter achieved a pitching record that has easily withstood all challenge. During that span he was unscored on in eight starting and relief appearances and amassed a record of fifty-six consecutive shutout innings.

His streak started with eight innings of scoreless pitching against the Yankees whom he held to seven hits and beat, 2 to 1, after they scored on him in the opening inning. His next start was a 3 to 0 shutout against the Yanks in which he allowed four hits. Four days later he blanked Boston, 6 to 0, with two hits. Two days later he pitched a scoreless one-inning relief shift against the Red Sox. On April 30 he blanked the Athletics, 2 to 0, on four hits. His next was a scoreless two and two-thirds inning relief appearance against Boston, and two days later he worked five scoreless innings against the Red Sox. In a complete game at Chicago he shut out the White Sox, 1 to 0, on two hits and needed only one more scoreless inning to surpass Jack Combs' record of fifty-three.

Johnson broke the record by striking out six of the first nine Browns he faced, using only his fast ball. With one out in the fourth, his streak ended at fifty-six innings when Gus Williams doubled and Derrill Pratt singled to get a St. Louis run home.

The gathering clouds of the First World War, and later its outbreak, had a sobering effect on the nation's capital in 1914, and the Senators suffered at the box office. Griffith had his "little ball club" in the first division throughout the season, and on June 6 and 7 it led the league, only to finish in third place behind the Athletics and Red Sox. Walter Johnson went into something of a slump, winning "only" twenty-eight games and losing eighteen, although he scored ten shutouts and had an earned-run average of 1.71.

But the club didn't boast a .300 hitter. Milan was tops with .295, and Gandil slumped to .259. Milan was lost to the club for thirty days after he and Moeller collided on a fly ball in Cleveland with Milan getting a broken jaw as a souvenir.

And then, just before the turn of the new year, the nation's capital was shocked. It was not by any mere development in the war. From Coffeyville, Kansas, came the flash that Walter Johnson had jumped to the Chicago North Side Club of the new Federal League after negotiations with Joe Tinker, league representative. Tinker's offer of a 16,000-dollar salary for Johnson plus a 10,000-dollar bonus for signing was accepted by him, Johnson confirmed.

Thus Griffith, the old player pirate whose ruthless raids on the National League had set the American up in business, now was confronted with the same tactics by a new league. He acted quickly and demanded that the Washington club meet the Federal League's offer to Johnson, and even offer more if necessary.

Griffith had warned president Minor long before that the Federals were angling for Johnson. "Johnson had a bad season this year," Minor commented. "He only won twenty-eight games. That doesn't warrant the 12,000 dollars we're now paying him. I'm going to write him a letter to that effect."

Griffith pleaded with Minor not to dispatch that type of letter to Johnson. He predicted correctly that Johnson would get furious and sign with the Federals.

Griffith, determined to regain his star pitcher, acted without further contact with president Minor. He wrote a letter to Fred Clarke, former Pittsburgh star and old friend of his National League days, who lived at Independence, Kansas, not far from Johnson's home, asking Clarke to make an appointment for him with Johnson. The appointment was made.

Johnson, though friendly with Griffith, was still furious with the Washington club, and refused to reconsider his jump to the Federals. Mrs. Johnson was with him. Griffith knew she preferred to live in Washington. In the midst of his talk with Johnson, Griffith asked Mrs. Johnson to "take a walk for an hour while we thresh this out." She did, and on her return Johnson was still unsigned by Griffith. She agreed to "take another walk." Griffith had her husband's signature on a new Washington contract before she returned the second time.

89

Johnson accepted the new offer of a 16,000-dollar salary from Washington, plus a 10,000-dollar bonus from the club for signing, the same terms the Federal League had offered.

But Griffith had exceeded his authority. He hoped he might persuade the Washington club directors to pay the 16,000-dollar salary he had given Johnson. But they would never agree to the 10,000-dollar bonus. Where would the 10,000 dollars come from?

Griffith thought he knew. Telephoning the American League headquarters at Chicago, Griffith inquired for League president Ban Johnson. He learned that Johnson was taking the baths at West Baden, Indiana, with Charles Comiskey, owner of the White Sox.

"I need $10,000 to retake Walter Johnson from the Federal League," Griffith phoned Johnson.

"What do you want me to do about it?" asked Johnson.

"I want you to give it to me from the league funds," said Griffith.

"It can't be done," declared Johnson.

Then Griffith pointed out that the American League boasted of a 450,000-dollar reserve fund which had always been used for such emergencies. "You've always called it our 'fighting fund,' and we've got a fight on our hands with the Feds," said Griffith hotly. "In the old days that's how we saved our league," he reminded Ban.

But Johnson was adamant. The Washington club would have to fight its own battles, he declared. The league wouldn't help.

"Let me talk to Comiskey then," Griffith shouted.

Getting Comiskey on the phone, Griffith said: "I want 10,000 dollars from you."

"For what?"

"To pry Walter Johnson away from the Federal League."

"That's your problem, not mine," said Comiskey, laughing.

"Oh no, it isn't, it's your problem, too," said Griffith.

"How do you figure that?"

"Well, you just bought Eddie Collins from the Athletics for 75,000 dollars, didn't you, Commy?"

"Yes."

"And the Federal League is giving you some competition over there on the North Side, isn't it Commy?"

"Yes."

"Well, then, how would you like to see Walter Johnson playing for the Chicago Feds on the North Side next season and drawing all those fans away from the White Sox park?"

"Holy Smokes!" ejaculated Comiskey, "how much did you say Johnson wants to stay in the American League?"

"Ten thousand from you will do it."

Griffith got Comiskey's check for the 10,000 dollars before the week was out, and turned the money over to Johnson, who promptly paid a 10,000-dollar debt of his brother Earl who had just been swindled by a worthless partner in a new garage business.

Griffith was handed a new managerial contract before the 1915 season opened, calling for 10,000 dollars a year for the next three years. It was an increase on the 7,500 dollars he had been drawing, but even the sensational success of his Washington clubs of the past three years didn't enable him to write his own ticket. He asked for a five-year contract at 10,000 dollars a year and was forced to accept one for a three-year term.

He wasn't satisfied with his outfield for 1915. Milan was his only solid outfield performer. Howard Shanks and Danny Moeller were an unexciting pair. Chick Gandil, at first base, was breaking training with great regularity, and Griffith was eager to replace him too.

In July, Griffith went to Buffalo to scout an outfielder named Charles Jamieson, who was for sale for 7,500 dollars. He was impressed with Jamieson, but he was even more impressed with a little first baseman who was clever around the bag and hit the ball sharply during the two days Griffith was at Buffalo. With his horse-trading technique, David Harum Griffith expressed little interest in Jamieson, but he told the Buffalo owner, "I might give you 5,000 dollars for him." He was laughed off and took a new tack.

"Throw in that young first baseman, and I'll give you 8,000 dollars for the pair of 'em," he said. That's the deal that was made, and that is how the Senators came up with Joe Judge, their regular first baseman for the next fifteen years.

The Senators came up with another rookie that season who was to have an even longer and more glittering career with the club. Griffith's habit of cultivating the friendship of small club owners paid off handsomely in this case. In the Spring of 1915, he had loaned the owner of the Portsmouth, Virginia, League club, 600 dollars "to help meet the payroll."

In July, the Portsmouth owner tipped off Griffith that the Virginia League was in financial difficulties and "soon will fold." He was sorry, he said, that he had been unable to repay the 600-dollar loan, "but I've got a pretty good pitcher down here who you ought to take as payment before the league collapses."

The Senators thus gained title to Sam Rice in payment of a bad debt. He came to them as a pitcher and stayed to star in the outfield.

The Senators were never in the 1915 pennant race though they finished fourth behind Boston, Detroit, and Chicago. Walter Johnson won twenty-seven and lost thirteen and had a typically good Johnson year, high-lighted by the day at Detroit when the Tigers knocked Bert Gallia from the box, and Johnson was sent to the mound. Manager Hughey Jennings put in three pinch hitters in a row and Johnson struck them all out—Bush, Kavanagh, and Vitt.

The Washington club on July 19 did write one record into the books, however. In Detroit, the Senators stole eight bases in the first inning, to the utter discomfiture of catcher Steve O'Neill, and heightened their reputation as a base-running club. The quartet of Danny Moeller, Eddie Ainsmith, Clyde Milan, and George McBride, achieved the eight steals in a single inning.

Moeller stole everything but first base. In succession, he stole second, third, and home. Milan stole second and third for the fourth and fifth thefts of the inning, and Ainsmith, a fast man despite being a catcher, later stole second, went

92

to third on an error, and stole home in a double steal with McBride before the inning ended.

John Henry was sharing much of the Senators' catching by this time. Ainsmith caught only Johnson, as a rule, because he claimed his catching hand was so beaten up by that chore he needed as much rest as the pitcher.

One of the Senators' defeats was a wicked 1-to-0 beating charged against Walter Johnson in New York when the winning run was scored on an outfield hit that rolled between Milan's legs. Johnson, however, was inured to that kind of heartbreak. His only comment in the dressing room was, "Goodness gracious, Clyde doesn't do that very often."

It was the season, too, when Johnson made a beanball pitch. He leveled a fast ball, head high, at Frank Baker, and Baker went into the dirt. Baker had been riding him, and Johnson was urged by trainer Mike Martin to "dust him off, or I'll think you have no guts." Johnson went pale after throwing the pitch and confessed, "I wished I had it back the instant it left my hand." He confided to roommate Milan that he was afraid he would one day kill someone.

Young Joe Judge had completely usurped Chick Gandil's first base job by the end of 1915, and before the start of the next season, the Senators sold Gandil to Cleveland. They also traded pitcher Joe Boehling and outfielder Danny Moeller to the Indians for shortstop Joe Leonard and outfielder Elmer Smith.

There were other new faces in 1916. Pitcher Joe Engel, released to Minneapolis, tipped the Senators off to a husky young catcher named Pat Gharity. Also bought was outfielder Mike Menosky. But the Senators, after leading the league in mid-May, took a fearful slump and finished seventh.

Johnson won twenty-five games, and he was charged with twenty-one defeats. There wasn't a .300 hitter on the club. The caliber of the Senators was apparent from the fact that Johnson could lose twenty-one games in a year when he had an earned-run average of 1.89 per game. He was nosed out for earned-run honors that year by a rising young pitcher with the Red Sox named Babe Ruth who had a 1.75 average.

It was the year Sam Rice quit the pitching ranks and

turned outfielder. Eddie Foster long had noted Rice's ability with the bat and admired his stylish flat swing. He repeatedly urged him to give up pitching and turn to the outfield. But Griffith was shorthanded for pitchers, and his lone concession was to use Rice as a pinch hitter. In fact, Walter Johnson and Rice, two pitchers, were the top pinch hitters on the club.

Rice's conversion followed a game he was pitching at Detroit against George Dauss. When Dauss, who couldn't bat his way out of a cellophane wrapper, banged one of Rice's pitches against the center field flagpole, Rice walked to the bench and announced: "I quit. If that guy can make a two-bagger off me, I'm no pitcher. Gimme an outfielder's glove." He demanded a knife from trainer Mike Martin and forthwith cut the toeplate off his pitching shoe.

In 1917, wartime Washington was an apathetic baseball town, and the Senators, after playing to the smallest opening-day crowd of their American League history, presented the stockholders with fifth place and a 43,000-dollar deficit on the year's operation. In fact, the team was held in such low esteem as a credit risk that the nine directors were borrowing operating funds from the National Metropolitan Bank. Only by the method of underwriting the loans with their nine personal notes was the cash made available.

The Senators were far out of the race in mid-May, and at the end of June were in seventh place with twenty-five wins and thirty-seven losses. Twenty-one of their thirty-seven defeats were by one-run margins, attesting the club's weakness at bat. Sam Rice, the reformed outfielder, was the only .300 hitter, and he had a mark of .302. The veteran George McBride slowed to the point where Howard Shanks became the regular shortstop. Joe Judge broke his leg sliding at Detroit in July, and catcher Pat Gharity was drafted to play first base. Mike Menosky was a regular in the outfield along with Milan and Rice. An outfielder named Burt Shotton was bought from the Browns along with shortstop Doc Levan for pitcher Bert Gallia and 13,000 dollars. Walter Johnson managed to win twenty-three games while losing sixteen, despite the handicap of his supporting cast. Eight of his victories were shutouts. Clark Griffith was trying to buy the controlling interest in the club despite the dark days at the gate, and had the backing of John Wilkins, prosperous Washington coffee company owner, until the war clouds gathered more thickly.

It was the year when the Senators achieved a special, if somewhat dubious distinction. They were the victims of the only tandem-pitched, no-hit game in major-league history. On the afternoon of June 23 in Boston, a pitcher named Babe Ruth walked the first man to face him and was chased out of the game, only to become party to a no-hitter.

Ruth walked second baseman Ray Morgan, the Senators' lead-off man in the first inning, and when umpire Brick Owen called the fourth ball, the Babe advanced to the plate in a rage.

"Get back to the mound, or you're out of the ball game," yelled Owen.

"If you chase me, I'll punch your face," shouted Ruth.

"You're out now," said the unintimidated Owen, whereupon Ruth swung a left to the umpire's head. Teammates halted further fisticuffs and rushed Ruth off the field.

The Red Sox called on Ernie Shore to finish the game, and as relief performances go, it must be considered the best in baseball history. Morgan, the man Ruth had walked, was thrown out stealing by catcher Sam Agnew, and not another Senator reached base for the rest of the day against Shore. Sixteen thousand Saturday fans saw outfielder Duffy Lewis save Shore's no-hitter in the ninth with a shoestring catch of John Henry's liner. It went officially into the record books as a no-hitter for Shore after a bit of deliberation by League president Ban Johnson.

Despite president Johnson's later reputation for cracking down on umpire sluggers, Ruth drew only a 100-dollar fine and ten days suspension for his action.

Shore's mastery over the Senators was of short duration, however. Three days later he went back to the mound against Washington and on the second pitch was tagged for a triple to the center field fence by lead-off man Joe Judge. They raked him for thirteen hits and beat him 7 to 6.

Baseball in the big leagues was quaking at the threat of collapse in 1918 with the nation now geared for war, but Griffith was hopeful that the leagues could play out the season. At his suggestion, the American League clubs requested that the Army assign drill sergeants to the baseball squads in spring training, and before each game the teams drilled in military fashion with bats across their shoulders instead of guns.

The blow that threatened to kill off baseball in 1918, fell in July. Secretary of War Newton D. Baker, in his famous "Work or Fight" order, designated baseball as a non-essential industry, and the owners were panicked.

Ban Johnson conferred with General Enoch Crowder, head of selective service, in an attempt to gain deferment for ball players, and was met with a stern no. Then Griffith telephoned Johnson that he would talk to "my personal friend, Secertary of War Baker." Griffith walked into Baker's office unannounced, and was well received. He pointed out to the Secretary of War that the leagues were already drilling their eligible players in war games and that physically they were ready for any call. He asked a deferment for the players until Labor Day and won it on agreement that the leagues close on that date, with a fifteen-day allowance for World Series play.

In appreciation of Baker's concession, Griffith immediately launched a fund-raising campaign to provide baseball equipment for the Army in France. By public subscription he raised more than 100,000 dollars, and the audit of the "Clark Griffith Ball and Bat Fund" still remains in the Congressional Library. Unhappily, however, the first shipload of equipment was torpedoed and sunk in the Atlantic.

The Senators lost Sam Rice, Mike Menosky, Doc Lavan, and catcher Val Picinich to the Army before the season closed, but Griffith did get a bit of service out of Rice. With the Senators playing in Boston, Rice slipped out of his army uniform at Fort Terry, Connecticut, after getting a two-day pass and was in the Senators' line-up for two games against the champion Red Sox.

As usual, Walter Johnson was the mainstay of the pitching

staff, and in 1918, for the ninth consecutive season, he won more than twenty games. He notched twenty-three victories—including five one-hit shutouts—and lost thirteen, topped the league with an earned-run average of 1.28 per game, and all but pitched the Senators into second place. They finished third behind the Red Sox and Cleveland, but only a half game in the wake of the Indians. Burt Shotton's muff of a pop fly in center field cost Johnson what might have been a decisive victory over Cleveland late in the season.

Frank Schulte, an old-timer from the Cubs, was in the club's outfield along with Milan and Shotton, and Jim Shaw did well with the pitching, winning sixteen. Harry Harper and Doc Ayers rounded out the pitching staff, although Nick Altrock also might be properly mentioned.

Altrock, then forty, and relegated chiefly to clowning and coaching by that time, did make one start on the mound for the Senators. Strapped for pitchers one day in Detroit, Griffith asked the ancient southpaw if he could take a turn on the mound, and Altrock grabbed the invitation.

He beat the Tigers that day, going the full route, and at the end of his afternoon's labors repaired to his favorite Detroit saloon to drink a dozen beers or so, as was his habit. Suffused with the beer and his triumph of the day, he sought to talk with the only other customer at the bar. Fishing for a compliment, Nick pointed to the score by innings posted behind the bar and said, preparatory to taking a bow, "I see where Altrock beat the Tigers today, with six hits."

It produced an effect, if not the desired one. His new companion squinted at the score by innings to confirm Nick's statement, and stared hard before saying: "Altrock? Jeepers, I never knew that old guzzler had a son pitching in the big leagues."

The stockholders of the Washington ball club lost some of their affection for Griffith by the end of 1919 after a third straight losing season. It was mutual. Griffith's club, never better than sixth in the last four months of the season, finished seventh. When he demanded a spending program to bolster the team for 1920 he was all but shown the door. So he bought the team, at least enough of it to move in as president. Actually, Griffith had more faith in Washington as a baseball town than he had cash in the bank when he made his purchase. His old friend, Connie Mack, knew of Griffith's long-time desire to buy control of the Senators, and steered him toward a backer.

Mack introduced Griffith to William Richardson, wealthy Philadelphia grain exporter and member of the Philadelphia Stock Exchange. Richardson also was a partner of Tom Shibe in the exporting business. Shibe was chief stockholder in the Athletics.

"Come back and see me after you've rounded up enough stock to give us a controlling interest," said Richardson, and Griffith hustled back to Washington.

At the 15 dollars a share he offered willing stockholders, Griffith discovered that he and Richardson could control 17,000 of the 20,000 shares in equal parts. Already Griffith owned 2,700 shares. Now where could get the 87,000 dollars he needed to swing his part of the deal with Richardson?

He walked into the office of president White of Washington's Metropolitan National Bank and put his case bluntly. Years before, when the other directors of the Senators had discontinued their accounts at the bank, angry at the failure to get a loan, Griffith had continued to bank at the Metropolitan National.

"Do you have confidence in me as a baseball man?" he asked the banker. White said he had long been an admirer of Griffith. "Thank you for that," said Griffith, "and now I'd like you to loan me 87,000 dollars to buy enough stock to make me president of the team." He got the loan within an hour.

From Richardson he got also the right to vote their combined shares at the stockholders' meetings and a pledge of noninterference in routine affairs of the club.

Griffith's first act as president of the Washington club was to place the business management of the club in the hands of a man of his own choosing—Edward B. Eynon, Jr. It was no sudden decision. He was impressed with Eynon's organizing and business ability as head of the Liberty Loan drives in Washington in 1917, and long had visualized Eynon as his business manager if he ever headed the club as president.

That 1919 season had been a rough one for Griffith. Walter Johnson went into something of a slump, winning only twenty games and losing fourteen. Jim Shaw won sixteen, but Harry Harper led the league in defeats, losing twenty-one and winning only six games. Sam Rice was the only player who batted over .300. Eddie Foster was slowing up at third base, and both McBride and Milan had left the team. Joe Leonard, the good-looking shortstop Griffith had bought from Cleveland, died in midseason of a burst appendix in New York.

Griffith was cheated on a deal that otherwise would have solved his third base troubles for a decade. He gave the Norfolk, Virginia, club three players for the opportunity to pick a player off that team on payment of 5,000 dollars, and his selection was a young third baseman named Pie Traynor. But the Norfolk club, with other offers for Traynor, now hiked the price to 10,000 dollars despite its pledge, and Griffith in righteous anger refused to do business on that basis.

It was the year when Sam Agnew joined the club under some apprehension. A month before, at Boston, Agnew was catching for the Red Sox and, irked by Griffith's riding from the coaching lines, walked to first base and slugged Griffith, whereupon Catcher Pat Gharity of the Senators flattened Agnew with one punch.

The incident didn't deter Griffith, though, when he had an opportunity to buy Agnew four weeks later. Agnew joined the club in Washington but gave Griffith a wide berth. He wasn't at ease until Griffith yelled to Agnew from a clubhouse window, "Hey, don't you shake hands when you join a new club?"

But balancing Griffith's ill-luck in missing out on Pie Traynor in the fall of 1919, was his stroke of fortune in another direction—Buffalo. He sent Joe Engel to that city to scout a young second baseman he had seen perform with a Baltimore shipyard team in 1918, and bought Bucky Harris for 2,000 dollars.

The Senators had a hitting ball club in 1920, but no pitching worthy of it. In a year when Walter Johnson, with batting

99

support, might have gone on to endless victories, he came up with a sore arm following eighteen days of sleeper jumps from the South, and had his worst season in the majors, winning only eight and losing ten. Southpaw Tom Zachary was the top pitcher with a record of sixteen to fifteen. Eric Erickson and Harry Courtney, when they could get the ball over the plate, managed twenty victories between them but lost a total of twenty-seven.

However, Griffith's club was showing signs of hitting power. Sam Rice, as usual, was top man with a lofty .338 average, Joe Judge hit .333, and outfielder Frank Brower hit .311. The young second baseman, Harris, broke in as a .300 hitter in his first full season, and the club led the league with 161 stolen bases.

At the finish they were a sixth-place ball club, though never better than fourth after May 1, and Griffith was wearying of his double duties as president and bench manager.

The paradox of the 1920 season was that the sore-armed Walter Johnson delivered the only no-hit game of his career, in a year when he won only eight games. July 1 was the date, Boston the locale, and the Red Sox the victims.

Johnson arrived in Boston scarcely an hour before the game. He was detained in Washington by the illness of five-year-old son Walter, Jr., and he took the mound on his son's birthday. Thirteen years after he introduced the fastest pitch in history to the American League, he fanned ten Red Sox, permitted only five of his pitches to be hit out of the infield, and beat the Red Sox, 1 to 0, with his no-hitter.

Only one man reached base against Johnson that day else he would have matched the perfect no-hit, no-run, no-reach-first performances of Cy Young in 1904 and Addie Joss in 1908. Bucky Harris was the culprit. The rookie second baseman muffed a soft grounder by Harry Hooper with two out in the seventh inning. But Harris atoned in a measure for that lapse. It was his single, one of the seven hits allowed by Boston's Harry Harper, that drove in the winning run for Johnson.

The Red Sox went all out to spoil Johnson's no-hitter. They sent in pinch hitters Karr and Eibel in the ninth, and

Johnson struck them both out. Now' he had to dispose only of Harry Hooper again. And then came a perilous moment. The dangerous Hooper slashed a fierce drive down the first base line. Joe Judge with a desperate mitt-hand grab came up with the ball, but was in no position to get to the bag. Johnson himself took care of that situation by racing to the bag for a bare-hand catch of Judge's throw, and saved his no-hitter. Judge went into a happy war dance. Hooper generously raced back to pump Johnson's hand in congratulation.

It was the year also, when Al Schacht, a New York kid out of minor-league ranks, managed to get on the Senators' pitching staff. In later years Schacht confessed he was the author of the letters sent to Griffith and signed "A. Fan," which extolled the skill of one Al Schacht and prompted Griffith to give him a tryout.

In the wake of Johnson's no-hitter at Boston, Griffith advertised the Big Train as the pitcher in the afternoon game of a July 5 double-header, and 18,821 whooping fans were in American League Park to greet Johnson's appearance against the Yankees. Before 7,490 fans in a morning game, Tom Zachary had beaten the Yanks, 4 to 3, and the city's fans were in gay holiday mood.

But unknown to the fans, Johnson wasn't even in the stadium that afternoon. In the morning he had telephoned Griffith that his sore arm had recurred after his Boston no-hitter, adding he could scarcely raise it to comb his hair. Griffith was panicked. He knew he would be accused of false advertising. He called a meeting of his pitching staff, explained his plight, and asked for a volunteer. Young Schacht, first to apply, got the job.

When announcer E. Lawrence Phillips boomed through his megaphone "Batteries for Washington: Schacht and Gharity!" the howls went up from the disappointed fans who had come to see Johnson. Cushions were thrown on the playing field. Griffith was called names, and Schacht was hooted at every step as he strode to the pitching mound.

In typical storybook style, Schacht won. He didn't allow the Yankees any kind of a hit until Babe Ruth singled in the fourth, and at the finish he had a seven-hitter, a 9-to-3 victory, and a nice contract from Griffith for the next season.

Thirty-four years in a baseball uniform, first as rookie pitcher, then as major-league star, manager, and president-manager of ball clubs, came to an end for Griffith in 1921. Bogged down by administrative work, player deals, and scouting trips, he turned over the management of the Senators to his veteran shortstop, George McBride.

McBride had been field captain of the Senators for six years, and when Griffith was off on scouting trips, he often had leaned on him to direct the club. Before he left, he used to tell the Senators, "McBride's the boss when I'm away, and I want you to know it. If he fines anybody, bear in mind I'll double it when I get back."

The Senators were a fourth-place ball club in 1921, losing third place to the Browns by only a half game, and Griffith was showing a profit in his operation. But the year was chiefly notable for two rookies who were acquired by Griffith. The club's weakness was a lack of left-handed hitting power, and Griffith was interested when the Columbia Club of the Sally League offered to sell him "a hard-hitting young outfielder who bats left-handed." Griffith dispatched Joe Engel to scout the fellow, but after no communications from Engel for a month, he lost interest.

While the Senators were on a Western tour, Griffith stayed in Baltimore for a week end of bridge and golf at the Suburban Country Club. Playing with a stockholder of the Baltimore Orioles, the talk naturally drifted to baseball. "Jack Dunn's club figures to do better pretty soon," the Baltimorean apologized. "We're dickering for a young outfielder who is going to be a sensation."

Griffith became interested. "Where's Dunn getting the boy?" he asked casually.

"The South Atlantic League," was the answer. "Dunn's paying 5,500 dollars for him."

Griffith wondered instantly if the outfielder were the same one of whom he had heard. If the shrewd Dunn were willing to pay that much for a Class B rookie to join a minor league club, the fellow must be some kind of a wonder. He valued

Dunn as an appraiser of talent, but he didn't pursue the subject until the next day.

Griffith, shrinking at the tactlessness of asking point-blank who Dunn's upcoming wonder might be, casually remarked to his Baltimore friend, "Those Orioles look as if they could win another pennant with more strength in their outfield."

"That's what Dunn thinks," was the answer.

"From what I hear about that Sally League outfielder, he seems to be just the fellow Dunn needs," continued Griffith. "You know the one I mean—that fellow what's-his-name, er-uh—" and Griffith snapped his fingers in disgust at his seeming inability to recall the name.

"You mean Goslin," the Baltimorean volunteered. "Yeah, Dunn likes him!"

That clue was sufficient for Griffith. That night he telephoned the Columbia Club owner, learned that Baltimore had not yet closed the deal, and bought Leon "Goose" Goslin for the Senators for 6,000 dollars.

Later in the year, with the club's infield bogging down, Griffith sent Engel on a hunt for an infielder. Engel's travels took him to Peoria, Illinois, where he liked the action of a young shortstop named Ossie Bluege. The Athletics also had been interested in Bluege, but scout Tom Turner of the A's rejected him for 5,000 dollars when Bluege suffered a knee injury before any deal was completed.

Engel, too, was distrustful of Bluege's knee, but he wasn't ready to give up yet. After a ball game, Engel intercepted Bluege on the way to the clubhouse and put a novel proposition to him. "The Washington club would buy you if we were sure of that knee of yours," said Engel. "Now, listen. You and I are going to race from here to the center field fence. If you can beat me to the fence, I'll buy you. I was on the track team at Mount St. Mary's, don't forget." Bluege won the race, luckily, and the deal was closed that night.

McBride didn't finish out the season as manager of the Senators. In August he was struck in the face by a thrown ball while batting to the infield, and what appeared to be a minor accident developed into a painful and trouble-giving mishap. Griffith retired him and reached in his ranks of veteran players again for a new manager, this time outfielder Clyde Milan, then in his fifteenth year with the club.

George Mogridge replaced Walter Johnson as top man on the pitching staff in 1921, with eighteen wins and fourteen defeats. Johnson won a game fewer and lost as many. Mogridge had come from the Yanks in a swap for infielder Bobby Roth, with Griffith also acquiring the veteran outfielder Duffy Lewis in the deal. Griffith's habit was to get two for one.

The Senators obtained Donie Bush from the Tigers on waivers to fill their infield gap at third base where Howard Shanks was slowing up. Bush alternated at shortstop with Blackie O'Rourke. The Senators had four .300 hitters: Rice .330, Gharity .310, Shanks .302 and Judge .301. But they were scarcely power hitters. In a season when Babe Ruth lifted the home run record to fifty-nine, the combined homers of the Senators' roster totaled only forty-two.

The first month of 1922, though, found Griffith making a big and expensive deal to improve his ball club. He knew his chief need was a capable shortstop, and he knew that Harry Frazee's Boston Red Sox had one in the veteran but still sprightly Roger Peckinpaugh. But how to get Peck?

Frazee wouldn't dare to sell Peckinpaugh to the Washington club outright for cash. Boston's newspapers and fans already were heaping continual abuse on Frazee for selling off Red Sox stars like Hoyt, Pennock, Bush, Schang, Scott, and Ruth to the Yankees for cash. Griffith had no star player to offer the Red Sox for Peckinpaugh. But he engineered a deal.

At Philadelphia, Connie Mack was having his troubles with "Jumping Joe" Dugan, his star third baseman who had a case of homesickness. Dugan had quit the A's a couple of times to return to his Boston home. If Griffith could swing a deal with Connie Mack for Dugan and turn him over to the Red Sox for Peck . . .

That's what he did. He gave the Athletics outfielder Bing Miller, infielder Frank O'Rourke, and pitcher Acosta, plus a check for 50,000 dollars, and came up with Dugan whose transfer to Boston fetched Peck for the Senators.

The 1922 Senators, however, did poorly and finished a la-

104

boring sixth under Clyde Milan. Peckinpaugh was a salary holdout in the spring and was late in reporting, and when he did show up Griffith was discouraged. Peck had a lame back.

In desperation in the South, Milan turned to rookie Ossie Bluege as a possible replacement for Peck at shortstop, and the first time Bluege got into an exhibition game, he clicked off six double plays with Bucky Harris against the Phillies at Leesburg, Florida. But by the start of the season, Peck was back on the job.

By the time the club started North, Goose Goslin was already something of a sensation. The rookie outfielder was stumbling a bit on defense, but at the plate he was whacking the ball like a natural hitter and for long distances. But long before his first payday, Goslin owed the club money. Twice he was fined for breaking training. After one all-night crap game in which the Goose wound up a big winner, he staggered down to breakfast. Milan led him back to his room, locked him in, took the key, and said, "I'll be back to talk to you in an hour." When he returned, all he found in Goslin's room was an open window.

But the Goose batted .324 for the Senators that year and was their only .300 hitter. Sam Rice and Joe Judge both hit .295, and the new second base combination of Peck at short and Harris at second was tremendously effective. They set a new record for double plays in the majors with 168. Bobby LaMotte and the veteran Donie Bush divided the third base job, the club's chief trouble spot.

George Mogridge, the southpaw obtained from the Yankees, replaced Walter Johnson as the top man on the pitching staff with eighteen wins and thirteen defeats. Tom Zachary turned in fifteen victories, and Johnson slumped to a record of fifteen to sixteen, and apparently had passed his peak.

The Big Train was plainly tired, but he was still the club's chief pitching attraction, still beloved by Washington fans. His teammates continued to marvel at the modesty of the man, and Joe Judge related the episode in St. Louis after Johnson had lost a 1-to-0 game.

"Walter was my roommate and we were going to the movies

after dinner at the hotel. I was trying to hustle Walter out of the lobby when some fan intercepted him and started to talk. I stood off until twenty minutes later, when Johnson finally broke away.

"I asked him why he had to stop and talk to every fan who approached him, and he said 'that fellow was from Kansas and said he knew my sister.'

"I told him it was news to me that he had a sister and Walter said 'I don't. But I had to be nice to the man.' "

Griffith wanted more aggressive management in 1923, and dispensed with Milan after a one-year term. The old outfielder quickly was taken by Minneapolis, and Griffith named Donie Bush as his new manager. Bush, even in his fading days as a player and handicapped by blurred vision, had retained the fiery spirit that marked his long career at Detroit.

A deal with the Red Sox during the winter, involving five players, brought the Senators their regular catcher of the next decade. In February they obtained catcher Muddy Ruel as well as Allan Russell, rubber-armed relief pitcher with a spitball. In this swap they sent catcher Val Picinich and infielders Howard Shanks and Eddie Goebel to Boston. In an effort to bolster third base, the Senators traded outfielder Frank Brower to the Indians for the veteran Joe Evans.

On the last day of the season, after being in the second division since April, Bush took the Senators into fourth place when they beat the Browns. Johnson staged something of a comeback winning seventeen while losing twelve, and a huge Texan named Fred Marberry who was bought from Little Rock late in the season was something of a sensation with four victories in a row without a defeat. Allan Russell did well as a relief specialist with ten wins and seven defeats.

Bluege started the year at third base and was beginning to stack up as something of a defensive genius, but he hit only .245. Ruel not only did the bulk of the catching, but lent a .316 average to the club's attack which, as usual, Sam Rice led, this year with .316. Judge hit .314 and Goose Goslin an even .300. Nemo Leibold, acquired from the Red Sox in May, hit .305 as an extra outfielder.

It was Griffith's best hitting club in a half dozen years, and

106

he thought it deserved better than fourth place. With Griffith there never was anything particularly sacred about a manager. He fired Bush and looked for a new man.

Chapter VII

STANLEY RAYMOND (Bucky) HARRIS, the Senators' 27-year-old second baseman, was the most flabbergasted young man in the United States one January morning in 1924. At Tampa, Florida, where he had gone for a month of golf before the start of spring training, he received a letter from Clark Griffith asking if he would take the job as manager of the Washington club.

"I think you can do a good job for us as manager, Bucky," Griffith had written. "If you want the job it is yours. But I must know quickly. I have told Kid Gleason I will give him my final answer on Saturday. Call me on long-distance telephone when you get this letter, if you'd like to manage our club."

Harris grabbed up the nearest phone and reached Griffith in Washington. "Hello, Mr. Griffith, I want that job," he blurted.

But he was talking into a poor connection. "I can't hear you," said Griffith. "I want that job," Harris was now screaming. Though he could hear Griffith, he couldn't make himself heard. When Griffith, impatient, cursed all the telephone poles from Washington to Florida and hung up, Harris was panicked. A big-league managerial job was his for the taking, and he was helpless.

Then he thought of a new tack. He dashed off to the telegraph office and wired Griffith: "I'll take that job and win Washington's first American League pennant." To the Western Union clerk he gave a twenty-dollar bill saying, "Send this telegram right away and repeat it every hour for the next four hours."

Harris had reason to be astonished at Griffith's selection

of himself as manager. He was only 27, had a scant three years of major-league experience, wasn't really an outstanding player, and actually thought he was in the doghouse with Griffith at the time. A few weeks earlier Griffith had caught him playing pro basketball in Pennsylvania in violation of a clause in his contract and threatened to fine him. Just before that, he had signed his 1924 contract with the Washington club calling for a 7,000-dollar salary. It was not a happy occasion, for after Harris had agreed to salary terms Griffith had told him, "We've got a chance to get Eddie Collins from the White Sox as manager. He'd play second base, of course. Do you think you could shift to third?" At that time, Harris wasn't sure he had a regular job with the club.

Bucky Harris wasn't born on a baseball diamond but he could say, in truth, that his birthplace was Ball Street, in Port Jervis, New York. His Welsh parents gravitated to the Pennsylvania coal fields where Grandfather Harris was a "Fire Boss," even as he had been in his native Wales. Into the mines he would sally every workday at 2 A.M. to test the safety of the chambers against the possibility of gas and fire hazards, and on his report would depend the operation of the mines that day. Miners worked or idled according to the sniffs of Bucky Harris' granddad.

Young Bucky worked in those mines, too, first as a breaker boy, one of the hundred kids who sat at the chutes making a funnel with their hobnailed shoes and picking out the chunks of dull slate that had sifted through the screens along with the shiny coal. From that job he graduated to the weighmaster's office at $4.30 a week, in Pittston, Pennsylvania.

Naturally enough, he played baseball. He was living in a mining sector of the state that was rich in baseball tradition. It gave to the big leagues Hughey Jennings and the O'Neills —Steve, Jim, Mike, and John. It gave as well Christy Mathewson, Mike McNally, Ed Walsh, Chick Shorten, Eddie Murphy, and the Coveleskies—Harry and Stanley. From Scranton, Wilkes-Barre, Shamokin, and Pittston they paraded into the big leagues. And many returned to the little mining towns at the end of their careers.

Three years before he was bought by the Washington club

108

from Buffalo, Bucky Harris was in a major-league training camp getting a tryout at the age of nineteen. Manager Hughey Jennings of the Detroit Tigers had seen the lad playing shortstop for the mine teams near Jennings' own home, and wired him to report to the Tigers' training camp at Waxahachie, Texas, in March, 1916.

His head swimming, Harris clambered off a train at Waxahachie on March 17, impressed first by the fact that he was in the same town with such big-league stars as Ty Cobb, Sam Crawford, Donie Bush, Harry Heilmann, and Jennings.

When he sought out Jennings, he received his first jolt. His sponsor was not even at training camp. An attack of blood poisoning had forced the Tigers' manager into an Oklahoma City hospital. Timidly, young Harris showed his telegram from Jennings to coach Jimmie Burke. Skeptically, and somewhat grudgingly, Burke issued the 140-pound kid a uniform.

It was a sad adventure for Bucky. Without Jennings, he was adrift. In his first two weeks at camp, he didn't even get a turn in batting practice. The Detroit veterans shooed him away from the plate when he tried to take some whacks, and he contented himself with playing around the infield. He impressed nobody, but it was an unfair test. He was playing on a grass infield for the first time. All his ball playing had been done on skinned diamonds dotted with clinkers, and he was baffled by the smoothness of the infield.

Bucky was with the Tigers when they opened the 1916 season at Chicago, but Jennings having heard the report of his coaches, was sending Bucky back to Pittston. The net result of Harris' trial with the Tigers was two tickets to that opening game which he saw from the grandstand. He was being dropped by the club that he was to manage thirteen years later.

Jennings remembered the boy, though. Later the same year, he wired Harris to report to Muskegon, Michigan, in the Central League, a club that needed a second baseman. Harris did, batted .185, couldn't make good, and was back in Pittston before the season closed. Jennings, though, didn't give him up. He found Harris a job with Norfolk in the Virginia League in 1917, and three weeks later the second baseman was out of a job again. The war came, and the league collapsed.

In midsummer, though, Harris got a job with the Reading Club of the New York State League, quite by accident. He wired every club in the league saying he was a second baseman with two years experience in organized baseball, hopeful that players going off to the service might leave a vacancy. Manager George Wiltse of Reading, needing a second baseman, asked his team in a dressing room meeting if any of them had ever heard of a second baseman named Harris from Pittston, Pennsylvania, who had wired for a job.

Bill Donahue, a big pitcher, said, "Sure, I used to play with Harris in the Canadian League. Swell fielder, and he may hit enough. He ought to do us some good." Bill Donahue had never seen Bucky Harris in his life. He was talking about Harris' older brother, Merle, and was merely extending himself for an old friend. He couldn't conscientiously recommend Merle as a good ball player, but he reasoned that the fellow needed a job badly, and it was little enough to do.

Wiltse was surprised when Bucky Harris reported, telegram in hand. "You're a kid. They told me this Harris was around thirty. Donahue must be crazy." Harris said he was sorry about the mistake, but pleaded for a chance to play second base for Reading. Wiltse, with misgivings, put him in the line-up, unsigned to a contract. A week later, he offered Bucky a contract at 135 dollars a month.

At the end of the season, the New York State League collapsed because of the war, as had the Virginia League, and Harris was again jobless. But Wiltse who had moved to Buffalo as manager was offering Harris a job in the Spring of 1918, at 175 dollars a month, and Bucky grabbed it eagerly. In midseason, he jumped Buffalo to play for the Baltimore Drydocks' team at 200 dollars a month and played in an infield in which he was the only minor leaguer. Joe Judge was at first base, Harris at second, Dave Bancroft at shortstop, and Frank Schulte at third base. The shipyard team did not lose a game that season, and three times whipped the Baltimore Orioles. Harris was playing with the best team of his career thus far.

Buffalo forgave him for jumping and in 1919, offered him a new contract at 300 dollars a month. His play around second base was causing favorable talk now, and he was hitting just under .300. Buffalo had a working agreement with the New York Giants, and Wiltse in midseason sent him to the Polo Grounds during an open date at Newark, telling him to report to John McGraw for a tryout.

McGraw told Harris to get into a Giants' uniform and take some batting practice and then get into the infield practice. Harris hit some pitches solidly, cavorted around second base for a half hour before the game and went back to the bench. McGraw had not spoken another word to him, and with an empty feeling he put on his street clothes and watched the game from the grandstand. The next time Harris was to speak to John McGraw would be five years later at Griffith Stadium when they would be opposing managers in a World Series.

On a Sunday late in August, 1919, at Buffalo, Clark Griffith walked into the life of Bucky Harris. Young Bucky didn't recognize the heavy-browed little bantam of a man who sauntered into a box seat near the Buffalo bench. But Buffalo manager George Wiltse whispered to Bucky, "He's here."

And Harris knew whom Wiltse meant. For days he was aware that Griffith was en route to Buffalo to scout him. This was the afternoon that might be the beginning of a big-league career. Buffalo was playing a double-header with Reading. Originally, the Senators had learned about Harris from Joe Judge who had played with him in the Baltimore shipyards. Later scout Joe Engel turned in a report on him, after a scouting trip to Buffalo.

Harris had wondered how he had impressed Engel. Just before Engel reached Buffalo, a line drive had crippled the third finger on Bucky's throwing hand. The finger was ugly and bloated, and Bucky could scarcely grip a bat, but he was determined to stay in the line-up while there were big-league scouts on the premises.

By the time Griffith reached Buffalo, Harris' finger was almost a hospital case. X-rays showed it was broken in three places, but to ease the pain Harris strapped the injured digit to his little finger.

Eight times Bucky went to bat in that double-header, with Griffith in the stands. He made three hits in each game, was hit by a pitched ball once, and another time he walked. That day Griffith saw Bucky Harris bat 1.000. When Griffith walked into the dressing room after the games, he found Bucky removing the tape from his fingers.

"Lemme look at that finger, son," said Griffith. "It looks nasty. You can't play ball with a finger like that. Better get some pictures taken. Ten to one it's broken," he was telling a man who already knew his finger was broken in three places. Griffith said no more to Harris, but that night Harris got a call from Wiltse.

"You're on your way up, Bucky," said Wiltse. "Griffith likes you. He's balking at the 5,000 dollars we're asking, but he'll pay it. He liked those hits you made and the way you stuck in there with that finger."

Wiltse told Harris something else. "Washington isn't the only club that wants to buy you. The Giants will take you for 5,000 dollars. So will Connie Mack. You can take your choice."

Where to go? Bucky appraised the situation. He wanted to play regularly for a big-league club. Who were the second basemen with those three teams? With the Giants it was Larry Doyle. Another Giant, Frankie Frisch, who they were saying was better than Doyle, was coming up. The Athletics' second baseman? He couldn't remember, but it didn't make any difference. The A's had finished in the cellar for four straight years, and they were again in eighth place. He didn't want to hook up with that kind of a ball club.

Washington? They were a better team and had finished third in 1918, and he wouldn't have to bat against Walter Johnson. Who did he have to beat for second base? There was only Hal Janvrin, who wasn't much of a hitter and was slipping in the field. "Gee, Mr. Wiltse, lemme go to Washington," said Bucky.

Harris joined the Senators late in 1919 and broke into the line-up on the day they were playing the Yankees in a double-header. He drove in two runs for Walter Johnson, but in thirteen innings Johnson was licked by the Yankees, 5 to 4. Harris caused the defeat of Johnson in the thirteenth inning and then learned about Walter Johnson.

A short fly into right center field was the winning hit, a cheap one. Sam Rice and Clyde Milan both called for the ball, but Harris, racing back from second base, waved them both from it. Then he misjudged it, and it broke up the game. Out in short center, Harris hung back as the players went to the clubhouse, ashamed of his busher stunt. And then he saw Walter Johnson, without so much as a shrug, fold his glove and stuff it into his hip pocket as if he were the winning pitcher. Then Johnson walked out to Harris, draped an arm around his shoulder and said, "Don't let it worry you, kid. It happens to everybody."

In his first full season, Harris became a fixture at second base for the Senators. He batted an even .300 and was good around the infield. In 1922, with the coming of the veteran Peckinpaugh to play shortstop, he was a sensation as a double play man and was the top-ranking second baseman in the league with 962 chances accepted. In 1923, he stole twenty bases to be fourth in the league, and his thirteen triples ranked him fifth in that department. His .282 batting average was eminently respectable.

As the newly named manager of the Senators in the spring of 1924, Harris was the youngest regular on the team. This was the time for tact. Fellows like Joe Judge, Peck, Rice, Johnson, Zachary, and Mogridge were big-league stars when he was a sand lotter. Harris sought out Johnson and Judge first, asked them if they would stick with him, and got an emphatic affirmative. They pledged everybody's cooperation.

At the first day of spring practice in Tampa, Harris made a short speech to the Washington players which was well received. "I didn't know I was going to be the manager of this club a month ago," he said. "Far be it from me to tell you fellows how to play ball—but what I'm asking is that you go out there and make me a good manager."

There was no indication at the outset that Harris would be any startling success in his first year as manager. In the early weeks the Senators floundered in the second division.

Baseball critics who had hailed Griffith's selection of Bucky as manager during the winter as "Griffith's folly" had their innings.

Then suddenly the Washington club seemed to find itself. Veterans like Judge, Rice, and Johnson, by what seemed a magic coincidence, began to enjoy their best seasons in years. Young Goose Goslin was becoming a terrific power with his big bat. Muddy Ruel was giving the club both smooth catching and timely hitting. Harris himself was playing second as if inspired. His managerial duties appeared to be no burden to his second base play.

The veteran Peck, seemingly on the downgrade a year before, caught the spirit, too, and he and Harris were a spectacular double play combination. Rookie Fred Marberry, who needed only a half dozen warm-ups pitched in the bullpen, was a sensation as a relief pitcher and on his way to setting a new record of appearing in fifty games in a season.

New York, Detroit, Philadelphia, Boston, and Washington held the league lead at various times in the first half of the season. Cobb, manager of the Tigers, lost no opportunity to jeer at Harris. He called him "Baby Face," "Snookums," and anything else that would imply Bucky was a boy among men, and from the third base coaching lines he would shout "Boot it! Boot it!" whenever a ball was hit to Harris.

Clark Griffith, scenting a pennant in July, was worried chiefly about the lack of outfield strength. Goslin and Rice were having good seasons, but little Wid Matthews in center field wasn't hitting much. Griffith dispatched Joe Engel on a country-wide search for a center fielder. Engel reported he liked only two players in the top minors, but added dolefully, "they're asking 65,000 dollars apiece."

"What're their names?" demanded Griffith.

"Billy Zitzmann who is with Newark, and a fellow named Earl McNeely, who's with Sacramento. Either one would help us."

Griffith jumped a train to Buffalo to scout Zittman who was with the Newark club, and came back unimpressed. "How about this McNeely?" he asked Engel.

"Are you serious about paying 65,000 dollars?"

"If it means a pennant, I am," said Griffith.

Engel suggested that Griffith himself scout McNeely. He didn't want to be responsible for recommending a player at that price. "Hell, by the time I get out to the Coast and bring McNeely back, two more weeks of the pennant race will be over. We need him now. I'll make the deal over the phone."

Eventually Griffith landed McNeely for 35,000 dollars cash, three players, and the loan of Wid Matthews to Sacramento for the rest of the season. He ordered McNeely to report to the Senators at Chicago.

Griffith, traveling with the team, waited for McNeely to check into the Senators' Chicago hotel, and greeted him with "So you're the fellow I paid all that money for," extending his hand in greeting.

"Sorry," said McNeely, shrinking from Griffith's handshake, "I can't raise my right arm above my hip. Dislocated my shoulder last week in a game at Frisco."

Griffith was furious and telephoned Baseball Commissioner Landis demanding the deal be canceled. Landis agreed to permit the Washington club to withhold payment until McNeely was given a chance to recover.

McNeely got into the game on the day he reported, but as a pinch hitter. Harris called on him in the ninth, and he rapped a two-bagger over third base with two on that won the game. Griffith was interested now. For seventeen days McNeely was used as a pinch hitter and delivered consistently. His arm, too, was showing improvement. Now the Sacramento club was demanding payment. Griffith was afraid to keep McNeely, afraid to turn him back. He gambled and kept him, and in forty-five games the outfielder batted .330 to help beat the Yankees in the down-stretch pennant drive.

The Senators were also favored by another development. When Harris' pitching threatened to go stale, he claimed sore-armed Curly Ogden, a right-hander from the Athletics, at the waiver price. Under the ministrations of trainer Mike Martin, Ogden's arm made a magical recovery. He won eight straight games for the Senators. But after each day's pitching he would walk the floor of the hotel suite he shared with

Harris and Muddy Ruel and hold his arm in pain and wonder if he could ever work again.

Up in New York the Yankees were anticipating a late August, four-game series with this upstart Washington Club, and it was clear enough what the Yankees were thinking. With their Babe Ruth, Bob Meusel, Pennock, Hoyt, Bush, and Schang, they'd murder these come-lately Senators who were audaciously trying to knock the Yanks out of their fourth straight pennant.

The Yanks went into the series with a half-game lead on August 29. In the series opener, Babe Ruth thumped out two home runs. But Ruth didn't hit enough homers. Sam Rice rapped out five hits in that game. The Senators gave Herb Pennock a fearful pounding, beat the Yankees 11 to 6, and took over the league lead by a half game.

Walter Johnson got the pitching job for the second game. He didn't go the full route, but he got a valuable lift from big Fred Marberry in the late innings. Joe Bush held the Senators to six hits. One of those was a home run by Goose Goslin. Two others were singles by Goslin. The Senators slapped the Yankees down, 5 to 1, for the second straight day.

The Yankees bounced back in the third game. It was a pitching duel between Curly Ogden and Waite Hoyt, with Hoyt the 2-to-1 winner despite the fact he was pounded for eleven Washington hits while Ogden was holding the Yankees to five.

This was the invitation for the Senators to collapse and again yield the league lead to the Yankees in the fourth game. They didn't. With 45,000 fans in the Yankee Stadium, George Mogridge got off to a sorry start for the Senators. Big Marberry relieved him in the eighth. Pitcher Sam Jones yielded a home run to Joe Judge to tie the score at 2 to 2 and send the game into extra innings. Bucky Harris was ejected from the game after a violent dispute with umpire Ducky Holmes over a fourth ball to Ruth. In the tenth, Sam Rice broke up the ball game with a two-bagger that scored Muddy Ruel and Nemo Leibold, for a 4-to-2 Washington victory.

Their mop-up of three games in that four-game series gave the Senators a 13-to-9 edge over the Yankees for the season.

116

At Washington's Union Station that night, 8,000 frenzied fans greeted the homecoming Senators, already hailing them as pennant winners, despite twenty-seven games remaining on the schedule. The Washington ball players were rescued by police from their admirers, and were shaken free only by use of the Presidential exits at the station.

The Senators had won sixteen of their last twenty-one games. Walter Johnson was on a new winning streak that had now reached eleven in a row. The fortunes of the Yankees and the Senators on the last western trip would tell the story. On September 15, the Yankees pulled into a tie for the lead, with each club showing eighty-two wins and fifty-nine defeats. But the next day Tom Zachary beat Cleveland while the Yankees had an open date, and the Senators were in front again.

That the Senators were the popular favorites in that race to the wire was always clear. Sentiment for a Washington pennant victory swept the nation, high-lighted of course by the general hope that Walter Johnson, at last, would find himself in a World Series. Bucky Harris was being hailed as a miracle man. He would be the youngest manager ever to win a pennant.

Harris cautioned his ball players against antagonizing the western clubs on the final swing. He was aware of the general good will toward the Senators. Now was no time for jockeying from the bench, against clubs that bore his team no ill will. The Senators during the season had been a lively, noise-making gang spouting defiance at everybody, but Harris was now taking a new tack.

"Let's not make any enemies if we can help it," Harris told his players. "Most of these western clubs would rather see us win the pennant than the Yankees. Let's beat 'em, but treat 'em nice."

Harris made it a point to mingle amicably with the western clubs before each series. He found them all sympathetic with Washington except the White Sox, for some reason. He sent Nemo Leibold, his White Sox alumnus, among the Chicago players and Leibold's report corroborated Harris' fears. The White Sox preferred to see the Yankees win the pennant.

117

Harris called a meeting before the White Sox series and told the story. "That's it," he said, "these guys would rather see the Yankees beat us for the pennant. There's nothing to be gained by being nice to the Sox, as long as they feel that way about it. Let's insult 'em first, and then beat their brains out."

That's what happened. The Senators beat the White Sox three games in a row. It was good because the Yankees were doing the same at Cleveland. Walter Johnson won his thirteenth straight in the Chicago series. It was the series opener, on September 22, and Johnson had not lost a game since July 11. In that series, Sam Rice carried his hot hitting streak to twenty-nine games in a row. Goose Goslin was on his way to a .344 batting year.

The Senators had gone into the West with a two-game lead. They came out of it with their margin unimpaired. The Yankees won nine of twelve games on their swing, but Harris' club matched that pace. The showdown would take place in the East, in the Yankees' four final games at Philadelphia and the Senators' last four games at Boston.

In the pennant-hungry nation's capital, a mild panic set in as the Senators dropped the first game at Boston and the Yankees beat the Athletics, 7 to 1, to cut Washington's lead to one game. Worst of all, the beaten Washington pitcher at Boston was Walter Johnson, whose thirteen-game streak was ended in a 2-to-1 duel with Alec Ferguson. Now was the crisis for the Senators.

In the second game at Boston, with 20,000 Bostonians openly rooting for the Senators, the first inning produced all the elements of disaster for Washington. George Mogridge started and surrendered four runs at the outset. Bucky Harris rushed Fred Marberry, Allan Russell, and Tom Zachary into relief shifts. They held the Red Sox to one more run in the last eight innings. The Senators got back in the ball game and won it, 7 to 5.

Over the wires from Philadelphia came the joyful news that the Yankees had lost to the Athletics, 4 to 3. Joe Bush's wild pitch was fatal in that game. Now the Senators had their two-game lead again, with only two games on the schedule.

They sweated out the next day, a Sunday, with blue laws forbidding baseball both in Boston and Philadelphia. On Monday, Tom Zachary and Fred Marberry teamed up to beat the Red Sox, 5 to 3. Down in Philadelphia, Eddie Rommel was beating the Yankees, and the Senators were the new champions of the American League.

Chapter VIII

THE nation's capital, inured to the excitement of Presidential inaugurations, calm in the midst of history-making legislation, and calloused to the fetes for visiting princes and potentates, went wild on Oct. 1, 1924, and exploded emotionally.

When Bucky Harris and his Senators detrained at Union Station, the city's first pennant clinched, they were swept up in a whirl of giddily happy fans. Total strangers pounded each other on the back. Storekeepers vied in dressing their show windows with baseball paraphernalia. Songs of Harris and the team mushroomed in the night clubs, and countless thousands lined Pennsylvania Avenue for the victory parade.

In shiny new open cars—with genuine four-wheel brakes provided by a reverent automobile dealer—the Washington team inched up the avenue behind a police escort that was hard pressed to fend off hysterical hero worshippers. The parade's destination was the White House, no less, and there President Calvin Coolidge greeted the team and promised to attend the World Series opening against the Giants three days later.

Only Washington could provide as brilliant a setting for a World Series as Griffith Stadium presented on that opening day. In the stands were 35,760 fans, taking every seat in the park and using temporary planking in center field. For the first time in World Series history a President of the United States and his First Lady were attending an opener. The United States Army Band played, and a military guard saluted the colors. Secretary of States Hughes, Secretary of War Weeks, Speaker of the House Gillette and Mrs. Gillette were in the White House box. Army and Navy bigwigs, senators, congressmen, and foreign diplomats were out in force. Walter Johnson and Roger Peckinpaugh were presented with sleek new motor cars in pre-game ceremonies.

And then Walter Johnson took the mound against the Giants—the great Walter Johnson in a World Series at last, seventeen years after he had first joined the Washington club. A nation was waiting to applaud his first World Series triumph.

Like all other Washington players, Johnson had been besieged by friends and late acquaintances for tickets to the series. He was reluctant to turn down any request. When he strode to the mound for his opening pitch, 360 dollars worth of World Series tickets were in Johnson's dressing room locker, paid for by him but unclaimed by the ingrates who had made the requests and then left the Big Train holding the bag.

Johnson's long deferred hope of pitching in a World Series turned bittersweet. In twelve innings, he lost to Art Nehf, canny little southpaw of the Giants, 4 to 3. Seven consecutive shutout innings Johnson pitched until the blow fell in the twelfth—Ross Young's single with the bases full.

Sadness mantled the capital that night. Johnson was still the hero of Washington fans, but they were roundly cursing the temporary bleacher seats in left field that encroached on the playing surface and left the Big Train the victim of cheap home runs by George Kelly and Bill Terry in the early innings.

From those two homers, the Giants took a 2-to-0 lead in the first four innings before Washington had a hit from Nehf. Kelly's drive, opening the second inning, hit on the playing field and bounced over the low fence into the temporary seats, a homer under the ground rules. Terry's smash that reached the seats on the fly in the fourth would have been an easy out ordinarily.

Nehf held the Senators scoreless until the sixth when Mc-

The Washington Baseball park where Connie Mack played in the 80's.

Opening Day, 1911. The park that was to become Griffith Stadium.

Clark Griffith as pitcher-manager of the New York Highlanders, whom he joined in 1903.

Clark Griffith and Connie Mack in 1920.

Manager Griffith (seated at right) matching wits with Germany Schaefer at spring training camp, 1916. Nick Altrock (center, seated) watches.

Manager Griffith mixes it up with an umpire.

Walter Johnson, the kid from Weiser, Idaho, as he appeared shortly after he joined the Senators in 1907.

Walter Johnson and his two famous battery mates. Above, with Muddy Ruel, and below with Gabby Street.

Walter Johnson pitching to Babe Ruth.

Clark Griffith and Judge Landis.

Sam Rice.

Stan Coveleski.

"Goose" Goslin.

The 1924 pennant winners parade down Constitution Avenue.

The 1933 pennant winners. *First row:* Rice, Stewart, Goslin, Schacht (coach), C. Griffith, Cronin (mgr.), Harris, Bolton, Altrock (coach), Mahoney (batboy, seated). *Second Row:* Russell, Thomas, Chapman, Travis, Burke, Kerr, Weaver, Myer. *Third Row:* Sewell, Berg, Whitehill, Prim, Schulte, Manush, McColl, Bluege, Kuhel, Crowder, Boken.

Two great Senators infields. *Above:* Joe Judge, Bucky Harris, Roger Pekinpaugh, Ossie Bluege. *Below:* Joe Kuhel, Buddy Meyer, Joe Cronin, Ossie Bluege.

Presidents at opening day. In the usual order: William Howard Taft, Woodrow Wilson, Warren Harding, Calvin Coolidge.

Presidents at opening day (*continued*). Herbert Hoover, Harry Truman, Franklin Roosevelt, Dwight Eisenhower.

The Senators' famous clowns, Nick Altrock and Al Schacht. The gentleman in the middle is Mr. John Quinn, at the time owner of the Boston Red Sox.

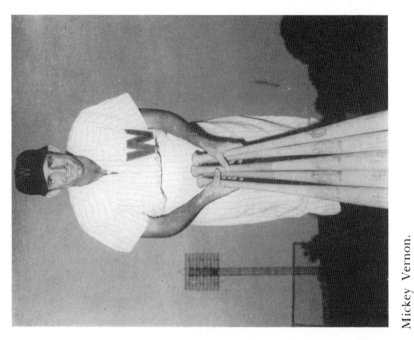

Mickey Vernon.

Conrado Marrero.

Bob Porterfield.

Bobo Newsom.

Clark Griffith in his office at Griffith Stadium.

Neely led off with a double to left. Nehf disposed of Harris and Rice, but Goslin singled to center to drive McNeely in and reduce the Giants' lead to 2 to 1.

Those were still the figures going into the last of the ninth, thanks to Johnson's mastery over the Giants since the fourth inning. And then the Senators tied the score. With his only hit of the game, Bluege singled to left with one out to put the tying run on base, and the veteran Peckinpaugh came through gallantly. He drove a long two-bagger into left field to score Bluege all the way from first with the tying run. Nehf tightened up to get rid of Ruel and Johnson at that point and send the game into extra innings.

Through the tenth and eleventh, the 36-year-old Johnson shepherded the Senators safely, but in the twelfth he weakened. A pass to Hank Gowdy put him in trouble. A bit later Nehf lifted a short fly that fell just beyond the grasp of McNeely in center field. When McNeely's return throw to the infield was wild, Gowdy raced to third and Nehf to second, with none as yet out.

Johnson, in this crisis, deliberately walked Jack Bentley who batted for Lindstrom, filling the bases. The tension eased a bit when Harris scooped up Frisch's grounder and threw to the plate for a force play on Gowdy for the first out. But Young delivered a clean single that scored Nehf, and on Kelly's long fly to left, the Giants' second run of the inning scored.

The Senators put possible tying and winning runs on base in their own half of the twelfth before they ran out of outs. Mule Shirley, batting for Johnson, reached base when Travis Jackson missed his high fly. McNeely flied out but Harris and Rice hit consecutive singles to score Shirley. Rice, however, was too ambitious. On his single that sent Harris to third with the tying run and only one out, Rice tried overzealously to take second and was thrown out. Goslin went out on an infield tap to Kelly, and the Senators were a beaten crew. In vain, Johnson had tied a World Series record by striking out twelve men in a single game.

Tom Zachary, the Senators' fifteen-game winner, was entrusted with the job of stopping the Giants in the second contest which attracted 35,922 fans—162 more than had seen the opener. He drew as his pitching opponent Jack Bentley, the former Washington sand lotter, who had gone on to fame with the Baltimore Orioles as a first baseman-pitcher before the Giants bought him for 100,000 dollars.

McGraw's strategy was plain. He was shooting left-handers at the Senators in an attempt to throttle the power department of the Washington batting order—the left-handed swinging array of Rice, Goslin, and Judge. Goslin had hit .344 for the year and beaten out Babe Ruth for the runs-batted-in crown. Rice was a .334 hitter, and Judge hit .324 for the season.

Bentley had two out in the opening inning when the Senators' big men opened up on him. Rice banged a single into center and quickly stole second, a maneuver that was quite superfluous in the light of the subsequent event. This was a fierce home run smash into right field by Goslin. Making it unanimous for the Senators' left-handed hitters was Joe Judge who followed with a single to center. That blow proved wasted, but the Senators had a 2-to-0 lead.

Bucky Harris personally lifted the Senators' lead to 3 to 0 in the fifth. During the 154-game regular season he had hit only one home run, but now he equaled that output. He smashed a Bentley pitch into the center field seats.

Zachary, meanwhile, was doing an artistic job on the Giants. For six innings he shut them out, yielding only three hits. In the seventh, Kelly drew a base on balls, and it became a run after Meusel followed with a single to center. Kelly scored from third while Bluege was grabbing Wilson's grounder and routing it around the base for a double play.

Needing two runs to tie the score in the ninth, the Giants got them. Zachary weakened and issued his third walk of the game, a pass to Frisch with none out. Young popped out, but Kelly singled to right and Frisch scored all the way from first base when the Senators handled the relay poorly. Meusel grounded out to Harris, but on the play Kelly raced to second with the tying run, and Hack Wilson deadlocked the game at 3 to 3 with a single to right.

Fred Marberry, who had been warming up since the sixth

inning, moved into the game at that point and eased the situation for the Senators by throwing three strikes past Travis Jackson on three pitches, preserving the tie.

The glumness of the Washington fans did not last long, however. Bentley lost his control and walked Judge on four wide pitches. Bluege sacrificed expertly, and the venerable Roger Peckinpaugh, hitless to that point, whacked a solid single into left field to score Judge for a 4-to-3 victory that evened the series.

At New York, in the third game, the Series reached the hectic stage. Peckinpaugh, the Senators' hitting hero of the first two contests, was forced out of the line-up by a painful Charley horse suffered in running out his decisive hit of the day before. Harris, in desperation, moved Bluege to short-stop and drafted the shoulder-heavy rookie, Ralph (Hack) Miller, for third base duty. Tommy Taylor, a better third baseman, was at the time incapacitated and wearing a splint on his throwing hand, a souvenir of his too enthusiastic cele-bration the night the pennant was clinched in Boston. Against the published report that Taylor had fallen down a flight of steps was the evidence that Taylor had smashed his hand on the head of a bellicose co-celebrant.

What started out as a supposed pitching duel between Fred Marberry and Hugh McQuillan lapsed into a parade of eight pitchers to the mound—four for each club. Marberry lasted only three innings, and the Giants managed a 3 to 0 lead. In a two-run second inning for the Giants, Terry and Gowdy rapped out clean hits, Harris dropped a throw from Bluege with a double play in prospect, Marberry made a wild pitch and later hit Frisch with a pitched ball.

McQuillan didn't last out the fourth inning. He was wild, and the Senators came up with two runs, one of them forced over, to cut the Giants' lead to 3 to 2. But in their own half the Giants came up with a surprise run of their own. Rosy Ryan, who had relieved McQuillan on the mound earlier in the inning, swung hard on a pitch by Allan Russell and, to what was surely his own amazement, hit a home run into the upper deck of the right field stands.

The Giants improved their lead to 5 to 2 in the sixth

against Russell with a run that stemmed from Miller's bewilderment on a ground ball by Gowdy. Miller stopped Gowdy's smash but lost track of it thereafter, and Gowdy was safe. Gowdy scored from second on Lindstrom's double to right.

Both clubs came up with single runs in the eighth inning, and in a futile bid to tie the score in the ninth the Senators at least maintained their record of scoring in each ninth inning of the Series. Harris' single, Goslin's bunt, and Judge's single put the tying runs on base with one out, and McGraw rushed Claude Jonnard to the relief of the fading Ryan. When Jonnard passed Bluege, forcing Harris home, Watson moved in as the Giants' fourth pitcher. There was no more trouble for the Giants. Hack Miller and Muddy Ruel grounded to Lindstrom for infield outs, and the Giants had a 6-to-4 win and a 2-to-1 lead in the Series.

The Series' fourth game was the Goose Goslin game. If Walter Johnson was number one in the hearts of Washington fans, Goslin was certainly number two. They had watched him come to the Senators in 1921 as the awkward young outfielder from the Sally League whose charm was supposed to be in his hitting. They forgave his malfeasances in the outfield, admired his contempt for the fences, and the sturdiness of his skull that was being put to almost daily tests by the Goose's crashes against the wall in his brave but futile chases for fly balls.

They oohed and ah'd at the power in his throwing arm and chortled when the Goose threw runners out from deep left and right. But it was at bat that they loved Goslin and the plate-crowding stance he took before fastening a murderous glare on the luckless pitcher of the moment. They knew the power in his big frame, and when he struck out their disappointment was tempered by the gusto of his swing and the massive pirouette that was much like Ruth's.

He had broken in with the Senators on a day when they were facing their long-time nemesis, Red Faber of the White Sox, and Goslin had tripled to right in both of his first two appearances at bat to drive in four runs for Washington. When Joe Judge remarked on the Senators' bench, "I didn't think we'd ever get a 4-0 lead on Faber," the Goose inquired blandly, "Is this Faber supposed to be good?"

But now it was 1924, and Goslin was solidly established as one of the league's better hitters, a real power hitter, and his outfielding, too, was smooth and smart. He was still using the same exaggerated closed stance with which he had begun at Washington, getting his tremendous power from a swing fuller than any other in the league. Actually, his back was nearly turned to the pitcher, and he stood poised for the pitch while looking over his own left shoulder, with his face in profile. The most prominent feature of that face was the Goose's big beak, and he wasn't sensitive on that point.

After he hit .344 during the 1924 season and led the league in runs-batted-in, Goslin was in the mood to quip a bit. "I don't see past my nose with my left eye when I'm up at that plate," he said. "I been hitting .344 as a one-eyed hitter, you know. If I could get two eyes on that ball, I'd hit .600 in this league."

Goslin didn't swing into action in that fourth game of the World Series until the second inning. By that time the Giants had a 1-to-0 lead from George Mogridge, the old Yankee southpaw whom Clark Griffith had picked up a couple of years before. Lindstrom, who drew a walk, crossed the plate on Frisch's infield out and a fumble by Bluege on Ross Young's grounder. It was in contrast to the one-two-three disposition of the Senators by the Giants' Jess Barnes in the first inning, and there was an obvious smugness among the Giant fans.

Goslin in the second inning hit a futile single, but in the third he connected and was rewarded. McNeely and Harris were on base with singles, and two were out when the Goose struck hard. A three-run home run boomed into the right field stands and the Senators had a 3-to-1 lead.

Barnes was still in there in the fifth for the Giants when the Goose struck again. Again it was McNeely and Harris on base with singles, and a wild pitch by Barnes moved them up. The Goose fetched them both home with a single to left that was his third straight hit of the game, and the Senators were in front, 5 to 1, with Goslin driving in all five.

Mogridge threw four shutout innings at the Giants before they cut his lead to 5 to 2 in the sixth, following Kelly's opening two-bagger to center. Kelly scored while shortstop Bluege was throwing out Meusel, Wilson, and Jackson on ground balls.

Goslin's fourth straight hit of the game produced nothing for the Senators, but in the eighth he made it five-for-five and ignited a two-run inning with a single. Bluege drove in both runs with a single to left, and the Senators had a 7-to-2 lead. Fred Marberry relieved the weakening Mogridge in the eighth, making his third appearance in four games, and the Senators pulled out with a 7-to-4 win to even the Series again.

Now it was time for Walter Johnson to return to a World Series pitching role. Even in the hostile Polo Grounds the fans rose from their seats and cheered as the Big Train trudged to the mound as the Senators' starting pitcher in the fifth game. He had Jack Bentley as his opponent, the left-hander who had outlasted him in the Series opener. But Johnson couldn't make it close this time. In regulation innings he went down to a 6-to-2 defeat, with the Giants shelling him for thirteen hits including a home run by Bentley himself.

Johnson held the Giants in check for two innings, and then they broke loose with a run in the third on singles by Jackson, Bentley, and Lindstrom. The Senators bounced back in the fourth to tie the score at 1 to 1 on Judge's single, Bluege's sacrifice, and a single to right by Hack Miller. But Johnson could not keep them in the ball game.

He wasn't the same well-rested pitcher who came up to the opener, went twelve innings, and struck out twelve men. This day, he had only three strike-outs to his credit, sure evidence that the Johnson fast ball wasn't smoking. The Giants tagged him for two runs and a 3-to-1 lead in the fifth. The big blow was Bentley's home run slam into the upper right field seats that followed a single by Gowdy.

Goslin blasted his third home run of the Series into the right field upper deck in the eighth to cut the Giants' lead to 3 to 2, and knock Bentley out, but McQuillan checked that rally. And in their own eighth the Giants ganged up on Johnson for three more runs after filling the bases with none out on Kelly's single, a pass to Terry, and Wilson's bunt that was mishandled by Johnson. Now the Giants had a 3-to-2 lead in games as the Series moved back to Washington.

Harris, now desperate for a winning pitcher in the sixth game, turned to Long Tom Zachary, the turkey-necked southpaw who had been his winner in the second game. McGraw's pitching choice was an easy one. He had available Art Nehf, Walter Johnson's conquerer in the twelve-inning first game.

The President and Mrs. Coolidge, watching their third game of the Series, were among the 34,254 prayerful rooters of the Senators. As Harris' club took the field for the game's start, a thunderous cheer acclaimed the figure of Roger Peckinpaugh limping toward the shortstop position. He was back in the Series after missing the fourth and fifth games, pain-wracked for three days with hemorrhages in his left thigh from an ugly Charley horse. Peck was strapped from ankle to waist to keep him upright, and had announced he'd be in the line-up "if I have to break a leg to get in there." How nearly prophetic was that crack, he was to learn later.

The Giants came out swinging against Zachary, and the 34,254 fans glumly watched them take a 1-to-o lead in the opening inning. Frankie Frisch, the second hitter, swatted a hard double into right field, but the scoring was temporarily stemmed when Zachary took Young's grounder and retired Frisch in a run-down between second and third. Young raced to second on the play and Kelly scored him with a solid single to center.

That was the last run the Giants were to get from Zachary. From that point, a pitching masterpiece unfolded. The veteran southpaw was never in trouble again. With each rise and dip of his pitching arm Zachary defeated the Giants' batting power. He held the Giants to a total of seven hits all day, and only one Giant reached second base after the first inning. Never did Zachary have a count worse than two balls against any hitter. He threw only ninety-seven pitches and kept the Senators in the ball game until they won it.

But the Senators were getting Zachary no runs, and the game rocked into the fifth with Nehf smartly nursing his 1-

to-o lead. And then in the fifth, Peck led off with a single to left and hobbled to first base. Ruel laid down the conventional sacrifice, and Peck made it to second. He scrambled to third as Zachary grounded into an infield out, and now the pressure was on McNeely. He drew a walk.

Now, with Harris up, the Senators gambled. McNeely dashed for second, hoping to originate a double steal with Peck, but Gowdy held the ball and made no play for him, Peck cautiously holding third.

Bucky Harris won the sixth Series game for the Senators; at least he drove in the winning runs. With a two-bagger to right, he ushered both Peck and McNeely home to put the Senators in front, 2 to 1, and that was the final score.

But the Giants were not beaten as yet. In the ninth they put a possible tying run on base with one out. George Kelly's single to right launched the Giants' last-ditch rally.

And then Irish Meusel connected. The victory for which Zachary had labored with such care, seemingly was being snatched from him as Meusel's swat tore through the pitcher's mound and streaked toward center field. But behind second base, the figure of Peckinpaugh, far out of his normal position, flung itself on the ball, and with a glove-hand flip Peck got it to Harris for a force play on Kelly.

It was Peck's last play of the Series. The old shortstop's leg collapsed beneath him even as he made the play. For a moment the infield appeared to be strewn with broken bodies of the Senators, for Harris' throw to Joe Judge at first base, in a double play attempt that was just a second late, had hit Judge on the leg and he, too, was down and in pain. But Peck was inert. Leg muscles that had been contained only by his bandages were now torn anew, and the blood soaked through his uniform.

Time was out as they carried Peck from the field. President and Mrs. Coolidge stood with the fans in tribute to the old warrior whose incredible stop and throw had kept the tying run off third base with only one out. Now the Giants had a man on first with two out.

But there was consternation on the Washington bench. Harris moved Bluege to Peck's shortstop post, but he was unwilling to chance the erratic Miller at third base. His alternative was Tommy Taylor, the fellow with his throwing hand in a splint. Harris was entitled to moan at his club's crippled state.

Now it was Hack Wilson menacingly at the plate who confronted Zachary. With him, Zach didn't dally. He threw three pitches, all strikes, and the Senators had the sixth game, as well as a 3-to-3 tie in the Series.

The President and Mrs. Coolidge were there for the seventh game in Washington, along with 31,677 fans. The packed stadium had no inkling of the drama they would see when umpire Bill Dinneen shouted "Play Ball!" Curly Ogden, who had been a flop with the Athletics before the Senators claimed him late in the season, was taking the mound for Washington. The first hitter, Freddie Lindstrom, he struck out. The next, Frankie Frisch, he walked. And then Ogden himself calmly walked off the mound into the dugout . . . but what was this?

It was boy manager Bucky Harris taking the lead in the battle of wits with John McGraw. Ogden's short-lived presence on the mound had been planned . . . something with which to dupe the Giants, Harris hoped. It had all been mapped out in Clark Griffith's office earlier that morning.

Harris had unfolded a bold plan to Griffith. He would start the right-handed Ogden and trick McGraw into putting his left-handed hitters into the line-up. Then, in the first inning, he would lift Ogden and insert the southpaw, George Mogridge, putting the Giants' left-handed hitters at a disadvantage.

"If the Giants switch to their right-handed batting order after that, I'll switch to Fred Marberry," Harris told Griffith. "By that time the Giants won't have any pinch hitters left, if McGraw has shifted with me. The guy I don't want to see in the Giants' line-up is Bill Terry. He has been murdering our pitching—made six hits in twelve times at bat so far. They'll put him in there if we start Ogden, but if they want to leave him in there against Mogridge that's all right with me. He doesn't figure to hit our left-handers. And the chances are that when we shove Mogridge in they'll lift Terry and we'll be rid of him. I'll feel a lot safer with Terry out. What do you say, Mr. Griffith?"

Griffith gave Harris the nod. And it happened, almost according to Harris' script. Mogridge, who had warmed up secretly under the stands, replaced Ogden in that first inning. McGraw went along with Terry, but only for five innings. In the sixth, Harris was rid of Terry, the Giants' .429 man of the Series, who was lifted for a pinch hitter.

It was a scoreless game for three innings. And then Harris hit his second homer of the Series in the fourth inning, against Jesse Barnes, with a four-base wallop into the temporary center field bleachers to put the Senators in a 1-to-0 lead.

But in the sixth, Mogridge faltered. He walked Ross Young and pitched a single to Kelly. Marberry was rushed into the box, but Irish Meusel batted for Terry and moved Young home with a long fly to tie the score at 1 to 1 . . . but the Giants were not through. Wilson cracked a single to center, Judge fumbled a grounder by Jackson, the reliable Bluege fumbled a grounder by Gowdy, and the Giants had a 3-to-1 lead when Barnes drove a long fly to Rice.

And then, in the eighth, the Senators bounced back. Nemo Leibold, pinch-hitting for rookie third baseman Tom Taylor, doubled down the left field line. Next man up was Muddy Ruel, a horrible liability at bat in the series thus far with his failure to make a hit in the first six games. At this point he got his first hit of the Series, a clean single. Bennie Tate batted for Marberry and drew a walk that filled the bases. The Senators' hopes sagged when McNeely's fly was easily grabbed by Meusel in left for the second out, and the issue was strictly up to the boy manager himself, Harris.

Bucky met the issue, and it might be added, the ball. He smacked a sharp drive down the third base line, and it skipped over Lindstrom's glove for a single. Both Leibold and Ruel scurried home with the two runs that tied the game at 3 to 3.

Now Harris needed a new pitcher. "We want Johnson!" was the chant from the grandstands.

In this crisis, Harris was willing to turn to Johnson too. And never was there such a baseball uproar in Washington as when Johnson trudged from the bench toward the mound. The fans knew what Johnson himself was thinking. Here was that one more shot at the Giants he had prayed for, after losing his two Series starts. He could yet win himself a World Series game.

Frankie Frisch jolted Washington out of its new satisfaction with a clean triple to the center field corner with one out in the ninth. Now, with Ross Young up, Johnson looked to Harris for instructions. He got them and gave an intentional walk to Young. Now he was facing Long George Kelly, and a long fly could beat Johnson. But there was no fly. There were three wickedly pitched strikes. Johnson had fanned Kelly. Then he retired Meusel on a grounder to third and Johnson was out of the inning.

In the eleventh, with southpaw Art Nehf pitching for the Giants, it was still 3 to 3. Pinch hitter Heinie Groh of the Giants singled to right with none out. Southworth ran for Groh and Jackson sacrificed him to second. Johnson dealt with Frisch, the triple-socker of two innings before, by striking him out. Now Young was at bat again, and again he passed Young deliberately to get at George Kelly. It was a repeat performance. Johnson again struck out Kelly and was out of the inning.

Into the twelfth the game went, still 3 to 3. There was more trouble for Johnson, as Meusel led off with a single to right. Hack Wilson was up, and Johnson struck him out. Meusel hit into a force play at second. Gowdy sent a soft fly to Goslin, and again Johnson was out of trouble.

In the Senators' half of the twelfth the Giants' sent in their fourth pitcher, Bentley. One out, Ruel lifted a pop fly to Gowdy behind the plate. Gowdy, set for the catch, stumbled, unaccountably it seemed, and dropped the ball. He had stepped on his mask. It was a break for the Senators. Ruel, reprieved, got his second hit of the Series, a double to left. Johnson was up, and he hit to Travis Jackson at shortshop. It was another break for the Senators. Travis fumbled, and Johnson was on first with Ruel holding second.

Earl McNeely was up at bat. A sharp grounder went toward Freddie Lindstrom at third base, and Lindstrom poised for a

131

routine play on the ball, and then came a funny bounce! A high, hopping bounce went over Lindstrom's head into left field for a freak single. The ball hit a pebble perhaps. It scored Ruel from second base and won the 1924 World Series for the Senators.

Out of the second million-dollar gate in World Series history, the Washington Club extracted a neat profit of 149,-511.47 dollars in 1924. Clark Griffith's treasury was fat, and he dealt generously with his boy manager, Harris. Bucky, who had signed a contract for 7,000 dollars for the 1924 season before he knew he would be the club's manager, was handed a new contract for 1925-26-27. It called for 30,000 dollars a year for the three seasons.

Chapter IX

HARRIS and Griffith agreed on their chief problem for 1925, and attacked it like a pair of realists. They were not deluding themselves about the state of the club's pitching, despite the triumph of '24. Johnson, their big winner, was now thirty-seven. Mogridge was pushing the same age. Zachary was aging, too, and aside from Johnson there was no guarantee of a starting pitcher who could win consistently. Marberry was young, but he was too valuable in relief roles. Curly Ogden, despite his eight wins in a row late in '24, was still troubled with that sore arm. Old Allan Russell was a gamble, and Joe Martina was almost finished. The rookies, Paul Zahniser and Byron Speece, were not impressive.

And they reckoned well. Mogridge, the venerable southpaw who had won sixteen games in 1924, collapsed by the next June and was traded to the Browns. Zachary was to slip from his previous record by winning only twelve games and losing fifteen. Ogden's attempt to stay on a big-league payroll was pathetic, and he drifted to Chattanooga. Martina was cut loose.

And who took up the slack? Griffith's solution was one of his greatest triumphs. With a pennant-defending club going for him, Griffith was not bent on any long-range planning. Patch and patch again was his theme. He had won his pennant with one of the oldest clubs in the league's history in 1924, and this 1925 team of his was to be even older.

He reached into the National League to claim Dutch Ruether on waivers from the Brooklyn Dodgers, and then he swung a deal with Cleveland for the even older Stanley Coveleskie, one of the last of the spitball relicts. To get Coveleskie he cheerfully gave up Byron Speece, of the accentuated underhand delivery, and rookie Carr Smith. When Griffith finally bought forty-year-old Vean Gregg, the strike-out king of the Pacific Coast League from Seattle, he was accused of going daft in his zest for old pitchers.

Griffith didn't stop there, though. Scanning his infield, he trembled at the broken bodies that were holding two positions, shortstop and first base. Roger Peckinpaugh had played for Griffith back in 1908 with the old New York Highlanders and had lasted out the 1924 season only with the daily ministrations of masseurs and club doctors. His left leg, which had collapsed during the World Series, was still a high risk. And at first base, Joe Judge, always a brittle fellow, was another gamble. .

Griffith obtained the veteran shortstop Everett Scott from the Yankees to help the aging, ailing Peckinpaugh. As a possible replacement for Judge, Griffith came up with the battle-scarred veteran of the First World War who had also served with the Braves, Joe (Moon) Harris. Griffith signed Harris for a double purpose. He could replace Judge at first base or play the outfield. And he could hit.

The Senators' infield was all set, Griffith and Harris assumed. Both Goslin and Rice had their greatest years in 1924, and the veteran Rice was showing no signs of slowing up. Rookie McNeely in center field had filled the bill nicely, and they foresaw no outfield troubles.

Back in the winter of 1923-24, Griffith had given thought to buying Coast League sensation Paul Strand from Salt Lake City for 75,000 dollars, and he was disappointed when Connie

Mack beat him to the buy. Strand failed as a major leaguer, but in the Athletics' spring training camp he had apparently justified Mack's purchase price. Joe Engel, Griffith's scout who had turned in an adverse report on Strand, was highly disturbed.

Engel was uncomfortable that March day at Tampa when the Athletics, with Strand, moved in for an exhibition game with the Senators, with Griffith still highly interested in the fellow. Engel hit upon a plan to get himself out of difficulty.

Before the game he went to Walter Johnson who was to pitch that day, and he spoke plainly to his old friend. He explained his predicament, with Griffith watching Strand. "If Strand gets hot today, I'm a bum in Griffith's eyes," said Engel. "I want you to do me a favor, Walter. When Strand comes up there, give him the works, please, for me." Anything for a friend was the Johnson creed. This one day he didn't loaf in a spring training game. At Strand's every appearance, Johnson buzzed his fast ball, and struck him out three times in a row—for Engel.

The Washington club that faced the Yankees in New York in the opening game of 1925 was exactly the same team that took the field in that final World Series game with the Giants the October before. Mogridge was the starting pitcher, and took a 5-to-1 beating.

Johnson, as usual, pitched the Washington opener. He allowed the Yankees seven hits and beat them, 10 to 1. President Coolidge, who had professed to be a Washington rooter, pulled the chief *faux pas* of that afternoon. He stood up in the visiting half of the seventh, until tugged back to his seat by Mrs. Coolidge, the number one fan of the Coolidge family.

The Senators, Cleveland, and the Athletics were in a three-club scramble for the league lead in the opening weeks, with the A's on top on May 9 with fourteen wins in their first nineteen games. The Senators were second with thirteen to six. McNeely wasn't hitting, and Joe Harris was now playing left field with Goslin in center.

The Yanks were out of it, far down in the second division, with Babe Ruth missing from their line-up because of a two-month illness. It was early established that the Senators' chief challenge would come from the Athletics. Connie Mack had come up with his sensational young outfielder, Al Simmons, his rookie catcher Mickie Cochrane, the young pitching wonder Sam Gray, and doing well too was Eddie Rommel. A fellow named Lefty Grove was throwing the fastest left-hand smoke ball in the league.

Griffith Stadium's right field wall now rose to a thirty-foot height after remodeling, and on May 1 Phil Todt of the Red Sox had the distinction of hitting the first home run over it.

The Senators were still the same deadly double-play team, and on May 28 against the Red Sox they equaled the league record of five twin killings in a single game. The Peck-to-Harris-to-Judge combination was the scourge of ground balls, and the ancient Peck was holding up nicely at shortstop.

The amazing Athletics, the seventh-place club of the season before, were setting a hot pace to hold the lead almost throughout June with the Senators never worse than second. The new pitching trinity of Johnson-Coveleskie-Ruether was clicking with consistency, and on June 19 Mogridge was traded to the Browns along with catcher Pinky Hargrave in a deal for Hank Severeid, the veteran catcher.

On that date of June 19, the rampaging Goslin whacked three home runs at Cleveland to tie the American League record. The last of his homers scored Sam Rice with the winning runs of a 7-to-5 game in the twelfth inning. Bucky Harris carried a twenty-four-game hitting streak into that contest. At that point Rice was hitting .361, Goslin was banging away at .353, Bluege was hitting .332, and the figures for Peck, Judge, and Joe Harris, were .312, .311, and .304.

Coveleskie was almost midway in a thirteen-game winning streak of his own, with six wins in his first seven starts. Johnson had ten wins to show and three defeats, and Ruether had won six out of nine games.

In late June the Senators beat the Athletics in a four-game series and then took over the lead. Goslin slammed a three-run homer surrendered by Lefty Grove in the seventh inning to win the opener, 5 to 3, and fittingly enough it was Johnson who finally pitched the club into the lead.

With a chance to move ahead of the Athletics by a half-game margin, Johnson took command on the afternoon of June 30, with 22,000 in Griffith Stadium. The Big Train not only shut the Athletics out, he outhit them! Johnson got two hits from Slim Harris, his pitching opponent, and was on his way to a no-hit game himself until the ninth inning when pinch hitter Wally French made an infield single for the A's only hit of the afternoon.

In that four-game series with the A's which the Senators swept, Johnson won the opener, 5 to 3, Ruether licked them on five hits, 6 to 1, and Coveleskie shut them out for eight innings in a 4-to-1 victory. Thus did the Senators' Big Three handle the A's.

Two weeks later the A's were back in the lead when the Senators lost three in a row in the West. But Coveleskie's streak was uninterrupted and reached eleven straight when he downed the Tigers, 2 to 1, on five hits. The Senators couldn't match a six-game winning streak of the A's, however. Harris lost the services of Goslin for nearly a week when he was suspended by League president Ban Johnson for a run-in with Bert Cole, Cleveland pitcher, whom Goslin had accused of trying to bean him.

For five weeks they were without Walter Johnson, who was bedded down with influenza, but Coveleskie and Ruether continued to win and the Senators were only a half game behind the A's after Coveleskie beat the Yanks for his thirteenth victory in a row.

When Coveleskie's streak did end, it was emphatic. The White Sox broke it on July 30, driving in four runs in the first inning and pounding out an 11-to-1 victory. On that day the A's moved into their biggest margin of lead, two and one-half games.

Johnson took the mound again for the Senators on August 2. That date was something special. It was on an August 2, eighteen years before that he had also faced a Detroit club in his first big-league appearance. In 1907, he lost to Detroit. On this 1925 date he won his ball game, allowing the Tigers two hits.

For a solid month the A's were out in front of the second-place Senators, but on August 20 the lead shifted, and Washington went on top. Tom Zachary and Fred Marberry teamed up in a twelve-inning pitching job that beat Walter Miller of Cleveland, 1 to 0. Goose Goslin's hit decided it. That same day the Browns came up with two runs in the ninth to beat the A's.

The A's the next day needed only a victory to go back on top, with the Senators losing a 1-to-0, eleven-inning affair to the Tigers, after Coveleskie had pitched scoreless ball for ten innings. But the A's were slapped down by the White Sox, 8 to 2.

The Senators never lost the lead in the last six weeks of the season. Old Joe Harris lengthened their margin to two and one-half games on August 26 with two homers, and a double against the White Sox on August 29. Sam Rice climbed among the league's leading hitters that day with an average of .371—the same day that Yankee manager Miller Huggins announced he was "tired of trying to make Babe Ruth behave," and fined the Bambino 5,000 dollars for misconduct, sending him home from St. Louis.

Washington and the Athletics came out of the West with the Senators leading by three and one-half games, and the A's in a six-game losing streak. They met in what appeared to be a last crucial series of two games. Roger Peckinpaugh doubled home three runs in the second inning and then stole home himself against Slim Harris. It was a 7-to-3 win for Johnson. The next day they beat the A's, 8 to 5. At Philadelphia on Labor Day, Johnson beat Grove in the morning game, 2 to 1, and the A's losing streak reached twelve in a row when the Senators won in the afternoon, 7 to 6. It was complete collapse for the A's, and Washington now had a nine-game lead.

From there it was easy for Harris' patchwork club. The oldest team in the league won the pennant with ninety-six wins and fifty-five defeats, better ball by five and one-half games than they had played in the pennant triumph of 1924. Their margin over the A's at the finish was eight and one-half games.

Coveleskie, the Cleveland castoff, had turned in twenty wins for the Senators, losing only five times. The rejuvenated

Ruether won eighteen and lost seven. Johnson had twenty wins and seven defeats and had actually led the club in hitting, with a .433 average that included two homers in his ninety-seven times at bat. Alec Ferguson, picked up from the Red Sox who got him as a Yankee castoff, turned in five victories and lost only once late in the season.

Now the Senators were scrutinizing the Pirates, their opposite numbers in the National League pennant picture.

The last week in September found the capital slightly heady and somewhat cocky in anticipation of a second straight world championship. Pittsburgh, Senator fans reasoned, wouldn't have a chance.

With the batting edge to Pittsburgh, the defensive advantage to Washington and the teams about evenly matched elsewhere, the balance of power might be found in the pitcher's box. And here the figure of Walter Johnson dominated any comparison. Thirty-eight years old, but still possessed of an indefatigable arm and a courageous heart which drove him to greater effort when his legs and his energy told him to quit, Johnson bulked large in the pitching plans of manager Harris. Surely he would pitch the opener, notwithstanding the fact that Coveleskie had a better season's record, the latter showing a 20-to-5 performance compared to Johnson's 20-to-7 record. Tom Zachary, Dutch Ruether, and Alec Ferguson would be other possible Washington starters, with Fred Marberry handling the relief chores. The Pittsburgh hurlers frightened no one. None of them came near the stature of Johnson or Coveleskie. Lee Meadows, Vic Aldridge, Ray Kremer, and Emil Yde were all good major-league pitchers, yes, but surely not to be compared with the Senators' mound aces.

One week before the Series started, three regulars among the Senators were injured. Manager Harris was by far the most seriously hurt, although it was expected that he would play. A spike wound suffered in a game with Detroit had not responded to treatment as rapidly as expected, but trainer Mike Martin was busy applying his ministrations and confidently predicted he'd be ready. Coveleskie's back was still aching in spite of Mike Martin's liniment massages. In addition, Peckinpaugh hurt his ankle sliding into second base, but he, like the rest of the ailing, was expected to play in the Series.

As the team prepared to journey to Pittsburgh for the opening game, manager Harris made a significant announcement. Joe Harris, he said, would be in the outfield, replacing McNeely, in an attempt to add offensive strength. Oh yes, he added, Johnson would pitch the opening game. All along the train route to Pittsburgh, the Senators were cheered. Whenever the train momentarily stopped, large groups were on hand to wish them good luck.

October 7 dawned cool and crisp in Pittsburgh. Forbes Field was festooned for the occasion with all the ceremonial trimmings. The bunting was everywhere, and 41,723 fans jammed every inch of the stadium to see the great Johnson duel with Lee Meadows, McKechnie's choice. Before the game, Muddy Ruel volunteered the information, for what it was worth, that Johnson never seemed faster. The crowd became conscious of Johnson's speed in the first inning when it gasped as one man as one of the Big Train's fast balls struck Max Carey in the side. But the crowd breathed a collective sigh of relief as Carey trotted to first with no apparent ill effects.

In the second inning Washington took the lead. It was Joe (Moon) Harris, least publicized of the Senators' offensive threats, who did it. In his first appearance at the plate in the Series he picked on a curve by Meadows and sent it into the temporary stands in left field. The ball struck a bench and bounced back on the field. Harris pulled up at second, thinking it was a ground rule double, but was waved around by the umpire who ruled it was a legitimate home run.

The Senators came back for more in the fifth inning. Joe Harris singled to left for his second straight hit. Bluege also singled to left, and when Peckinpaugh smacked an infield hit, the bases were loaded. Meadows, who was sacrificed to Johnson's pitching ability, was weakening. But then he demonstrated that he, too, could call on pitching reserve. He whipped three straight strikes past Ruel, the Washington catcher watching all three go by. Walter Johnson watched two strikes and a ball, then swung viciously for Meadows' second strike-out. Up came Sam Rice with the last chance to boost Washington's 1-to-0 advantage. Meadow's first pitch was a ball and then came two strikes. Carefully Meadows pitched the next one, but Rice sent it on a line into center field for a single, scoring Joe Harris and Bluege. Washington scored its final run in the ninth inning when Goslin singled, advanced to second on Judge's infield grounder, and scored on Bluege's single to center. The game was a Washington victory, 4 to 1.

It was Johnson's day. Fast, sneaky, and courageous, he was master all the way. It mattered little that Pie Traynor homered to score the Pirates' only run. Ruel actually had trouble holding the ball, so fast was Johnson. His performance that day was reminiscent of the years when, much younger, he smoked the ball past opposing batters with monotonous regularity. He was the Johnson of old, striking out ten and allowing only five hits. In winning, Washington acquired eight hits. The Senators had won the opening game. Their joy was great, tempered only by the news of the death of Christy Mathewson that same day in Saranac Lake, New York.

If the first game proved anything, it was certainly the fact that so far the forecast had proven correct. Johnson's pitching held the balance between two evenly matched teams. But what would the Senators do when Johnson wasn't pitching? Perhaps the next day would be a real test of comparative strength. Coveleskie, his back taped, was Harris' pitching selection while McKechnie countered with Vic Aldridge, another right-hander.

The early pattern of the game pointed to another Washington victory. The Senators once again took the lead in the second inning, again by a home run, this time by Joe Judge. The irrepressible Traynor came back in the fourth for his second home run of the series, and the score was tied, 1 to 1.

Coveleskie and Aldridge were engaged in a great pitchers' duel, with the score still 1 to 1 in the last half of the eighth. But then came disaster from an unexpected quarter. Roger

140

Peckinpaugh had been a great shortstop. His fielding had won him acclaim of friend and foe alike, and his batting, although not of the slugging variety, was steady. But what happened to Peck in the last of the eighth can be answered only by the fates which guide such misadventures. Moore was the first batter, and he sent an easy grounder to shortstop. Peckinpaugh reached for the ball, but it bounced off his glove and rolled against his sleeve. It was an error, Peck's second of the series. After Carey grounded to Harris, Cuyler drove a home run over the temporary right field fence and the damage was done. The Pirates had taken a 3-to-1 lead. After Cuyler's homer Barnhart singled, and Traynor grounded to Peckinpaugh who once again fumbled for his third error. Fortunately for Washington, it was able to retire Wright and Grantham to prevent further damage.

The Senators rebounded in the ninth to bring the score to 3 to 2 but fell short of scoring the tying run. Joe Harris walked and Earl McNeely was sent in to run. A single and another walk filled the bases, with none out. A hit would tie the score. In this situation manager Harris sent Bobby Veach to bat for Ruel. With the crowd holding its breath, Veach lifted a fly to Carey, and McNeely scored with the second run. Ruether, who had relieved Coveleskie, struck out, and Rice grounded out to end the game, Pittsburgh winning, 3 to 2.

The second game was costly to Washington, for in addition to losing, it also temporarily had to dispense with the services of Ossie Bluege, its third baseman. Bluege was beaned by Aldridge in the third inning. Bluege, after being carried from the field, was taken to Johns Hopkins Hospital in Baltimore for two days of observation. The Washington club was informed the next day that Bluege had not suffered a fractured skull. "In fact," the doctor told Clark Griffith, "we believe that Mr. Bluege's skull is the thickest we've ever X-rayed at Hopkins, for which he can be fortunate."

Bluege's replacement at third base that day in Pittsburgh was a rookie named Buddy Myer, acclaimed a year before as the finest baseball player ever to perform for Mississippi

Agricultural and Mechanical College, the school that sent Hughie Critz to the majors. The Senators bought Myer late in the season from New Orleans as a second baseman for 25,000 dollars, after refusing to give him a 1,000-dollar bonus for signing that spring when he wrote the club asking for a tryout.

After a day's postponement because of the rain, the Series shifted back to Griffith Stadium. President Coolidge rushed back from his Massachusetts home to be on hand, and with him came other dignitaries, including Secretary of State Kellogg and Attorney General Sargent. Manager Harris' pitching selection was Alec Ferguson, right-hander, opposed by Ray Kremer of the Pirates. For the first time in the Series, the Pirates scored first, going ahead in the second inning on Traynor's triple and Wright's long fly to Goslin. But the Senators quickly rebounded in their half of the third to tie the score. Rice singled to center, Bucky Harris sacrificed, and Judge doubled. Back came the Pirates to take the lead again in the fourth. Cuyler doubled and Barnhart singled him across. The Pirates made it 3 to 1 in the sixth, once again capitalizing on Peck's shoddy fielding. His fourth error permitted Wright to get on first and score on singles by Smith and pitcher Kremer. Goose Goslin put the Senators back in the game in their half of the sixth simply enough. He just hit one over the right field fence.

The Senators won the game in the seventh inning like champions. One run behind, Harris sent little Nemo Leibold to bat for Ferguson with instruction to wait out a walk. He did. After Rice flied out, Bucky Harris smacked an infield hit, his first of the series. Goslin was up. Everybody, including the Pirates, expected him to swing from the heels. Their belief was substantiated when he swung—and missed—at the first offering. Then, with the infield playing far out, Goslin surprised everybody by placing a perfect bunt down the third base line, filling the bases. Judge then lifted a fly to center, and Earl McNeely, who was running for Leibold, scored with the tying run. Joe Harris, a hero throughout the entire Series, came through again with a sharp single to left to score Bucky Harris with the winning run.

That's the way it ended, 4 to 3, Washington. But it didn't end before some dramatic baseball had been played. To the cheers of the fans Fred Marberry went to the mound in the eighth inning. Making his first appearance in five weeks, the cannon-ball relief hurler added to his glory by striking out the first two Pirates. Then Earl Smith stepped to the plate and drove a long fly to right center field. Rice backed up as far as he could against the wall, and then suddenly the player, the ball, and the crowd all merged into one confusing picture. Sam Rice had fallen into the bleachers. That was sure, but did he catch it? There was a delay by Rice in getting out of the stands, and manager McKechnie charged out of the dugout, protesting that Rice had dropped the ball and that it had been recovered for him by a spectator.

After long debate, the four umpires announced unanimously that Rice had caught the ball before falling into the bleachers and held onto it. But McKechnie wasn't satisfied. He strode angrily to Judge Landis' box and asked if a protest could be filed. Landis said "No", and McKechnie retired crestfallen to the dugout. In the Washington dugout, Rice was asked about the delay in getting out of the stands. With a straight face, Rice said he was choking when his Adam's apple hit the head of a spectator.

To add to the confusion in the eighth inning, the Senators batted out of order in their half of the inning. When Washington took the field for the eighth, McNeely, who had run for Leibold batting for Ferguson, went to center. Rice moved to right and Marberry went to the mound. Under the rules, McNeely should have batted ninth, but in his place Marberry came up. The Pirates were caught napping, and when they realized the error, it was too late to do anything about it. Sam Rice, the next batter, was already batting.

From the time that Bucky Harris announced Walter Johnson as Washington's pitcher in the fourth game, there wasn't much doubt as to the outcome. His opponent was a southpaw, Emil Yde. Neither team scored until the third, when Washington pushed across four runs in one offensive outburst against Yde. With Rice and Harris on base, Goslin delivered his third home run of the Series, tying a World Series record and putting Washington three runs ahead. The next batter was Joe Harris, and he too smashed a home run into the left field bleachers. Those four runs were all Washington ever got, but with Johnson pitching superbly, they didn't need any more. They won, 4 to 0.

But is was a very costly victory for Washington. For in that same third inning good luck was tempered by misfortune. Walter Johnson singled to left to open the inning but tried to stretch it into a double. In so doing, he severely strained his leg muscle. He limped off the field and was told to quit by trainer Martin. But Johnson begged to remain in the game and ordered Martin to bandage the muscle. Johnson could scarcely walk, but proved himself the best pitcher in baseball on one leg as well as two. In the six innings following his injury, he faced only twenty batters. All told, he yielded six hits in capturing his second game of the Series, the third for Washington, which now led, 3 to 1.

The night before the fifth game Harris wrestled with his pitching decision for the next game. Should it be left-handers Ruether or Zachary, or should he send Coveleskie back? Sensing victory, the youthful Harris gambled on Covey. It was a bad choice, for the Pirates, who had already beaten the ailing Pole, slashed out a 6-to-3 triumph to bring themselves within one game of a tie.

As in the second game of the series, Covey drew Vic Aldridge as his pitching opponent. Bluege, whom Aldridge had beaned in the second game, returned to the line-up. The Senators started off with intentions of ending the Series, scoring in the first inning on Rice's single, a sacrifice by Harris, and a double by Goslin. The Pirates went ahead in the third on two walks, a single, a stolen base, and an outfield fly, good for two runs. The Senators came back in the fourth to tie the game with Joe Harris' third homer. But a walk to Moore in the seventh, followed by three singles, produced three runs. The Senators reduced the Pirates' margin in the seventh to 5 to 3 on Leibold's double and Rice's single, but the Pirates clinched their 6-to-3 victory in the ninth on a walk and two singles after two were out.

The Pittsburgh victory threw manager Harris' pitching

plans into turmoil. Expecting to win the Series with Coveleskie, Bucky now scoured his staff for an available pitcher for the sixth game in the smoky city. Against the pitcher's own wishes, he decided to return Alec Ferguson to the mound. Taking no chances, McKechnie sent Ray Kremer to pitch, as he did in the third game. But Harris had other worries. For, in addition to his pitching problems, he was worried about his spiked hand. He was playing with a taped hand, which gave him great pain. He was of little value to the team at bat, but played well enough in the field.

The sixth game was a near duplicate of the second, with Pittsburgh winning, 3 to 2. With neither team hitting, the game resolved itself into a defensive battle, with Traynor's bunting and Wright's fielding giving the Pirates the advantage. The Pirates scored twice in the third inning.

In the fifth Moore drove a homer into the temporary bleachers to give Pittsburgh a 3-to-2 lead, which turned out to be the final score. Washington had scored its two runs earlier on Goslin's homer in the first and on a single by Judge and a double by Peckinpaugh in the second. Both pitchers hurled well, but Kremer deserved his victory, yielding seven hits to Ferguson's six.

With the Series knotted at 3 to 3, Pittsburgh fans were certain that the Pirates had the necessary offensive impetus to win against the Senators who had suffered defeat in their last two meetings. While Harris pondered his pitching selection (only Harris pondered apparently, for everyone else knew it would be Walter Johnson), the rains came again and postponed the Series for one day. Now Harris' pitching selection was certain. It would have to be Johnson. The day of rest would aid his injured leg.

There was rain and cold in Pittsburgh on October 15, 1925, and few of the assembled crowd thought the game would be played. But Judge Landis was insistent and ordered the teams on a muddy field. Johnson was opposed by Vic Aldridge. Each was making his third start. Throughout the steady rain the players were vague and shadowy figures. Never had a ball game been ordered to proceed under such circumstances.

145

But Landis was the law, and the Series, now in its ninth day, went on as scheduled. Knowing that Johnson's leg was none too steady, the Senators went out to pile up an early lead. They scored four runs in the first inning. Rice singled to center and immediately went to second on a wild pitch. After Harris flied to Barnhart, Goslin walked and both runners advanced on a second wild pitch as Aldridge experienced difficulty in gripping the wet ball. Joe Harris walked to fill the bases, and Judge walked to force in Rice. Bluege singled, scoring Goslin and leaving the bases filled. On the next play catcher Smith tipped Peckinpaugh's bat, and a catcher's balk was called, forcing in Joe Harris with the third run. Morrison succeeded Aldridge on the mound, and the Senators had their fourth run from him when Moore fumbled Ruel's grounder, allowing Judge to score.

But the Pirates weren't out of the game. Pitching with excruciating leg pains, Johnson permitted three singles and a double in the third inning, and his lead was cut to 4 to 3. In the fourth inning, Washington stretched its lead to 6 to 3 when Rice and Goslin singled and the valuable Joe Harris doubled to bring in the two runners. Back bounced Pittsburgh in the fifth to make it 6 to 4 on doubles by Cuyler and Carey. The Pirates were hitting Johnson freely, but Harris dared not take him out as long as Washington led.

In the seventh the Pirates finally tied the score, after trying for six previous innings. Once again, however, they needed Peckinpaugh's errors to do it. Moore grounded to Peck, who once again fumbled the ball. Carey doubled and Traynor tripled to make it 6 to 6. On the quagmire that passed for a baseball diamond the Senators forged ahead in the eighth. As if to atone for his grievous fielding, Peck blasted a home run high into the left field stands. If the Senators had been able to hold that 7-to-6 lead, all of Peck's errors would have been forgiven.

Pitching carefully in the eighth, Johnson disposed of Wright and McInnis on fly balls, then whipped two straight strikes on Smith. But the next pitch was to his liking, and he rapped it into center for a double. Yde ran for Smith. Bigbee batted for Kremer and doubled to right, scoring Yde with the tying run. The Pirates rubbed it in. Moore walked, the first base on balls Johnson had issued all day in the rain. Carey grounded a double-play ball directly at Peckinpaugh, but, horrors, his throw to second was wide and all runners were safe. It was Peck's eighth error, a new Series record. With the bases loaded, Cuyler delivered the finishing touch with a double which slithered under the canvas in right field, scoring Bigbee and Moore. It was 9 to 7, and that was the way it ended, with Goslin expressing Washington's futility in the ninth by watching a third strike go by.

In the dressing room the gloom was everywhere. Saddest of all was the weeping Peckinpaugh, the unmistakable goat of the Series. A telegram from League president Ban Johnson to Harris didn't help. In it he criticized Bucky's use of Walter Johnson for three games for "sentimental" reasons. "Sentiment," he wired, "has no place in a World Series." Bucky made the only logical defense of his position: "He was my only choice. I'd start him again."

Landis, too, was furious at Harris. Some of the players had turned journalists for the Series, but Landis didn't like what he was reading, especially by the Senator authors. He promptly called Bucky Harris, Ruel, and Peckinpaugh, among others, and ordered them to apologize to the umpires for some allegedly derogatory remarks which appeared in print. The players attended the meeting, but Bucky left the high commissioner in high dudgeon with a reply that he was too busy to attend.

After the game many Pittsburgh fans came to the Washington dressing room, searching out Walter Johnson. Always their message was the same: "We're glad Pittsburgh won, but we're sorry it had to be you." Only the post-mortems remained. The batting averages reflected some of the reasons why the Senators lost. Only Joe Harris, with an amazing .440 average in the Series, and Sam Rice, who hit .367, were consistent hitters. Ruel was the only other hitter above .300, batting a surprising .316. Bucky Harris, playing with a badly damaged hand that prevented his gripping a bat, swung for a miserable .087.

Returning to Washington, where a large crowd of youngsters greeted them at the station, the Senators divided their spoils before scattering for home. Full shares of about 3,800 dollars were voted twenty-four players. Coveleskie and Marberry were given 1,000-dollar bonuses by Griffith for outstanding performances during the season. Trade talk struck the Senators immediately. The name of Goose Goslin figured prominently, but Griffith, in a characteristic pronouncement, declared: "I wouldn't trade Goose for the whole Yankee Stadium. And I mean it."

Chapter X

ONLY by the margin of Joe Judge's home run in the final game of the 1926 season at Chicago, did the Senators avert a drop from two-time pennant winners into the second division. Judge's swat landed the club in fourth place, a game and a half ahead of the White Sox.

The club's pitching sagged dismally that season. Johnson turned in fifteen victories, but he showed his worst earned run average (3.51) since earned run records began to be kept in 1913. He lost sixteen games. The veteran Coveleskie was feeling the weight of his years too, and he slipped from the top ranks of the league's pitchers in 1926, by a record of fourteen wins and eleven defeats. Fred Marberry, both starting and relieving, won eleven and lost seven, and rookie Al Crowder won seven and lost four.

The finger pointed directly at the impotency of the Senators' pitching staff, since the club led the league in hitting. The Senators had a team batting average of .292 to take team hitting honors.

Young Myer had replaced the fading Peck as the club's regular shortshop despite having played only second and third base in his one year in the minors. At bat he pounded out an estimable .304 average. The club had a complete .300-hitting outfield with Goslin .354 in left, Sam Rice .337 in right, and Earl McNeely .303 in center. Little catcher Muddy Ruel swung a .299 bat.

There was no indication in the opening game of the season that Johnson wasn't going to have a good year. The 38-year-old Big Train, now a nineteen-year veteran of the major leagues, took the mound against Eddie Rommel of the Athletics at the Griffith Stadium opener on April 13, and at the end of fifteen innings was the winner by a classic 1-to-0 score.

Batters were still wary of Johnson's speed despite the fact he was nearing forty, and the customers always gasped in fear of tragedy on those rare occasions when the Big Train did hit a batter. One day early in 1926, with the White Sox in Washington, Eddie Collins took one of Johnson's fast balls in the leg.

Collins went down instantly, and briefly it was feared that he had a fractured leg. Johnson raced to the plate where Collins was groveling in anguish, and stood there with grief on his face while first aid was given the injured player. Eventually, Collins got up, still hugging his leg in pain. When he decided to stay in the game, Johnson patted him gratefully on the back. Given his base, Collins limped to first, and the fans applauded the gameness of the White Sox star who was apparently torn with pain. Johnson, relieved that he hadn't broken a man's leg, went back to his pitching. And from the trusting Johnson, Collins, the fraud, stole second on the first pitch!

Old Dutch Ruether, a big winner in 1925, was of so little help the succeeding season he was sold to the Yankees at the waiver price. Tom Zachary went to the Browns in a cash deal. At second base, Bucky Harris was getting no younger, and Stuffy Stewart was brought up from the Southern Association to fill in. Bobby Reeves, a football star at Georgia Institute of Technology, was also getting a tryout at third base and shortstop. But without pitching, the Senators were a second division club until the last day of the season.

Tragedy hit the Senators a month before they opened their 1927 season. At Tampa, Florida, Walter Johnson, pitching

149

in batting practice, was hit on the right leg by a line drive from the bat of his roommate, Joe Judge.

Like other pitchers, Johnson had been struck many times by batted balls. A few moments of sharp pain, a swelling, ice packs, a couple of days limping, and the pitcher generally is little the worse for his accident. Traditionally, ball players like to poke fun when pitchers are nicked and apparently not badly hurt. On this occasion, as Johnson toppled to the ground, clown-coach Al Schacht rushed out to the mound and went into high jinks, counting ten over the fallen Johnson in the manner of a fight referee.

Neither Schacht, nor Harris, nor the thirty-odd Senators on the scene could know at the time that the club's clown actually was counting ten over the pitching career of the greatest hurler in American League history. Johnson's leg was broken, and he came back from the South on crutches.

In that spring training camp of the Senators was the distinguished figure of Tris Speaker, wearing a Washington uniform after a long career with the Red Sox and Cleveland. Griffith had grabbed up the Gray Eagle after his voluntary retirement from the Indians, following Dutch Leonard's unsubstantiated charges that both Speaker and Ty Cobb had bet on fixed games.

Griffith paid Speaker 30,000 dollars on a one-season contract as insurance in the Washington outfield. Earl McNeely was no longer a batting power in center field, and his throwing arm was dismal. Griffith envisioned Speaker as a powerful addition to an outfield otherwise comprised of Goose Goslin and Sam Rice.

The Senators in 1927 were guilty of the most colossal error in the trading market in the history of the club. In May, they dispatched the promising young infielder, Buddy Myer, to the Red Sox in a straight swap for the veteran Topper Rigney, who had previously been with the Tigers. It was a deal they rued.

The deal wasn't originated by Griffith, and he made it reluctantly. Bucky Harris pressed the old gentleman to make the trade, after letting Speaker talk him into it. Speaker sold Harris on the idea of a Myer-Rigney swap by vowing that "this club can win another pennant if we can get a third base-man like Rigney and let Bluege play shortstop."

Rigney flopped dismally for Washington, batting only .271 in 46 games, and he was slow in the field. He was released after midseason. Myer became a sensation at Boston with his hitting and fielding, and in 1928 led the league in stolen bases. In later years Griffith admitted it was "the worst deal I ever made."

Johnson was useless to the Senators for seven weeks, but with the aid of an iron brace fitted to his leg from the ankle to the knee, he kept in shape by pitching in batting practice. On Decoration Day he made his first start of the season, against the Red Sox. He shut Boston out with three hits.

Admiring Washington fans celebrated on August 2, for Johnson was to start against Detroit, the club that, twenty years before to the day, had beaten him in his first major-league start. Twenty thousand fans were in the park for the Johnson anniversary. The two clubs honored him by giving him the day's gate receipts of $14,476.05, and gifts from the fans, including $1,500 in cash, were heaped high around home plate.

On his twentieth anniversary day with the Washington club, Johnson was sharing the front page of the newspapers with President Calvin Coolidge, who came into the limelight that day with his famed statement, "I do not choose to run."

Secretary of State Frank Kellogg delivered a testimonial speech at home plate, paying Johnson tribute by saying, "Your name stands for what is best in sports and your personal life is held as an example to the youth of our country." For four innings Johnson didn't allow the Tigers a hit. Then they got six hits and four runs in the fifth and drove him out in the eighth to beat the Senators, 7 to 6.

The Senators were in the first division all season, and finished third behind the Yankees and Athletics. Speaker earned his 30,000 dollars or most of it, by hitting .327. Goslin as usual led the club in batting with .334, and the club got timely pinch hitting from Bennie Tate. But the veteran pitchers bogged down. Johnson could win only five games and he lost six. Marberry had ten wins and seven losses. On the top of the pitching staff were a pair of rookies, Bump Hadley who won fourteen and lost six, and Horace Lisenbee, another Southern Association graduate who won eighteen and lost nine. Coveleskie was given his outright release and Crowder was sold to St. Louis.

Save for the tremendous relief work of Marberry and Garland Braxton, the latter a southpaw obtained from the Yankees, the Senators would have finished in the second division. Braxton set a new record for appearances by a pitcher in a single season, figuring in fifty-eight games. He had an earned-run average of 2.94. Marberry pitched in fifty-six games.

At the Tampa, Florida, training camp the next Spring, the 1928 Senators got two staggering jolts. Walter Johnson came down with a severe case of influenza, was rushed back to Washington, lost thirty pounds in a prolonged illness, and never was to pitch another inning for the Senators. Goose Goslin, star of their batting order, came down with a sore arm that became famous.

Two specialists accompanied Johnson to Washington from Florida, and he was not discharged from the hospital until two weeks after the season started. He was still a patient when his retirement from the Washington club was announced. He had signed a two-year contract to manage the Newark club of the International League, owned by publisher Paul Block.

Goslin, the perennial problem child of the Senators at every spring training, got into deep trouble in the spring of 1928. During one of the workouts, he swaggered over to an adjoining part of the Tampa Fair Grounds where a high school track team was practicing, and watched the kids throw the sixteen-pound shot. The temptation was too much for the Goose. He grabbed up the shot, flung it twenty feet farther than anybody else, and for the next half hour was having a huge time at this new kind of fun.

The next day Goslin couldn't raise his left arm to comb his hair. One of the best throwing arms in the majors was useless. At first it was regarded as just another sore arm, but

152

when the club came North for the opener with the Red Sox, everybody in the league knew the Goose couldn't throw a ball one hundred feet.

But the Senators needed Goslin and his big bat in there. He played left field with the assistance of shortstop Bobby Reeves who, on every ball hit to Goslin, would dash into the outfield to take what was little more than a lob from the Goose and relay it in. Bucky Harris called Goslin "the only outfielder in history with a caddy." But with Goslin hitting more than .400 for half the season, there was no great temptation to get him out of there.

The Senators were fortunate to have Reeves around in that crisis. At Georgia Institute of Technology, his football fame exceeded his baseball reputation, but he did have a tremendous throwing arm. In the infield practices, first baseman Joe Judge, his hand raw from taking Reeves' hot shots from across the diamond, actually was driven to casting off his first baseman's glove and warming up with a catcher's mitt to save his catching hand from further punishment by Reeves.

The team Bucky Harris brought North had a heavy Southern Association accent. The regular center fielder was Sammy West, who had come up from Birmingham late the preceding season. He had been recommended as a good hitter who was clumsy in the field, and what a false lead that was. In thirty-eight games in 1927, he demonstrated that he was wonderful in the outfield with a tremendous throwing arm, but his batting average was a mere .239. But in the '28 training camp he clinched the center field job with his hitting.

A pair of former football stars at the University of Alabama who had teamed up to beat the University of Washington, 20 to 19, in the Rose Bowl game of 1928 were now members of the Senators. Grant Gillis, who had thrown a pass sixty yards through the air for the winning touchdown, was with the Senators as a shortstop. Red Barnes, who had caught Gillis' pass just over the goal line had come to the Senators as an outfielder from the Southern Association.

Without Walter Johnson for the first time in twenty-one seasons, the Senators' pitching staff bogged badly. The vet-

153

eran Sam Jones, a fortunate purchase from the Yankees, took up a lot of the slack with seventeen wins and seven defeats, but he was the only pitcher to win more than he lost, with the exception of Garland Braxton, another old Yankee, who won thirteen and lost eleven. Horace Lisenbee, an eighteen-game winner of the year before, turned in only two victories. Irving Hadley and Fred Marberry were in-and-outers.

But the Senators finished fourth, behind the Yankees, Athletics, and Browns, three games ahead of the White Sox. They got out of the second division with a late season spurt that saw them win seventeen of their last twenty-seven games. Braxton had the best earned-run average in the league (2.52). Bucky Harris was slowing at second base, and Jackie Hayes was his chief replacement.

George Sisler was a member of the Senators briefly, in the Spring of 1928. Griffith bought him cheaply from the Browns. Sisler was already complaining of the sinus trouble that eventually was to drive him from baseball, but Griffith gambled he would make a comeback. In Florida Sisler hit well, but Bucky Harris was concerned with his fielding. Heavy-legged and slow, Sisler proved no threat to the fancy-fielding Joe Judge, and in May he was sold to the Boston Braves on waivers.

A shortstop named Joe Cronin broke into the Washington line-up late in July. Bobby Reeves was wearied from his arduous duties as shortstop and assistant left fielder to Goslin, and he welcomed the rest when Bucky Harris benched him in favor of Cronin, who came from Kansas City.

Harris must have liked what he saw in Cronin because on the Senators' next western trip he was playing the young Irishman with regularity in Reeves' shortstop job. Griffith, however, was pleased with Reeves and unimpressed by his early look at Cronin. He wired Harris in the West: "Reeves will never be a ball player if you don't play him."

Harris, an independent soul if prodded too much, promptly telegraphed Griffith a curt reply: "Neither will Cronin be a big leaguer if we don't play him." Harris had his way. Cronin was in sixty-three games before the season ended.

154

He batted only .243, but he was making all the plays around shortstop.

Goose Goslin, sore arm and all, was the big noise of the 1928 Senators, however. He was in the race for the batting championship from the start, and at one point was hitting better than .400. In the closest batting race in American League history, he nosed out Heinie Manush of the Browns for the title by one point, .379 to .378.

First it was Al Simmons of the Athletics who challenged Goslin for the lead, but the Goose spurted over a long stretch to dispose of him. In August, Lou Gehrig took up the chase, but Goslin was maintaining his steady pace. A week before the season closed, Manush actually was in front of him, and the championship was decided on the last two days in a head-to-head battle between the opposing pair as their clubs closed out the season.

In that final four-game series with the Browns, Goslin made seven hits in fifteen times at bat, to take a two-point lead into the final day. Sam Jones, the ace of the Senators' pitching staff, volunteered to work out of turn in an attempt to deflate Manush's average. But Manush in four times at bat singled twice for two of the Browns' seven hits.

Goslin, though, collected two hits himself, from the pitching of George Blaeholder, of the Browns. His first was a three-run homer that decided the ball game. His two-point lead was cut to one point at the finish, but the Senators had their first American League batting champion since Ed Delahanty's .376 in 1902. The Goose was also third to Babe Ruth and Lou Gehrig in homers, with his total of seventeen.

It was Bucky Harris' worst year in the big leagues, however. He was slowing up alarmingly around second base, and played only ninety-nine games. His batting average sagged to .204. Forgetful Washington fans who had acclaimed him so uproariously after the pennant-winning years of 1924 and 1925 were now jeering from the stands and unfeelingly shouting "Take him out!" when Harris booted the ball.

Rumors flew that Harris had gone ultra-social and high-hat following his marriage and Paris honeymoon at the end of the 1926 season. He had married Elizabeth Sutherland, daughter of the senator from West Virginia. Also, Harris was being blamed for the trade that sent Buddy Myer to the Red Sox.

Harris blamed his slowness on the beating his legs had taken on the hardwood basketball floors before he quit that game for baseball exclusively. But to the finish there was no lack of determination about Harris' play.

Red Ruffing was still with the Red Sox when Harris demonstrated he wasn't above anything to win a ball game. Ruffing was battling the Senators into extra innings, and the day was darkening when Harris from the bench pleaded with his next hitter to get on base in some way. "If we can fill the bases, I'll get the winning run in somehow," Harris announced, "even if I have to take one in the ribs and force it over."

That's what happened. The Senators did fill the bases, and on Ruffing's first pitch to Harris, Bucky feigned an attempt to get out of the way and took a fast ball under the arm, even as he had announced he would. The winning run was waved home from third.

That night Harris was at dinner with his new bride and her father when Mrs. Harris remarked, "Stanley, it looked to me as if you deliberately got hit by Ruffing's pitch to get the winning run in."

Before Harris could admit it, the senator interjected, "Ridiculous, Liz. That would be unsportsmanlike. You know that Stanley wouldn't do a thing like that." And Bucky didn't disillusion him.

On Oct. 1, 1928, Harris was out as the Senators' manager. Clark Griffith called him in, pointed out that he was losing popularity, and suggested he resign. But Griffith knew of another place for Bucky. "Frank Navin, of the Detroit club, wants to hire you as manager," said Griffith, "and you can have the job tomorrow." Harris had the job ten minutes later, by long distance telephone, replacing George Moriarty as manager of the Tigers.

Walter Johnson wasn't Griffith's ideal as a manager. He wanted another man in the image of Bucky Harris, who had gratified Griffith so much with his hell-for-leather leadership in those years before Harris had become jaded with the whole business. Griffith liked to think that he had schooled Harris in his own aggressive style, and he pined for another of the type. He scanned his roster in vain. The veterans Joe Judge and Sam Rice he rejected as uninspiring. Bluege, his good young third baseman, also lacked spark. Griffith succumbed to sentiment and named Johnson.

Against the fear that Johnson was too nice, too gracious to fling himself into the hard business of managing a big-league ball team, Griffith staked the hope that the Big Train's year of managerial experience at Newark had helped to fit him for the job. Washington fans may have shared Griffith's misgivings about Johnson, but they didn't voice it in their appreciation of the fitness of things—Johnson managing the Washington club after giving his powerful best from the pitching mound for twenty-one seasons. Certainly no manager ever took a job with more well-wishers.

Johnson's debut season was a hard one. After five consecutive years in the first division under Harris, the Senators fell into fifth place under Johnson in 1929, eight full games behind the fourth place Browns, and were never a pennant factor.

But Johnson did make one tremendous contribution to the club in that year. He took a cold view of the infield he inherited from Harris, and particularly was he dissatisfied with Reeves at shortstop. Also, he was not impressed with Jackie Hayes or Stuffy Stewart, the rookies who were supposed to replace Harris at second base. He well remembered young Buddy Myer, the kid from New Orleans, whom the Senators had traded to the Red Sox in 1927, and he wanted Myer in his ball club. He would shift Bluege to shortstop and replace the light-hitting and erratic Joe Cronin. He wanted Myer at third base where he had made good for the Red Sox in 1928 and had led the league in stolen bases. He'd gamble on his second baseman.

At Johnson's urging, Griffith made a deal that fetched Myer from Boston—a whopping five-player delivery to the Red Sox during the winter of 1928-29. With what must have been a breaking heart, Griffith turned over to the Red Sox shortstop Bobby Reeves, infielder Grant Gillis, the hard-throwing rookie pitcher Horace Lisenbee who in 1927 had won eighteen games, the veteran right-hander Milt Gaston, and the big rookie outfielder Elliott Bigelow.

Now Griffith could total up the staggering cost of Myer to whom, back in 1925, he had refused to pay a 1,000-dollar bonus for signing when the lad came out of Mississippi A & M looking for a baseball job. Later that year the Senators bought Myer for 25,000 dollars from New Orleans. The five players turned over to Boston Griffith appraised at 100,000 dollars. "It cost me $125,000 to get the man I could have signed for almost nothing," he moaned.

Actually, Griffith found himself twice blessed in the Myer deal. Not only was Myer to become a key man of the Senators for the next decade, but the Washington club at first had balked at the trade with Boston on one disputed point. The Red Sox held out for Reeves to be included in the deal. The Senators tried to appease them with Joe Cronin. The Red Sox wouldn't take Cronin, who had hit only .243 in contrast to Reeves' .303 average in 1928, and Griffith found himself stuck with the lad who was to become the greatest shortstop of his time and a pennant-winning manager.

Johnson's 1929 Senators never clicked. Sam Rice was the only .300-hitting outfielder. Tris Speaker, after a one-year stay in Washington, had moved on to join Ty Cobb on the Athletics. Earl McNeely had been traded to the Browns. Young Red Barnes, the Alabama football star who had batted .305 the year before, slumped to an even .200. Goslin, the league batting champion of 1928, slumped from .379 to .288 and was having a foul season. Sammy West gave the club slick center fielding but hit a meager .267.

The two relief men, Marberry and Garland Braxton, were the top pitchers on the club, the only men to win more than ten games. Ad Liska, the submarine baller from Minneapolis where he won twenty, won only three for the Senators. Sad Sam Jones was fading and won only nine of eighteen decisions. Little Lloyd Brown, a southpaw from Memphis, won eight against seven defeats. Strong-armed Bump Hadley pitched often, won only six and tasted sixteen defeats.

Johnson shuffled his infield almost weekly. Bluege made the move from third base to shortstop gracefully enough, but second base was still Johnson's chief worry, and in desperation he transferred Myer from third to that spot where Myer was to remain for the next decade. But the season produced a regular shortstop in young Cronin who was conquering his weakness with softly hit ground balls. Cronin revealed himself to be the owner of a sensational throwing arm, and he batted a creditable .282.

But it was no use. When the Athletics won eleven in a row in May, on their way to the pennant, nine of those victories were against the Senators and implanted them firmly in the second division. In July they lost twenty games, won only ten. In August they bumped into an eleven-game losing streak that dumped them in sixth place before they finally beat the Tigers for fifth.

The Senators of 1930 could qualify as a tough-luck team in one respect. They won two more games, ninety-four, than the Washington team that won the 1924 pennant, yet finished in second place. In vain they pursued the still strong Athletics who were on their way to a second straight pennant with Jimmy Foxx, Al Simmons, and Mickey Cochrane giving a big lift to the pitching of Grove, Earnshaw, and Walberg.

Johnson's club got off to a sizzling start with ten wins in its first thirteen games, and it appeared they were pennant bound if all they had to do was beat the Athletics. They slapped down the A's in seven straight meetings in late May and early June, and then it was a complete about-face. The next seven times they met, the A's won.

The Senators were a dismal road club. On their first swing into the West they won only five out of thirteen. Their second venture was worse—seven out of nineteen. On a third western trip they dropped seven out of thirteen. Two eight-game winning streaks at home, and a ten-victory skein were offset by the club's utter inability even to break even on the road.

The Senators-A's engagements produced one of baseball's bitterest feuds. Big Fred Marberry and big Al Simmons carried on a pitcher-versus-hitter vendetta all season. Simmons accused Marberry of trying to bean him, and Marberry confided that was exactly his idea. He sent the Athletics' slugger collapsing to the ground with high hard ones every time he faced the A's. A half-dozen times Simmons advanced to the pitcher's box, bat in hand, to lay waste to Marberry, who was willing to chance it. Cooler headed teammates always averted mayhem, however.

In Marberry Simmons was tackling the Senators' tough guy on the ball field. Off the field, the big Texan was a gentle, smiling fellow who wanted trouble with nobody, but in his rookie days under Harris he had established his willingness to get tough with the tough hitters. Up in Yankee Stadium a couple of years before when the Yankees were riding him from the bench, Marberry paused on the way to the showers to challenge the Yankees one by one or en masse. "You, Ruth, can be first," roared Marberry, "and you'll need all the help you can round up." The Yankees looked over the giant Texan and silence fell among them.

It was the year that Griffith was in one of his lustiest trading moods. He was envisioning a pennant for his club in early June, and two days before the trading deadline he surprised Washington fans by disposing of Goose Goslin to the Browns in a swap for outfielder Heinie Manush and pitcher Alvin Crowder. The same day he traded Red Barnes to the White Sox for outfielder Dave (Sheriff) Harris. Minutes before the deadline fell he engineered a third deal: pitcher Garland Braxton and catcher Bennie Tate to the White Sox for first baseman Art Shires.

The trade of Goslin, who was popular with the fans and a personal favorite of Griffith, occasioned something of a heart wrench, but he wasn't hitting and Manush was. Anyway, Griffith had long berated himself for trading Crowder away to the Browns three years before, and he was never stubborn about recognizing a mistake. The records are choked with episodes of Griffith's reclaiming of players he traded.

160

It wasn't chiefly with an eye to showmanship and color that Griffith obtained the unusual Art Shires from the White Sox, although the old gentleman was never averse to stimulating fan interest by that medium. Griffith long complained that his veteran, Joe Judge, didn't spur himself to his best job "unless he has got competition around. I have to keep two first basemen on the payroll to get the best out of Judge."

Shires' presence spurred Judge, all right. The old timer's batting zoomed to a lofty .326 while Shires got into only thirty-eight ball games for the Senators. The self-styled "Great Man," with his fancy luggage and low-cut roadster, both emblazoned by "Arthur The Great" labels, sat it out on the Washington bench while Judge gave him a lesson in playing first base and hitting.

The Senators' Man Of The Year was the once-scorned Joe Cronin, the rookie from Kansas City in whom Bucky Harris had originally perceived greatness. Young Cronin was now a four-alarm sensation with his shortstopping, and suddenly he turned into one of the most dangerous hitters in the league. He finished up with a .346 average, one of the three Senators to hit better than .340. Manush topped them with .362, and the ageless Sam Rice hit .349.

Griffith had traded wisely. Crowder finished up the season with fifteen victories as the club's leading pitcher. Sheriff Harris hit .320 in a utility role and was driving in more runs than his outfielding let in. The Senators never did catch the Athletics, but Griffith was bolstering his club, and in August in a piece of long-range planning he separated himself from 65,000 dollars to buy Joe Kuhel, Kansas City's hard-hitting first baseman, for the day when Judge would fade.

Joe Engel scouted Kuhel for Griffith and turned in a glowing report. Engel, with no authority to spend Griffith's money in any such hefty amount as 65,000 dollars, expressed doubt that Kuhel was worth that figure. "You're inconsistent," said Griffith. "If he's half the ball player you tell me he is, he's worth more than $65,000. We're buying him, and you start praying you've told the truth."

The Senators always did believe their fate in that 1930 race turned on one day's events—on July 4 at Philadelphia

161

when they were battling the A's for the lead. Al Simmons, with a lame ankle, wasn't in the A's line-up. He sat it out on the bench until the ninth inning. Then he pinch-hit with the bases full and homered against Bump Hadley to win the morning game. In the afternoon he came off the bench again and beat Ad Liska with another home run.

Johnson's 1931 Senators were a lively crew with a solid .300-hitting oufield led by Sammy West's .333 and supported by the consistent hitting of Sam Rice, Dave Harris, and Heinie Manush, but they never could catch the Athletics who drove to their third straight pennant. The Washington club matched the ninety-two victories of the pennant-winning Senators of 1924, but landed only in third place, behind the Yankees who nudged them out of second in the final series of the season.

Al Crowder, the old Army sergeant who had served in the Philippines before discovering he could make more money pitching ball, led the 1931 pitching staff with eighteen wins and eleven defeats, but Fred Marberry was the workhorse of the outfit. Pitching in and out of turn, starting and relieving, Marberry figured in forty-five games and emerged with a scintillating record of sixteen wins and four defeats.

Crowder, though, was the big man on the staff. He was throwing a fast ball that didn't look fast. What it had after Crowder came out of his lazy delivery was considerable "sneak." And what Crowder had otherwise was considerable shrewdness and a motion to first base that discouraged base stealers.

Rarely did players steal on Crowder, and rarely did he even throw to first base to keep them close to the bag. Crowder explained: "I'm like Sam Jones. We don't have to throw to first to keep a runner on. They know we know how to pitch and they can't take a big lead on us. When they do, they're dead ducks."

Crowder amplified his technique: "I just take a look over there at any runner who's on first. When I look, I cock my head the same way every time and just shift my eyes. If I see the runner, I don't worry. He's not far enough off the bag to hurt me. He hasn't got any jump. But when I look and I can't see him, he's too far off, and he's mine."

In the club's Biloxi, Mississippi, training camp, manager Johnson fell out with his old first baseman, Joe Judge, who had saved his no-hit game for him that day in Boston in 1920. Johnson took a dim view of Judge's brittleness and showed a high preference for the rookie Kuhel. He was differing, too, with Clark Griffith, who still had faith in Judge and insisted the veteran was the more solid ball player. Judge outplayed Kuhel in camp, and Griffith won his point.

The Senators opened the season with Judge at first base, with Kuhel farmed out to Baltimore at Griffith's suggestion, on April 26. Four days later it was a new deal at first base for the Senators. Judge was stricken with appendicitis at Fenway Park and rushed to a hospital. The recall of Kuhel was rushed from Baltimore, and Johnson had his rookie first baseman on the job. Kuhel hit a somewhat weak .269 for the season, but defensively he was brilliant.

Lou Gehrig of the Yankees had reason to remember that 1931 season of the Senators. That was the year when he missed the American League's undisputed home run championship and was forced to be content with a tie with Babe Ruth at forty-six homers. Save for what happened in Washington on April 27, Gehrig would have dethroned Ruth as home run king.

That was the day Gehrig hit the famous home run that wasn't a home run, yet met all the specifications. It was a tremendous blast into the center field bleacher seats a dozen rows deep. Gehrig was the victim of as cruel a turn of fate as any man who ever hit a ball out of the lot.

Lynn Lary of the Yankees was on first base with two out at the time and was off at the crack of Gehrig's bat, head down and racing toward the plate. Between second and third Lary looked up to see—of all things—center fielder Harry Rice making a catch of the ball.

What Lary didn't know was that Rice, twenty feet in front of the bleacher stands, was catching the ball on the rebound out of the seats. It came out of the bleachers in a high arc, and Rice was simply grandstanding it for the fans, taking the ball while still facing home plate.

Lary, presuming it was merely a long out, raced across third base into the Yankee dugout. He was compounding his mistakes. Manager Joe McCarthy was coaching at third base, and Lary interpreted McCarthy's sign to slow down as a signal that it was no use running because the ball had been caught. Gehrig, oblivious to what Lary was doing, rounded third base on his way home and was called out by umpire Bill McGowan for passing a base runner. Gehrig received credit only for a three-bagger. Joe McCarthy did not reappear on the coaching lines for the Yankees that season.

Later in the year, the Senators themselves made history of a kind. Specifically it was Bobby Burke, the slender left-hander, who barged into the record books with an astonishing no-hit game against the Red Sox, the first ever recorded in the city's American League history.

That Burke turned in a no-hitter from the same mound from which Johnson had pitched for years and failed in such a feat was truly amazing. The tall southpaw was never held in high regard by either the Washington management or Washington fans. In four previous years with the Senators, he had won only fourteen games and lost eighteen, and was displaying no particular genius.

But this day he was something special. He mowed the Red Sox down with his fast ball and got his no-hitter on August 8 by buzzing a third strike past Earl Webb, the last Boston hitter. He walked five men and struck out eight, but his no-hitter was in no way suspect. There was not a hard chance for his supporting cast.

To that point, Burke was having a great year. He had won eight games and lost only two. It must be recorded, however, that he didn't win another game in the last two months of the season. He was to serve six more years with the Senators without distinction and was retained on the basis, it was alleged, of that no-hitter. Burke never did quite make good.

164

Bucky Harris later referred to him as "the kid who got an 11-year tryout."

Griffith was still scenting another pennant for his ball club and viewed the pitching as his chief weakness. To bolster that department he bought Monte Weaver, a big winner at Baltimore, for 25,000 dollars for spring delivery in 1932. Also, he signed Ed Linke, the chunky, fast-balling strike-out king of the Davenport, Iowa, team of the Mississippi Valley League, who had fanned 228 men in 240 innings.

His infield of Kuhel, Myer, Cronin, and Bluege left Griffith content, and to bolster his outfield he shipped pitchers Bump Hadley and Sam Jones along with second baseman Jackie Hayes to the White Sox for outfielder Carl Reynolds, catcher Moe Berg, and infielder Johnny Kerr. Reynolds, the giant Texan, was the chief consideration in the deal. He had hit well for the White Sox despite his reputation as a spring hitter, and the fact that he was right-handed gave the Senators' outfield a balance between Manush and Sammy West, the southpaw swingers.

Dave Harris, despite his high batting averages, was not the solid type of outfielder Griffith liked, and Harris knew his own shortcomings. He made light of them. "I can drive more runs across the plate than you smart guys can think across," the Sheriff used to say. When Johnny Kerr was cast as his roommate, the Sheriff entered a joking objection. "I don't want to room with a .240 hitter," he said. "And I don't like to room with a .240 fielder," rejoined Kerr.

Dave had the determined shoulders of a sheriff, and he looked like a sheriff but actually wasn't a sheriff at all, he would confess. "A deputy deputized me to help track down some mule thieves in Carolina once—they were not even horse thieves, just mule thieves, mind you—and I guess that's where I got the name of Sheriff. I ain't no sheriff a-tall."

Harris drew as his roommate in the Biloxi training camp and on the road Moe Berg, the new catcher. Never was there a more incongruous pair. The Sheriff, a North Carolina hillbilly of informal schooling, found himself the buddy of the game's most educated ball player. Berg had come out of

Princeton where he had hit the longest home run in Princeton history while playing shortstop, not catching. After taking a law degree, he rounded out his schooling in Paris and graduated from the Sorbonne. Berg was master of seven languages, and he could boast that at the time he joined the Washington club his thesis on Sanskrit was listed as a reference work in the Congressional Library.

And they were pals—Berg and the Sheriff. To Dave, the kindly Berg represented all things. "He knows everything," the Sheriff boasted. "Only man who takes two suitcases on the road—one full of clothes and the other full of books and magazines. The only thing I can teach him is how to hit."

They kidded about each other's hitting. Berg had a very real respect for Dave's ability to connect with the ball, particularly his skill at coming off the bench at any time and banging away as a pinch hitter. Berg privately was convinced that the Sheriff's profound lack of imagination helped him to hit. "The Sheriff has nothing else on his mind. All he sees is a pitcher out there with a round ball, throwing to him with a round bat, and he thinks every pitcher is in the hole the minute he walks to the plate."

Berg watched the Sheriff line three balls out of the Biloxi park in batting practice and in genuine admiration asked, "Where do you get that power?" The Sheriff grinned as he walked away from the plate to let Berg get in some hitting licks. "Listen, Moe," he said, "I just wanna tell you something. All of them seven languages you know ain't gonna do you no good when you go up there with a bat in your hand. What you need then is a genius like me."

When a St. Louis taxicab strike forced the Washington players into a chartered bus for the trip from the park to the hotel, Harris was angry. "These blankety-blank cab drivers want all the money in the world," the Sheriff commented. "It's a blankety-blank note when a team of big leaguers has to take a blankety-blank bus to the park just on account of some blankety-blank no-good cab drivers."

Berg chided him for that expressive manner of speech, but good-naturedly. "Now, Dave, that's not nice," he said. "Don't

166

you know that profanity denotes lack of vocabulary? Can't you use anything but a two-syllable word?"

And the Sheriff inquired naïvely, "What kind of a word is that, Moe?"

Nobody was smarter than Berg, the Sheriff averred. He pointed Moe out to fans and visitors as the smartest man in the world, and he believed it. Thus it was that at Biloxi that Berg was disturbed when Harris failed to put in an appearance at breakfast, a meal he never missed. Moe discovered the Sheriff in the lobby later, in civilian clothes while the rest of the team was in uniform for the ride to the ball park. He inquired what the matter might be.

"Believe it or not," said the Sheriff, "but I ain't feeling well. First sick day I ever had in my life. Don't know what's wrong. My stomach's jumping. Johnson told me to take the day off."

Berg scanned him with a serious manner. "Let me see your tongue," he said professionally. Obediently the Sheriff stuck out his tongue. Berg looked long and profoundly, backed away and then told Harris: "You'll be all right. Just lay off the heavy food and get some rest today and tonight. In the morning you'll be your old self. You just got a slight touch of intestinal fortitude." Without batting an eye at anybody except a baseball writer, Berg said that.

The next morning Harris bounced down to breakfast in excellent health, just as Berg predicated. "Feel great, Moe," he said. "You were right. That little touch of intestinal fortitude I had is all gone."

Berg shared the club's catching duties with Roy Spencer that year. His .236 batting average lent little to the club's attack, but both Johnson and Griffith valued him for his smart handling of pitchers and his superb throwing arm. His slowness on the bases was a souvenir of a broken leg he had received while playing shortstop for the White Sox a couple of years before.

That Berg ever became a major-league catcher was purely accidental. He had no catching ambitions even when he first donned the mask and protector. He was the White Sox's utility infielder in Washington one day when manager Ray

167

Schalk came out of the game with a broken finger, suffered from a foul tip. Crouse, the White Sox's second catcher moved in and Schalk commented, "With McCurdy hurt there goes our last catcher. If anything happens to him, we're sunk."

Then Berg spoke up: "Stop your worrying, Ray. You have a good catcher sitting right here on the bench." If Schalk heard him, he said nothing. But two innings later a foul tip broke a finger on Crouse's throwing hand, and now Schalk wheeled toward Moe. "Okay, Berg, you asked for it. Now let's see what kind of a catcher you are."

Thus was born Berg's major-league catching career. He was a stranger to the mitt and mask since his high school days. Schalk was giving him a job he didn't ask for, but now was no time to explain that he wasn't boasting about himself when he said the Sox had a good catcher sitting on the bench. Actually Moe was talking about Earl Sheely, the big first baseman who had been a catcher in the Coast League before joining Chicago!

It fell to the lot of Dave Harris to make the Senators' most sensational hit of the 1932 season despite the fact it fell thirteen runs short of tying the score on the afternoon of August 6 at Detroit. Tommy Bridges was bidding for a no-hit game that day—the perfect no-hit, no-reach-first game. For eight and two thirds innings he didn't permit a Senator to reach base. Detroit fans were praying he'd get past the last man.

Due at bat for the Senators was pitcher Bobby Burke, but manager Walter Johnson waved him down as Burke started for the plate, bat in hand. Out of the Washington dugout strolled the husky figure of Sheriff Harris. Johnson, who so often himself had been on the brink of a no-hitter, wasn't going to make it easy for Bridges despite the fact the Senators were in a hopeless state, trailing 13 to 0, with none on and two out in the ninth. But his selection of Harris appeared to be pushing things somewhat. For years Harris had boasted, "Bridges is one of the pitchers who is keeping me in the league." His faculty for hitting Bridges' pitches was well known.

And it was reaffirmed on the first pitch. The Sheriff swung, and a clean single streaked into center field to cheat Bridges of his no-hitter, the only safety he allowed. After the game, Johnson defended his move with the blunt comment: "Nobody is going to get a cheap no-hitter if I can stop him."

Those 1932 Senators got powerful pitching from freshman Monte Weaver and (General) Crowder. Weaver was a graduate of Emory-Henry College and a mathematics professor who had obtained his Master's degree with a thesis on the science of railroad curves. He won twenty-two, lost only ten, and was the prize product of the season. Crowder produced twenty-six wins and thirteen defeats.

They lost second place to the Athletics by only one game in finishing third, and were the most dangerous club in the league during the last month of the season when they came up with twenty-four wins in their last twenty-eight games. But the Yankees, with Ruth and Gehrig functioning, outdistanced the rest of the league and won one hundred and seven games to get a clear thirteen-game margin over the second-place A's.

It might have been closer except for the events of July 4 in Griffith Stadium when the Senators and Yankees staged one of the most riotous affrays in the stadium's history. Carl Reynolds, scoring from third base, knocked catcher Bill Dickey down, causing him to drop the ball. Reynolds picked himself up and was proceeding toward the dugout when Dickey regained his feet, rushed at Reynolds from behind, and smashed a hard right to the face, breaking Reynolds' jaw in two places.

It had been, apparently, just another case of a base runner knocking a catcher over. But in Boston a few days previously, the same thing had happened to the slender Dickey, and now he was outraged, particularly when hit by the 210-pound bulk of the solid Reynolds who was never gentle in his slides.

Dickey was fined and suspended for his attack, but the Senators lost the services of Reynolds for six weeks at a time when he was hitting more than .360 and justifying grandly the trade that brought him from the White Sox. On his return to the line-up, he failed to recover his batting form, and his average slumped to .305. For nearly two months Reynolds' jaw was wired after being reset, and he was on a soft food died that left him pounds underweight when he did resume play.

Chapter XI

THE Senators were making money. Only once in the last ten years had they finished out of the first division. But there had been no pennant in seven years. Griffith wasn't content. He had tried for the flag with that 1932 club that finished behind the Yanks and A's, and he wasn't satisfied with Walter Johnson's leadership. Johnson, he felt, was too easygoing, and the contrast with Bucky Harris' aggressive piloting of 1924 and 1925 was great. He fired Johnson at the 1932 season's end.

There was no great outcry by Washington fans. They still revered Johnson as a pitching idol of yore, but they had seen him bring no inspirational leadership to the club. Griffith was easily able to square his act with his conscience. He wasn't showing Johnson the door without regard for the old pitcher's future. Johnson was more than a moderately wealthy man. Griffith had paid him the highest salary of any pitcher in the league from 1912 to 1928, and during one considerable span the figure had reached 25,000 dollars a year. Johnson now owned a vast farm at near-by Germantown, Maryland. Griffith had given him a four-year shot at the Washington managerial job, and they parted friends.

The next week was one of wild speculation concerning the new Washington manager and his identity. Griffith, close-mouthed, would say only, "Maybe I'll manage the club myself. I'm not too old. I won a pennant in this league once, you know." Nobody took that hint seriously. More credence was given the report that Griffith was trying to talk Connie

Mack into selling him Al Simmons for 100,000 dollars, with Simmons to be named playing-manager of the Senators.

Indications pointed to the probability that Griffith would name a man from his own ball club as his 1933 manager. The sixty-four-year-old club owner often voiced his pride in the fact that ever since he had given up the managerial reins in 1920 he had dipped into his own playing ranks for each new manager. They were, in succession, McBride, Milan, Bush, Harris, and Johnson.

As it was suggested in 1928 when Harris took his leave of the club, the names of the veterans Joe Judge and Sam Rice were put forward as probable appointees of Griffith. He refused comment until October 8 when he disclosed his choice. It was Joe Cronin.

Even as Griffith had startled the baseball world back in 1924 by fetching twenty-seven-year-old Bucky Harris out of the playing ranks to give him the managerial job, he had come up with a new surprise. Cronin was only twenty-six, the youngest man ever to become a major-league manager.

Griffith had his reasons and told them proudly: "Cronin's a scrapper. He thinks nothing but baseball. I like these young fellows who fight for everything. I made no mistake with Bucky Harris. I think I have another Harris."

For Griffith, the change in managers had its economic aspects, too. He was getting rid of Johnson's 20,000-dollar salary. Cronin, in his new job, was getting a 2,500-dollar raise, a clear saving of 17,500 dollars for Griffith on the transaction.

For the young Irishman Cronin, his elevation to the managership of a major-league ball club at the age of twenty-six was a dream come true. It wasn't his first stroke of high good luck. Back in San Francisco he realized the ultimate dream of all school kids. His schoolhouse, Mission High, burned down, and at fourteen he was free to play baseball in all the daylight hours.

Later he did transfer to Sacred Heart School where he was the bigshot shortstop of the team which boasted another pretty good ball player in a lad named Wally Berger. Berger was to go up to the majors and set home run records with the Braves. Cronin was good not only on the ball diamonds of San Francisco. He was the city playground tennis champ, a tall kid who could get tremendous leverage with a racquet. But tennis he rated as a minor sport.

Joe Devine, then scouting for the Pittsburgh Pirates before starting a long term with the Yankees, spotted Cronin playing semi-pro ball around San Francisco in 1924 and was apparently intrigued. He offered him a Pittsburgh contract, and Joe jumped at it. His parents signed the papers for seventeen-year-old Joe.

Pittsburgh, however, proved to be just a name on Cronin's first professional contract. The Pirates promptly optioned him to their Johnstown, Pennsylvania, farm to start the 1925 season. But that fall, after he had hit .313 in ninety-nine games, they expressed a new interest in him. They brought him up, let him have his picture taken with the pennant-winning Pirates of that year, and let him sit on the bench in a Pirate uniform during that World Series with the Senators. Cronin's name was not on the Series eligibility list, and little did Clark Griffith dream that seven years hence the nineteen-year-old Irishman on the Pirates bench would be his manager.

The Pirates then sent him up to New Haven in the Eastern League in '26, and brought him back that fall after he finished the season with a .320 batting average for New Haven. He was in thirty-eight games with the Pirates, hit .265, impressed nobody, hung around for twelve games in 1927, and then was dispatched to Kansas City with no strings attached.

Joe Engel, Griffith's scout, was foraging in the American Association in July, 1928, with vague orders to pick up any likely looking shortstop if the price was reasonable, and had no idea that at Kansas City he would make a rich strike.

He had seen Cronin play, and his liking for him was tempered by a game-losing boot Joe made that day. George Muehlbach, owner of the Kansas City club, was entertaining a half-dozen major-league scouts in his brewery that night. Muehlbach mentioned Cronin's name in disgust. "I'm sending that crazy kid to Wichita," he said. "I could have gotten $15,000 for him a week ago, now I'll take ten."

"Give you $7,500," said Engel.

"It's a deal," said Muehlbach, thereby stunning Engel who had no final authority to make a deal for Griffith. But in the company of his fellow scouts he was embarrassed to call it off, and the transaction was made.

When Engel advised Griffith of his purchase, the old gentleman was furious. "Seventy five hundred for a kid shortstop who is hitting .245 in the minors. Are you crazy?" he said over the phone to Engel.

Engel decided on a cooling-off period for Griffith, and revised his plan of returning to Washington immediately with Cronin. He kept Cronin with him in the Midwest for a week on the pretense of doing more scouting, and shared his suits and clean laundry with his "find" who had sent all his funds to his mother in California and was traveling light.

When they did come to Washington, Engel took Cronin into the Griffith Stadium office but bade him wait downstairs until he could get more intelligence as to Griffith's current frame of mind. Meanwhile he introduced the rookie to a comely brunette named Mildred Robertson, in the outer office. She was Griffith's niece and his secretary. Engel's introduction was typically breezy. "Hi, ya, Millie," he said. "Been scouting for a husband for you and just brought him in from Kansas City. Meet Joe Cronin."

Griffith's first glimpse of Cronin in a Washington uniform was none too reassuring. What he saw was a skinny-legged, gangling kid with awkward arms and elbows who had the grammar school habit of dipping one knee toward a ground ball. At bat, Cronin was just as unorthodox, with a Heinie Groh stance that left him facing the pitcher almost squarely, with no sign of power in his stroke. Griffith glared at Engel and threatened to fire him.

Cronin saved Engel's job and in the ensuing years got him a bonus besides. He hit a mild .243 for the Senators in sixty-three games in 1928, but in 1929 he was the club's regular shortstop, a .282 hitter who was getting distance, and a fellow who could make all the plays from deepest short with a superior throwing arm.

173

He was the league's best shortstop in 1930 with his average zooming to .346. And his Irish temper had risen completely to the surface. He squabbled with umpires, stuck his big jaw in their faces, and blew emotional gaskets to give hovering photographers some of their finest shots of an angry ball player. He had made good grandly.

Three years in a row Cronin gave the Senators a spectacular job at shortstop and banged out averages of better than .300. Washington fans were completely taken with him. It was with huzzahs that they greeted Griffith's announcement that Cronin was the club's new manager.

Griffith, who had come up with a boy wonder in Bucky Harris in 1924, was now pressing his luck in gambling on the even more youthful Cronin as a playing manager—at least that was the opinion of the baseball realists in the winter of 1932-33. But Griffith was always pleased when he could toss off one of these little surprise bombshells.

He called Cronin to Washington from San Francisco on December 1, and the pencils flew over note-pads in his little stucco office as the pair of them plotted the new Washington team of 1933, a week before the winter trading sessions of the club owners in New York. If Cronin was surprised to find himself managing a big-league club, then Griffith was equally flabbergasted at the first demands of his young manager.

"I'd like to have these ball players," said Cronin, handing Griffith a slip with the names of three pitchers written thereon. "We'd have a chance to win the pennant, I think."

Griffith scanned Cronin's list. On it were the names of Earl Whitehill of the Tigers, Jack Russell, right-hander of the Indians, and Walter Stewart, left-hander of the Browns.

"Whoa," said Griffith, "you just don't go taking ball players off other clubs simply because you'd like to have 'em. Those clubs don't part with solid pitchers like them just because you want 'em."

"Well," said Cronin coyly, "they always told me you were a pretty good baseball trader. I thought if anybody could swing a deal for 'em, you could."

If Cronin was attempting to appeal to the old gentleman's

174

vanity, he succeeded. Griffith turned back to the list and hummed.

Cronin was talking fast. "These pitchers I named—tell you why I picked them out, especially. Right now we're a better ball team than the Athletics. To win any pennant, we have to beat the Yankees. That's who we're shooting at. We need some pitchers who can beat the Yankees. Whitehill and his left-handed stuff gives them fits. So does Walter Stewart with his southpaw pitching. They'd get us a lot of wins over the Yankees."

Griffith inquired about Russell, the Cleveland right-hander. Why did Cronin like him? Russell had no reputation for beating the Yankees.

"No, but he has a good reputation for beating us," said Cronin. "He was death on our team all last year. If we can get him pitching for us instead of against us, and if we have Whitehill and Stewart to shoot at the Yankees, we ought to be loaded."

They moved into the New York meetings, and Griffith swung quickly into action, reveling in the horse-trading role on which he long prided himself. He sent Cronin into the lobbies to stalk whatever game was about, and bird dog Cronin presently shooed president Alva Bradley of the Indians into Griffith's suite.

Bradley emerged minus pitcher Russell, now the property of the Senators. He balked at Griffith's original offer of first baseman Harley Boss, the promising rookie from Chattanooga, and held out for cash in addition. The Indians needed a first baseman, Griffith knew, and he played on that need. Griffith's counteroffer expanded the deal. He'd toss in catcher Roy Spencer if the Indians would also give him catcher Luke Sewell. That was the deal that was made.

"Well, it's a start, Joe," said Griffith. "Now for the big men, Whitehill and Stewart."

Griffith went high to get Whitehill. The Tigers demanded no less than Fred Marberry in the swap, and Griffith was loath to part with the big Texan who for a decade had been the work horse of his staff. When he did capitulate with respect to Marberry, the Tigers held out for something more. Griffith tossed in his left-handed rookie, Carl Fischer. Thus within two hours, the Senators had two of the men they sought, plus the veteran catcher Sewell. Now Griffith turned his charms toward the Browns who had Stewart.

But now Griffith had more expansive ideas. Ever since the dismissal of Johnson as manager in October, he had been pestered by Goose Goslin who went to the Browns in that 1930 trade for Heinie Manush. Goslin wanted to go back to Washington, but not under Johnson with whom he had had differences. The same day Johnson was let out, Goslin telephoned Griffith and pleaded with him to "buy me back." The Goose reminded Griffith, "You've never won a pennant without me."

For two days Griffith negotiated with the Browns. They talked of Stewart for Sammy West. Griffith offered to include Carl Reynolds if the Browns would toss in Goslin. The Browns held out for a pitcher, too, and Griffith outlined a new deal, a six-player swap.

They swung it. Stewart, Goslin, and outfielder Fred Schulte went to the Senators for West, Reynolds, and Lloyd Brown, the good left-hander who had won fifteen games for the Senators the past season. Now Cronin had all he asked for, plus catcher Sewell, and the pair of outfielders, Goslin and Schulte, with the latter representing right-handed hitting strength.

In the 1933 training camp at Biloxi, Cronin made the same kind of appeal to the older players that Bucky Harris had submitted nine years before, admitting his managerial inexperience and asking their loyalty.

He got their pledge, and with the exception of one day at Detroit he was popular with all of the Senators. That was the day Al Crowder balked at Cronin's decision to take him out during a Tiger batting rally. Crowder in disgust threw his glove from the mound into the dugout on the fly.

"That'll cost you $25," said Cronin.

"Twenty-five bucks is a bush-league fine," Crowder snarled.

"And that was a bush-league trick," said Cronin. There was no more trouble.

176

Beating the Yankees was the big objective, and that Cronin's Senators did. But it was hectic in the doing. Yankee-Senator feuds punctuated the season. They batted it out as ball teams and also with their fists. Tempers ran short and bad blood spilled over. At the finish, Cronin's Senators had whipped the Yankees in fourteen of the season's twenty-two games between them to wrest the pennant away from Joe McCarthy's club, meeting every Yankee challenge and pulling away to clinch the flag by a seven-game margin. As Cronin had reckoned, it was Whitehill and Stewart with their effectiveness against the Yanks who were vital factors in tipping the scales.

The Yankees won their first seven games in a row before the Senators started closing the gap. The opening Yankee-Senators series in Washington was an explosive battleground. Ever since the Dickey-Reynolds episode of the year before, the two clubs bristled at each other. Buddy Myer slid into Lou Gehrig knee-high at first base, and literally cut the pants from big Lou who, no bellicose sort, was content to watch Myer bounce on his head fifteen feet toward the Washington dugout.

Even Babe Ruth was infected by the bitterness between the two teams. When the Yankees opened in Washington he crashed into Cronin covering third base and almost undressed him. Cronin challenged him, and a battle on the spot was narrowly averted.

Three days later in the same series, on April 25, it was a riot. Ben Chapman, the hot-tempered Alabaman, slid into the Mississippian, Buddy Myer, at second base to break up a double play and cut a swastika with his spikes on Myer's thigh. Scrambling to his feet, before Chapman could rise, Myer lashed out with his spikes and booted Chapman with a dozen swift kicks. Players of both teams streamed off the benches. Washington fans piled out of the stands swinging at everybody wearing a Yankee uniform. Lefty Gomez, armed with a bat, was thrashing wildly.

Police scrambled on the field. A plainclothesman attempted to disarm Gomez and was solidly clouted. Dixie Walker, Chapman's roommate who was warming the Yankees' bench, selected Myer as his personal target, and with a running jump bore Myer down from behind, pummeling him as he fell. Police shooed the Yankees and Senators back to their dugouts ultimately, and hauled five fans away under arrest.

That fight was over, but it was only part of a double feature. The umpires threw Chapman, Walker, and Myer out of the game, but to reach the Yankees' dressing room Chapman was compelled to use the exit that skirted the Washington bench. There on the dugout steps, fiery Earl Whitehill described the approaching Chapman in unflattering terms.

Chapman swung a right to Whitehill's chin and missed the chin but not Whitehill's left eye. The punch caved Whitehill in, and a dozen Washington players battled Chapman and Walker down the long steps to the dressing room. Police broke that one up too. The Senators got a newspaper decision out of the fisticuffs, but they dropped the ball game to Russ Van Atta, 16 to 0, one reason for their boiling tempers.

President Will Harridge of the American League suspended Chapman, Myer, and Whitehill for five days and fined them 100 dollars each. Griffith screamed at the leniency toward Chapman, but it fell on ears long deafened to Griffith's screams.

The Athletics weren't figuring heavily in the pennant race. The winter before, Connie Mack had traded Simmons, Haas, and Dykes to the White Sox, and the Yankees were the team to beat. The Senators were doing that dramatically all season.

They didn't catch the Yankees until June 23, but in the first month of the season they served notice it was to be no Yankee runaway. In Yankee Stadium on April 29 occurred the unforgettable play of the season.

Monte Weaver had the Yankees beaten that day, 6 to 3, going into the last half of the ninth, and now the Yankees were challenging. Gehrig and Dixie Walker banged out hits before anybody was out, putting runners on first and second, and bringing Lazzeri up. Thirty-five thousand fans roared as Lazzeri drove a tremendous line smash between Goslin in right field and Schulte in center with an extra-base label written all over it.

Seemingly everybody in the ball park knew the drive would

fall safe with the exception of Gehrig. He played it cautiously, hugging second until the ball dropped. Dixie Walker, playing it smarter, was dashing into second when Gehrig finally took over. Walker was almost running up Gehrig's back as they lit for home.

Meanwhile Goslin was making a quick retrieve of the ball in deep right center, and with one of the most powerful throwing arms in the league whipped it on the fly to Cronin who had raced far out for the relay. Now it was in the hands of the best relay man in the league, and Cronin didn't dally, but cut loose a meteor throw to Sewell at the plate. On the fly, too, the ball plunked into Sewell's mitt, and he tagged Gehrig sliding in.

Sewell did a pirouette from the force of the tag, but he was alive to the rare possibilities of the play and dove back across the plate, ball in hand, to tag Dixie Walker, too. A double play at home plate on the same batted ball! Lazzeri ended up on third with a useless triple, and the Senators won the ball game one play later.

Cronin himself was a ball of fire. With his managerial responsibilities apparently no burden, he made three hits against the Yankees in a July 4 game and took over the league batting lead from Babe Ruth with a figure of .367. Manush had just been on a twenty-six-game hitting streak, and Luke Sewell was the only regular who wasn't hitting .300 in midseason.

On July 4, the winter trading script of Griffith and Cronin was working out beautifully. The Senators took on the Yankees in a double-header at Griffith Stadium, nursing a league lead of a half game. Whitehill started the first game, and the Senators won it in the tenth, 6 to 5, when Cronin singled Manush home. Walter Stewart started the second game and went all the way for a 3-to-2 victory.

In August again, the Senators moved into Yankee Stadium for a crucial series and dropped two games in a row, their lead dwindling to one game. And then they bounced back. Whitehill beat the Yankees 5 to 1, with a five-hitter, and Weaver followed with a seven-hit victory to mop up the last two games of the series and beat off what proved the last Yankee challenge.

The Washington pitching was standing up smartly. White-hill, Stewart, and Russell, the three men Cronin had plotted to get, were on their way to sensational seasons. Whitehill ended up as a 22-game winner. The trio, at the finish, had pitched fifty-six victories and only twenty-eight defeats. The veteran Crowder was the biggest winner with twenty-four to his credit. Weaver won ten of his fifteen decisions.

As a precautionary measure in August, Griffith bought Sam Gray, the veteran right-hander who had drifted to the Browns from the Athletics. That deal produced a rare sequence. Gray, with a chance to detach himself from a last-place team and cut in on a generous World Series share with the Senators, telephoned Cronin in Chicago after the sale was announced. "Don't buy me, Joe. They're trying to unload a sore-armed pitcher on you. I can't do you any good, make 'em call off the deal," Gray told the flabbergasted Cronin.

Griffith did protest the deal, and Commissioner Landis, on the evidence, called it off. Cronin called Gray "the most honest man I've ever known."

Buddy Myer was the Senators' lead-off man, hitting .302 and getting on base otherwise. With Manush, Cronin, and Goslin batting behind him, Myer complained, "they've got my tongue hanging out. When we're not putting on the hit-and-run, they're banging the ball anyway and I have to run." He summarized his complaint by adding, "It's wonderful."

In bottle-legged Cliff Bolton, the good-hit, no-catch catcher, the Senators had a deluxe pinch hitter. Rarely used behind the bat, he swatted sixteen hits in thirty-three batting appearances, mostly in a pinch role. Luke Sewell and Moe Berg divided the bulk of the catching.

In early September, only a miracle could keep the Senators away from the pennant. On September 10, they had a nine-game lead over the Yanks. In consecutive games against the last-place Browns, they missed their chance to clinch it, but on September 20, they were in first place to stay. Walter Stewart beat his old mates in a 2-to-1 duel. Another ex-Brownie, Heinie Manush, made the big last putout on a fly by Oscar Melillo, under difficult circumstances. His sun glasses had slipped to the ground, and he was hunting them when Melillo hit the ball. It was a duel in the sun between Manush and the fly, and he emerged the winner with a staggering one-hand catch.

Again it was the Senators versus the Giants in a World Series after a nine-year lapse, and again Washington was pitting a boy manager against the National League pennant winners. Joe Cronin was matching managerial minds with Bill Terry.

The nation's capital was hailing Cronin as a miracle man, but not quite with the fervor that it saluted Bucky Harris in 1924. Unlike Harris, Cronin wasn't winning Washington's first pennant. The town would explode, of course, if Cronin would win the World Series. If there were any misgivings about the Senators' ability to beat the Giants, they centered on the presence in the Series of Carl Hubbell, the Giants' left-handed master of the screwball. All year Hubbell had been the most invincible pitcher in either league with his twenty-three victories and twelve defeats. His screwball was particularly effective against left-handed hitters, and the Senators were loaded with that type in Myer, Manush, Goslin, and Kuhel.

Cronin was secretive as the Series opener in New York approached. With Terry proclaiming a week before that Hubbell would pitch and win the first and fourth games of the Series, Cronin refused to divulge his first-game pitcher until the morning of the game. His choice was a surprising one. He passed up Alvin Crowder, his twenty-four game winner, and Earl Whitehill, his top left-hander, and played a hunch. He started southpaw Walter Stewart.

The Senators took a 4-to-2 beating. Hubbell was their master, allowing only five hits and fanning ten. The Giants pounded Stewart out of the box in the third inning, taking a 4-to-0 lead. Jack Russell and Al Thomas bravely attempted to keep the Senators in the ball game by pitching shutout ball from that point.

Buddy Myer, a nervous fellow that day after witnessing a

fatal truck-pedestrian accident on his way to the park, gave the Giants their first opening by booting his first chance of the game, an error on Joe Moore's grounder. By the game's end, Myer's error total was three. With two out, Mel Ott crashed a home run into the right field stands, and the Giants had a 2-to-0 lead in the first inning.

Cronin could rue his choice of Stewart as early as the third inning. Hugh Critz, Bill Terry, and Ott whacked out singles that fetched the Giants their third run. With one out, Russell replaced Stewart, and fanned Davis, but the Giants got their fourth run home when Jackson grounded out.

Back in their own first inning, the Senators were initiated into the shape of things to come that day. Hubbell calmly struck out the first three Washington hitters he faced, Myer, Manush, and Goslin—all of them left-handers. The Senators came up with lone runs in the fourth and ninth. Myer led off the fourth with a single and scored on two infield outs and Critz's muff of Goslin's grounder. In the ninth, Manush was safe on Ryan's error and was pushed around on singles by Cronin and Schulte, and Kuhel's infield out. They could have gotten better breaks. Myer was robbed of a hit by Blondy Ryan's leaping stop at shortstop, with two on base. Goslin made a bid to tie the score with two on, but his tremendous line drive into the right field seats was foul by a foot. On the next pitch, Terry leaped high in the air to haul down another Goslin liner.

Cronin turned to his veteran right-hander, Crowder for the second game. For five innings he was superb, and the Senators took a 1-to-0 lead into the sixth. With Hal Schumacher pitching for the Giants, Goose Goslin put the Senators in front in the third inning with a home run smash into the right field upper deck, over the NRA sign "We Do Our Part." Crowder was pitching two-hit ball going into the sixth, and then came the deluge.

Into that sixth, the Giants packed all their six runs to win the ball game 6 to 1. Moore opened up with a single to left. Critz forced Moore, but Terry doubled Critz to third. Ott was purposely passed to fill the bases and permit Crowder to face the weak-hitting George Davis, but Terry had other plans.

Terry called time and motioned toward the dugout, whence emerged the familiar figure of Lefty O'Doul, the old pitcher who had turned outfielder and won a National League batting championship. Rotten luck hounded the Senators. Crowder had O'Doul struck out momentarily, but Sewell dropped the foul tip into his mitt. Reprieved, O'Doul singled sharply to center for the tying and winning runs.

The Giants weren't through, though. Jackson singled scoring Ott. The slow-footed Gus Mancuso caught the Senators' infield flat-footed with a squeeze bunt, and O'Doul scored from third. Schumacher singled to center scoring Jackson. Moore singled scoring Mancuso before Al Thomas was rushed to the relief of the helpless Crowder. At the finish, the hits duplicated the first game's totals: ten for the Giants, five for Washington.

When the Series scene shifted to Washington for the pivotal third game, President Franklin D. Roosevelt and the greatest congressional delegation ever to see a ball game, took a pre-game drenching, as did the 25,727 cash customers. Showers held the crowd to slim proportions for a World Series, and those two defeats in New York had tempered the enthusiasm of Washington fans.

Earl Whitehill put the Senators back in the Series, with the only shutout performance that was to be pitched. He held the Giants to five hits and beat them, 4 to 0, holding hitless the three men who in New York had belabored Washington pitching so vigorously: Terry, Moore, and Ott.

Cronin herded his men into the clubhouse before the game and announced he was going to give them the only pep talk they had heard all season, from him. He said he hoped they were as ashamed of what had happened in the first two Series games as he was. He told them they were a better ball club than the Giants, and now was the time to show it to a city that had supported them all season.

And they didn't dally. The Senators hopped on Freddie Fitzsimmons for three hits in the first inning. Buddy Myer opened up with a single to right, and Goslin answered the pleas of the 25,727 with a vicious double off the right field wall. Manush popped up, and while Fitzsimmons handled Cronin's grounder, Myer scored from third base. Solid Fred Schulte exploded a double into right and Goslin pranced home.

They improved their 2-to-0 lead to 3 to 0 in the second inning. Bluege opened up with a two-bagger against the left field wall, and Sewell laid down the conventional sacrifice, the need of which was obviated when Myer rapped out a two-bagger that scored Bluege.

Fitzsimmons was still in there for the Giants in the seventh when Buddy Myer's third hit of the game produced the Senators' fourth run. It was a single that scored Luke Sewell who had preceded him with a single and stolen second.

At last, the Senators had in Whitehill a winning pitcher in the Series, and the Giants' threat to sweep it in four games was stemmed. But the spectre of Hubbell pitching for the Giants on the morrow was clouding the hopes of Washington fans.

Monte Weaver faced the task of opposing Hubbell in that fourth game. The battle that ensued was the highlight of the Series. Undaunted by the immensity of his assignment, Weaver matched Hubbell out for out in the first three innings. Not a man on either team reached base until the fourth. And then manager Terry punctured the scoreless duel with a soaring home run deep into the temporary seats in center field to put the Giants in a 1-to-0 lead in the fourth. Weaver bent anew to his task.

Scoreless for six innings, the Senators managed to kick up a fuss in the sixth, nevertheless. With Myer on third base and two out, Manush swatted a ground ball between first and second. Both Terry and Critz broke for it in a frenzy to protect Hubbell's 1-to-0 lead, and Critz scooped it up. Terry was in no position to take a throw to first base, but Hubbell raced over to the bag for Critz's toss in a race with the steaming Manush.

Umpire Charley Moran of the National League called Manush out, nullifying Myer's dash for the plate. Manush ranted at Moran and was joined by Cronin and the entire

184

Washington bench. Losing the argument, Manush brushed his hand across the back of Moran's neck as he started for the dugout. Whether it was accidental or intentional only Manush knew. The umpire wheeled and thumbed Manush out of the game. Manush paid no heed and trotted out to his left field position. Moran attempted to wave Manush out of the game before he would permit play to resume. The angry Manush merely waved back with an uncomplimentary gesture. Not until umpire-in-chief George Moriarty walked into left field and talked earnestly with Manush did the big outfielder make a move toward the dugout. When he started the long walk, the crowd urged him to defy the umpires and stay in.

Weaver blanked the Giants in the seventh, and then the Senators got the tying run for him. Joe Kuhel beat out a bunt, Bluege sacrificed him to second, and Luke Sewell delivered a run-scoring single to center to deadlock the game at 1 to 1.

Into the ninth and through the tenth, Weaver battled Hubbell on even terms. In the eleventh, the Giants broke through. Travis Jackson beat out a bunt, Mancuso sacrificed, and Blondy Ryan, weakest hitter in the Giants' regular line-up, banged a single to center to move Jackson home.

Joe Kuhel, whose bunts during the regular season had helped him to hit .322, answered the prayers of the Washington fans in the eleventh by laying one down against Hubbell and beating it out to put the tying run on base with none out. Bluege sacrificed him to second, and Terry went into conference with Hubbell on the mound. With the left-handed Cliff Bolton standing by to pinch-hit for the Senators, Terry left Hubbell in.

The Giants had no line on Bolton as a hitter, and were playing him straight away. But as Hubbell rubbed up the ball, coach Charley Dressen bolted out of the dugout to confer with shortstop Blondy Ryan. He told Ryan he knew Bolton was a pull-hitter in the Southern League, and ordered him to play closer to second base.

Those orders were quickly rewarded. On the next pitch, Bolton hit a wicked smash toward second base, and Ryan was in position to grab up what might have been the game-tying hit. Not only that, but he flipped it to Critz whose throw to Terry beat the slow-footed Bolton for a double play that delivered a 2-to-1 victory to Hubbell.

For the Series' fifth game that would close the Senators out if the Giants won it, Terry sent Hal Schumacher to the mound. Schumacher was striving to match the two Series victories of Hubbell. The backs-to-the-wall Senators put all their hopes on the veteran Crowder.

As in three previous games of the Series, the Giants broke in front, with a two-run second inning against Crowder. Embarrassing to that pitcher, too, was the fact that the runs were driven in by his pitching opponent, Schumacher. With two out and Jackson and Mancuso in scoring position by virtue of a single, a walk, and a sacrifice, Schumacher lined a single into center field.

And from the pitching mound, Schumacher was heaping more woe on the Senators. He took his 3 to 0 lead into the sixth inning, and with two out the Senators still had nothing. But Manush and Cronin revived Washington hopes with consecutive singles, and then along came Fred Shulte. With one stroke Schulte tied the score at 3 to 3, striking a home run into the center field bleachers. Kuhel and Bluege followed with singles that were futile, but they did serve to rid the scene of Schumacher. Luque, the venerable Cuban, moved in to pitch for the Giants.

Jack Russell succeeded Crowder in the sixth, and now it was Russell and Luque in a superlative relief pitching duel that carried the 3-to-3 stalemate beyond the ninth, into the tenth. With one out in the tenth, Mel Ott hit a long fly ino deep center. Schulte drifted back, got his gloved hand on the ball, failed to hold it as he crashed into the shallow, retaining wall, and the ball dropped into the laps of the first-row bleacher fans. Ott dashed around the bases but was flagged down at second base by umpire Pfirman, and manager Terry bolted out to the field in violent protest that it was a home run, not a ground-rule double. Pfirman reversed himself with the approval of umpire-in-chief Moran, and amid the boos of the 28,454 Washington fans Ott completed the circuit with the run that put the Giants in front, 4 to 3.

The Senators' tenth produced only a dying gasp. With two out, Cronin singled and Schulte walked, but the crafty Luque worked the count to 2 to 2 on Joe Kuhel and then added the final fillip to the Giants' triumph by striking him out on a called strike.

One year after their pennant triumph, it was complete collapse for the Senators in 1934. They set a new American League record for collapsibility, in fact. Their defense of the pennant was a farce. After the first few weeks they were never a factor and skidded farther than any pennant winning team in history. They finished seventh.

They weren't sunk without a trace, though. The clues were plentiful. Misfortune dogged them at every step in the form of injuries. Cronin rarely could put a healthy club on the ball field. The Senators' travail began with Luke Sewell's broken finger in training camp that kept him out of the line-up until mid-June.

Ossie Bluege reported to Biloxi wearing glasses for defective vision. Rookie Cecil Travis, from Chattanooga, who had won the regular third base job with his hitting, was beaned by Thornton Lee of the Indians on May 5, and was in a hospital for three weeks. Hal Trosky spiked Buddy Myer in late May and put him out for two weeks. Manager Cronin had reason to curse his luck. In that same game Travis and Jack Russell collided in attempting to field a bunt, and Russell was rendered *hors de combat* by Travis' spikes.

Moe Berg was benched with a Charley horse. Walter Stewart came down with a facial paralysis. Joe Kuhel broke his ankle in June sliding into second base awkwardly to avert a collision with Charley Gehringer. Heinie Manush came up with a sprained ankle the day Kuhel returned to the line-up, and the next day Johnny Stone was a victim of an ankle sprain. Dave Harris came down with a Charley horse in July and late that month Ed Linke became a medical curiosity when his pitching hand mysteriously went dead, with no pulse in the fingers.

In mid-August, Red Kress broke his thumb and was out for the rest of the season, and a few days later Myer was out again for a month with spike wounds. On September 3, Cronin broke his wrist in a collision at second base and had his hand in a cast for the rest of the year. The Senators finished the season with catcher Luke Sewell playing first base, rookie outfielder Jake Powell playing some second base, and Bluege moving to the outfield.

Goslin was out of the ball club. He was at odds with Cronin who the season before had benched him against certain left-handed pitching, to the great disgust of the Goose who recognized no difference in any kind of pitching. The Senators got outfielder Johnny Stone in the deal that sent Goslin to the Tigers.

Cronin traded Al Crowder, too, to Detroit. They had also had words. Crowder was objecting to Cronin's practice of playing the rookie Travis at third base instead of the reliable Ossie Bluege. From that date Cronin was finished with him.

Back in the fag end of 1933, Cronin had his first look at the tall Travis kid, and was impressed. In his major-league debut against Cleveland pitching, Travis rapped out five consecutive hits, all of them to left field despite the fact he was a left-handed hitter. Lucky hits, they might have looked like. But throughout 1934 Travis got the same kind of hits and a .319 batting average. After thirteen seasons at third base, Ossie Bluege was being replaced.

Travis had cost the Washington club 300 dollars. Kid Elberfeld found him playing sand-lot ball around Atlanta and brought him into his baseball school. He sold him to Joe Engel at the Nats' Chattanooga farm, and Travis was a fixture from the first day he played his first game of organized ball. He hit .351 in his first year in the Southern Association.

That Travis had a nice type of courage was demonstrated after he was beaned by Thornton Lee and sent to the hospital for recovery. It was feared that Travis would be bat-shy when he returned to the line-up. The first time he did get to bat after convalescing, circumstances found him hitting against the Cleveland club and the same pitcher, Lee. Travis was so bat-shy he tripled to left center.

188

With his ball club going nowhere but not quite threatened by an eighth-place finish, Griffith resorted to showmanship. Purely as a diversion he signed Allen Benson, a bearded pitcher from the House of David team, whom scout Joe Cambria had towed into Washington for a tryout one day. He proved a gate attraction and drew a big crowd when Griffith ordered him started on a Sunday against the Tigers. Brother Benson was pounded out early, but not quite disgraced.

When Griffith promised him another chance to start a ball game, Benson pleaded with Cambria to be allowed to shave his beard. "Nothing doing," said Cambria, "you're staying only if the beard stays." Benson wound up with a .000 record after a second start in which the Browns beat him, and was dispatched to Albany in hand with Cambria, the club's part-time scout.

If the Senators were wilting in 1934, romance at least was budding for Cronin. The dark-eyed miss to whom Joe Engel had introduced him in Griffith's outer office the day he came to Washington six years before, was now his betrothed. On September 27, after the cast was taken from his wrist, he took as his bride Mr. Griffith's secretary and niece, Mildred Robertson.

In those last waning weeks of the season, Cronin turned the management of the club over to his number one coach, Al Schacht. Assuming his new role as acting manager on September 27, Schacht immediately called a pep meeting of the seventh-place club and made a somewhat notable address:

"Listen, guys," he said, "Anything can happen in baseball. Washington ain't out of the race yet. Figure it out for yourself. If we win all our 27 games and Detroit loses all their 26 games, we finish in a tie with the Tigers. Now that's worth fighting for, ain't it? And don't forget the team that can't be beat won't be beat. Am I right or am I right?" Then he ducked a barrage of wet towels.

Before the season ended, Washington fans did have the distinction of seeing Babe Ruth bow out in his final appearance as a Yankee regular after twenty-two seasons in the league. On September 30, 12,000 paid him tribute with a signed testimonial presented at home plate. Also at home plate was the St. Mary's Industrial School of Baltimore Band.

For the occasion, manager Schacht sent Rookie Orville Armbrust to the mound. In Ruth's first three appearances the rookie forced Ruth to ground out, walked him, and retired him on a pop-up. Fearful that Ruth might be walked by Armbrust on his final appearance, Schacht waved Al Thomas to the mound with orders to pitch to Ruth. He did, and Ruth's fade-out as a Yankee regular went into the books as an easy fly to rookie Jake Powell in center field.

Chapter XII

IN a negative sort of way, those 1934 Senators were sensational, but their biggest sensation was reserved for late October when Clark Griffith pulled his most astounding deal. "I have never sold a ball player for cash," had been his proud boast during the first twenty-three years of his connection with the Washington club. He was excluding the piddling 2,000- and 3,000-dollar transactions and the waiver price deals. He meant that no star Washington player had ever been sold by him with cash as a prime consideration. He always demanded players in exchange.

But when Griffith was ready to scrap his boast, he didn't trifle. For the record baseball price of a quarter of a million dollars he sold to the Red Sox, Joe Cronin, his wonder boy manager and nephew by marriage.

The deal was not Griffith's idea. He had never intended to sell Cronin. When, in August, a Washington newspaper published the report that millionaire Tom Yawkey, Red Sox owner, was angling for Cronin, Griffith denied it heatedly.

"It's ridiculous," he snorted. "I wouldn't dare to sell Cronin. I wouldn't be able to face the Washington fans after a deal like that, and anyway no club would pay what Cronin is worth."

He suspected Eddie Collins, general manager of the Red

Sox, of inspiring the story. He got Collins on the long-distance phone and cracked down hard. "Stop talking about my ball players," he warned Collins, who denied he had spread the tale.

At the World Series in Detroit, Griffith met with Collins again, still incensed at the Boston man. Collins reiterated his innocence. But that night the phone rang in Griffith's Book-Cadillac Hotel and a voice said, "If you're going to be in, I'd like to talk to you." It was Tom Yawkey.

Yawkey asked Griffith bluntly if Cronin were for sale and Griffith said, "No, and consarn it, I don't like these stories that the Red Sox are going to buy him."

Yawkey smiled, and then he purred, "Would $250,000 bring him, Griff?"

"You can't offer that much, no ball player is worth $250,-000," said Griffith, "you're just wasting your time. Anyway, I don't want to sell Cronin."

Griffith had become angry, and Yawkey took his leave, saying he was sorry he had brought the matter up. He was apologizing for offering a quarter of a million dollars for a ball player.

Returning to Washington, Griffith realized he was being gnawed by a doubt in his own mind. Certainly he had never considered selling Cronin, but now he was wondering. Was he doing the right thing for Joe? Cronin had married into the Griffith family, and, in the late weeks of the 1934 season with the Senators hopelessly in the ruck, the grandstand wolves were already making pointed cracks. Cronin's neck had reddened at the boos. Perhaps, after all, it would be wise to sell Cronin. At Griffith Stadium there would always be that troublesome family angle for Cronin to contend with if the team were down.

Yawkey called him again. "That $250,000 still goes, Griff," said the Red Sox owner. "Let's talk about it in New York this week." Griffith was wavering. He agreed to see Yawkey in New York.

With him went his business manager, Ed Eynon. They saw Yawkey in his deluxe offices in the Tower Building, where Yawkey directed his maze of lumber interests and corporation directorates. With Yawkey was business manager Eddie Collins of the Red Sox.

Yawkey made the 250,000-dollar offer again.

"Maybe I'll make the deal if you'll toss in Lyn Lary, your shortstop," said Griffith.

"That's murder!" shouted Collins. "We just paid the Yankees $35,000 for Lary." "I don't care if you paid 35 million for him, we've got to have Lary for shortstop," insisted Griffith.

"No deal, then," said Collins.

Griffith and Eynon started to walk out, and Griffith was feeling vastly better, now that the deal was off. He was pleased now that he wasn't going to lose Cronin. "We've forty minutes to make our train," Eynon said.

Yawkey interrupted. "Let's talk some more," he said.

Turning to Collins, Yawkey added, "What do you say, Eddie, let's give 'em Lary and make it a deal?"

"If you want it that way, all right," said Collins sourly.

Yawkey grabbed up the handiest piece of paper, wrote out a bill of sale, signed it, and handed the paper to Griffith. "Well, I guess that ends that," he said.

"Not yet, Tom," said Griffith soberly.

"What do you mean? Lord, man, what else is there to do?"

"It's no deal unless it's all right with Cronin," said Griffith. "I'll have to call him first."

"All right then," said Yawkey impatiently, "get your pet on the phone."

That night on his return to Washington, Griffith telephoned Cronin who had just completed his honeymoon trip to San Francisco through the Panama Canal. He told of Yawkey's offers.

"But it's no deal, Joe, unless you're satisfied," he added.

"Never mind me," came Cronin's answer. "You take the money. I'll go to Boston. You tell 'em it's a deal."

"They'll give you a five-year contract at more than I'm paying you, Joe, and it's ironclad with no release clause," said Griffith.

"I knew you'd look out for me. And now that's all settled.

I'm hanging up before these telephone charges eat up all the profits. 'Bye."

There never was any question about the identity of the next Washington manager. Yawkey had made it clear that Cronin would be installed as playing manager of the Red Sox, thus ousting Bucky Harris who had moved to Boston from Detroit for a one-year term. Harris was available, and Griffith promptly signed him to manage the 1935 Senators.

Thus he kept intact his record of naming only his former ball players as his managers over a span that embraced seven managerial appointments. Griffith had never been reluctant to reclaim ball players he had traded. Without any show of embarrassment he had bought back Buddy Myer, Goose Goslin, Al Crowder, and others he had shipped away over the years, and he could bring back a former manager, too, if it pleased him.

His fondness for Harris was well known. He conceded that Harris, after his first flush of success in 1924 and 1925, had been lax in disciplining his ball players, but Griffith frequently voiced one favorite statement: "Bucky Harris can get more out of a ball team between the hours of 3:00 and 5:00 o'clock, than any man in baseball."

Harris was eager to work for Griffith again. "I'm complimented when Mr. Griffith wants me to manage his team again," said Harris. "He can be the toughest man to work for, and the best. A manager can always alibi to other club owners who aren't baseball men. He can tell them they lost because so-and-so couldn't hit a curve ball or this guy can't go to his left for a ground ball, but you can't give Griffith that stuff. He knows more about baseball than his manager. He knows why you win and why you lose. With Griffith, you don't have to alibi. He knows all your mistakes. If he's hiring me back again, he must think I'm pretty good, and I'm flattered."

For the next eight seasons, Harris labored with the Senators' collections of fading veterans and rookies unrefined by high minor-league experience, and only once did he land a Washington club in the first division. But if the Senators' position at the end of each season was undistinguished, they were not an unexciting ball club.

They produced a batting champion in 1935. Little Buddy Myer gained that distinction—the third Washington player ever to lead the American League in hitting. He joined the company of Ed Delahanty who in 1902 led the league's hitters with .376, and Goose Goslin who in 1928 topped them all with .379.

On the last day of the season, Myer was leaving his Washington hotel for the morning train that would take him to Philadelphia where the Senators were playing the A's in the finale. Accompanied by Mrs. Myer, he stopped suddenly in the lobby and stooped to pick up a safety pin he spotted on the floor.

"What's that?" inquired Mrs. Myer as Buddy stuffed the object in his pocket.

"I just found a two-base hit," said Myer, displaying the pin. "Find a pin and it always means a two-base hit."

Joe Vosmik of the Indians was leading the league batting race by a point on that last day of the season, with Myer runner-up. At Cleveland, where the Indians were winding up with a double-header, Vosmik was being withheld from the first game to protect his lead. And then the wires started telling of a batting rampage by Myer in Shibe Park. Hurriedly, the Indians moved Vosmik into the second-game line-up. He got one for four.

Up in Philadelphia, Myer hit a bunt in his first time at bat, singled to center in his second, grounded out his third time up, then singled to left for his third hit. He needed one more hit to clinch the batting crown. In the eighth inning he got it, the two-bagger he had talked about that morning, despite the fact he had to reach for an outside pitch to prevent Bill Dietrich from walking him.

Myer nosed out Vosmik by six-tenths of a thousandth of a point, .3495 to .3489.

The Senators finished sixth, but they were taking on personality. Griffith, desperate for pitching, unloaded 40,000 dollars and bought Buck Newsom from the Browns. And now playing regularly in the outfield was Jake Powell, the local boy from the sand lots. Handsome young Buddy Lewis showed up from Chattanooga and commenced a twelve-season stay with the club.

Like Travis, who had preceded him from Chattanooga, Lewis scarcely cost Griffith a cent. Lewis, seventeen-year-old Junior Legion sensation in his native Gastonia, North Carolina, was headed for the Giants, he thought. For being voted the outstanding player in the Junior Legion series, he was rewarded with a trip to New York and a three-week stay with the Giants. He wore a Giant uniform, but manager Bill Terry ignored him, shooed him off the field when the club was practicing. In disgust, young Lewis quit the Polo Grounds and for the rest of his New York stay contented himself with playing sand-lot baseball in Central Park.

Joe Engel found him playing sand-lot ball around Gastonia the next fall and invited him to try out with Chattanooga. He played third base in all of Chattanooga's 154 ball games in 1935, batted .303, and was moved up to the Senators. He was a .291-hitting third baseman in his first full year in the majors.

The veteran Red Kress was hanging on in the Washington infield, after getting a dramatic reprieve from Chattanooga in midseason of '35. Reporting to the park one day, Kress got his release to Chattanooga. He was at home packing when he got a hurry call on the phone. They wanted him back at the stadium, in uniform. Buddy Myer had just been thrown out of the first game of a double-header, and was ineligible for the second game. They wanted Kress to play second base.

Kress hustled out to the park and canceled his release to Chattanooga by pounding out four straight hits in the second game, against Cleveland. They never did get him out of the line-up after that, shifting him to shortstop when Myer returned.

Griffith was now patching again, and he traded Heinie Manush to Boston for Roy Johnson and Carl Reynolds, another of his rebuys. Before the 1936 season, he switched Johnson and Bump Hadley to the Yankees for right-hander Jimmy DeShong. Never a solid pitcher with the Yankees, DeShong proved Washington's big winner in 1936, gained eighteen victories, and was highly instrumental in pitching the club into fourth place, only a fraction of a point behind the third-place White Sox.

A trade with New York brought Ben Chapman to the Senators for Jake Powell. Even Griffith was pained by Powell's ruthless tactics on the bases, and his fate with the Senators was determined that day in May when Jake somewhat deliberately crashed into Hank Greenberg at first base on a routine play and broke Hank's glove-arm, incapacitating him for the rest of the season. "Protect yourself," Jake muttered unsympathetically.

In Yankee Stadium later in the season, Powell as a Yankee all but gave first baseman Joe Kuhel the same treatment, but the more agile Kuhel was merely brushed. Then he started a battle with Powell on the baselines. From the Washington bench rushed substitute catcher Walter Millies who jumped on Powell from behind. Jake shook free and aimed a punch at Millies' jaw, to his own great pain. Catcher Millies, before joining the battle, had affixed his catching mask to his face.

There had been trouble with Powell in Spring training in Orlando, Florida, the club's new spring base. Harris fined him once for late hours, and when the club started north on the only train out of Orlando, Powell wasn't on it. But mysteriously Powell showed up in time for the exhibition game the next day at Cordele, Georgia. How did he make it? He had chartered an airplane from Orlando. That was fine, except that Harris learned a few days later that Powell had chartered the plane at the club's expense. Another fine for Powell.

With the Yankees, Powell came back to Griffith Stadium an unpopular figure. When the left field bleacher fans booed him and he talked back, they threw bottles at Jake. Jake threw the bottles back, and the police broke up their bottle-heaving party.

In 1936, for the second straight year, Newsom was dividing his time between the pitching mound and the hospital. In his second start for the Senators in '35, he was struck on the knee by a line drive by Earl Averill and went into the act

196

of a man hit over the head. It looked like grandstanding as Buck collapsed and was taken to the bench for treatment. The game was held up, and Newsom returned to the mound to pitch the rest of the contest. At the finish it was learned how badly he had been hurt. His knee cap was broken in that second inning, and he had pitched the rest of the game on one leg. He was on crutches for six weeks.

In the spring of '36, young Buddy Lewis was the sensation of the training camp with his hitting, and Ossie Bluege himself advised Harris that Lewis couldn't miss being a great third baseman. The opening-day line-ups against the Yankees were announced by Harris, with Lewis playing third. But when the team took the field, it was the veteran Bluege, not Lewis, at third base. With President Roosevelt, much of the Cabinet, the Army band, and dignitaries all over the premises, plus 31,000 in the park, Lewis got an attack of jitters on the bench and admitted to Harris, "I'm too scared. Better play Bluege at third."

That was the confession of the lad who later was to fly 352 missions over the Hump in India during the Second World War."

That opening game of 1936 was distinguished, however, by what might be called Buck Newsom's second most important injury. He had talked himself into the opening pitching role, always a highly desirable honor for a Washington pitcher who traditionally gets himself introduced to the President of the United States before the game and sometimes, as in Newsom's case, swaps autographs with the Chief Executive.

Newsom found himself pitching against Lefty Gomez of the Yankees before the Presidential party and 31,000 paying fans. In the first inning, he started after a bunt laid down by Ben Chapman, then reconsidered and permitted Bluege to field the ball. At that point, however, Newsom became lost in thought, or something, and stood transfixed in the path of Bluege's throw to first base. Bluege's rifle throw traveled fifteen feet before it cracked Newsom solidly on the skull.

The ball dropped, but Newsom didn't. He went into a

drunken stagger, hands to his head, and reeled off balance in a wide circle toward the Presidential box, before setting a new course back to the pitching mound. Buck was proving he wasn't dead; he could take it. The only concession he would make was a trip to the bench for a cold towel. Then he went back to his job, pitched the full nine innings, and beat Gomez and the Yankees, 1 to 0.

When he approved the deal for Newsom a year before, Bucky Harris knew what he was taking on but he was willing. "I know all about the big blow-hard and his showboating, but if he can keep throwing that ball hard and wins us some games I'll take the headaches that go with managing Newsom," Harris said.

That Newsom could throw hard was one of his boasts that had to be accepted. He won sixteen games with the sixth-place Browns of 1934, and in that season Harris saw Buck pitching nine hitless innings against Harris' Red Sox before losing a 2-to-1 decision in the tenth on Boston's only safety. He worked in and out of turn and proudly bragged that he never had a sore arm. He qualified for another superlative. He had the most abused arm in baseball. In the hope of sneaking in credit for another victory he'd rush to the bullpen unordered to warm up and volunteer to take over for a losing pitcher.

He was an eight-year man in organized ball before the Senators took him. He came up out of Hartsville, South Carolina via Raleigh, Greenville, Wilmington, and Macon, before the Dodgers showed an interest in him in 1929, and lost it the next season. He drifted to Jersey City, back to Macon, to Little Rock, and was captured by the Cubs in 1932. He was working for Albany the next season, and then the Cubs shipped him to their Los Angeles farm in the Coast League. Buck was the best pitcher in the Coast League, won thirty games, was named the most valuable player, and was bought by the Browns.

Before joining the Senators he established himself at St. Louis as "The Voice." Commissioner Landis called Newsom and Dizzy Dean, of the Cardinals, to his Chicago office and censured them for not confining their activities to baseball during the season. They were being paid by a furniture store owner in St. Louis for personal appearances at his shop. When they went before Landis, even the voluble Dean couldn't insert an edgewise word. Newsom did all the talking for both.

Harris called him "the Hartsville Squire." Newsom liked to prate about the thirteen-room mansion he said he owned in South Carolina. "You oughta see my den," he said. And he rode with the hounds and grew cotton and made more money from his plantation than he did out of baseball. At least he said he did.

Newsom was always a little bit sensitive about his baseball salaries anyway, and fancied himself as the top wage earner on the Washington club. He was dismayed when one reporter referred to him as "The Senators' $14,000-a-year-pitcher," after he had lasted only two innings. The next day he took the miscreant aside and talked frankly to him. "You shouldn't call me a $14,000 pitcher," Newsom said. "I wouldn't work for any cheap dough like that. My contract calls for $18,000." That was fine, except later intelligence gained by the reporter from the business office revealed Newsom's salary for that year to be 13,000 dollars.

When Joe DiMaggio was breaking in so sensationally for the Yankees in 1936, Newsom announced he wanted to start against the Yanks. "Watch me against DiMag," he boasted. "I know that guy's weakness." A week later, Newsom was facing DiMaggio. Buck did expose Joe's weakness all right. DiMaggio displayed a weakness for two-baggers. He tagged Buck for no less than three of them.

Newsom had one standard alibi. He never threw anybody an easy pitch. At least he never admitted it. When DiMaggio one day banged a three-and-two Newsom pitch for one of the longest home runs ever hit into the center field bleachers in Griffith Stadium, Buck accepted no blame. "I never threw a better pitch in my life. Stuff on it and it was breaking to the outside. He had no right to hit that kind of a pitch for a home run. I'd throw it to him, or anybody else, again."

Buck credited himself with all kinds of record feats, i.e., when he said he won thirty-three games that year with Los

199

Angeles. It was pointed out to him that the record books said thirty.

"Who you going to believe?" he demanded, hurt.

During one of Newsom's salary holdouts when he was threatening to sit it out in Hartsville unless Griffith gave him a big increase, Bob Considine stopped by Hartsville to interview him on his way to Florida. Newsom instructed Considine to tell Griffith he would never pitch another ball for the Washington club.

Considine reached Florida in his automobile the next day and found Griffith in the lobby of the Senators' hotel. Before he could blurt out the news of Newsom's threat to Griffith, the Washington club owner said:

"Here's some news for your paper. Newsom just drove in a couple of hours ago and signed up."

Very often, though, Newsom was a stickler for the truth. One time he said he could go 100 miles an hour in his new Ford in second gear. Earl Whitehill bet him 100 dollars he couldn't and lost. How could Whitehill know that Buck had built a special second gear into his new car?

Newsom was one of Griffith's favorite pinochle companions in the off-day sessions, but the Washington owner's love for pinochle was topped by his love for a better ball team, so he traded Newsom to the Red Sox in mid-year of 1937. With him went outfielder Ben Chapman in a swap for the Ferrell brothers, Wes and Rick, and the California Spaniard, outfielder Mel Almada.

Newsom had completed term one in Washington, before bouncing and rebouncing on and off Griffith's club until he had racked up five terms in Washington, surpassing the record of F. D. Roosevelt.

If Griffith was tolerant with Harris, it was understandable. The Senators had no farm system worthy of the name. And there was evidence, too, that Griffith had lost his trading touch. In desperation he signed fat Shanty Hogan, ex-Giant, to bolster his catching staff, and Hogan ate himself out of the club in spring training of 1938, after helping the Senators to finish sixth in '37.

200

The two kids from Chattanooga, Cecil Travis and Buddy Lewis, were teaming with Johnny Stone to take the Senators as far as they did go in '37, all of them hitting .300. Monte Weaver was their only winning pitcher. DeShong faded badly, and the Senators finished fifth somewhat valiantly in '38, with the help of the .350 hitting of Taft Wright, the rotund outfielder gained from Atlanta in a deal for Dave Harris.

The Senators took a tough blow early in '38. After playing only fifty-six games, Johnny Stone was out of the line-up. He had slowed mysteriously, and jokingly he was being called just a lazy Southerner. Then, in Detroit, the truth came out. Stone was a victim of a lung disease, and was ordered by doctors to give up the game.

Toward the end of the year, Griffith fired Wes Ferrell. It was outright. Griffith didn't even attempt to swing a deal for him. He gave Ferrell ten days pay and told him to leave. Ferrell's unforgivable crime was his crack in a Philadelphia railroad station when he said, "This cheap Washington club won't even pay our taxi fares." Somebody went to Griffith bearing tales.

Griffith took Al Simmons in 1937, buying the veteran from the Tigers, and fired him at the end of the 1938 season despite the fact he had hit more than .300. He didn't like Simmons' actions on the last day of the season. Heckled by some box-seat fans, Simmons called time and directed a stream of curses at the customers. Griffith, within earshot, promptly fined Simmons 200 dollars and said, "No ball player of mine can act like that toward my fans." Simmons took another view of the fine, declaring it was a low trick of Griffith's to reclaim a 200-dollar bonus for which he had qualified by hitting .300.

For the Senators, it was the beginning, too, of their Cambria-sponsored era Cuban prospects, whose advance guard was already on the club and the coming and going of Zeke Bonura. After Joe Kuhel slumped to a .283 figure in '37, Griffith traded him to the White Sox in a straight swap for Bonura the next spring, in an attempt to inject some more hitting power into the club. The Bonura Story with Washington thus began.

Griffith never made a worse deal, and the paradox is that he never made one more profitable financially—the Cronin sale excepted. Bonura was a dismal flop with the Senators, but Griffith, with his shrewd trading in baseball flesh, turned him into a neat profit.

Big Zeke, a bumbling first baseman with an infectious enthusiasm and an overrated batting capacity, stuck the '38 season out with the Senators, and in December was peddled by Griffith to the New York Giants for 25,000 dollars and two minor-league players despite the mere .289 batting average he compiled.

Zeke played for the Giants in 1939—when he wasn't riding the bench—at a salary of 15,000 dollars. Manager Bill Terry could scarcely wait until the season ended to place him on the waiver list. None of the National League teams would bite. But Griffith the next spring said he'd be glad to take Zeke off Terry's hands for 7,500 dollars. Griffith reasoned that his own rookie first baseman, Jimmy Wasdell, wasn't showing anything and Zeke couldn't be much worse. In effect, Griffith had rented Bonura to the Giants for 17,500 dollars for one season.

By the next July, though, Zeke had taken his leave of the Nats again, being sold by Griffith to the Chicago Cubs for 10,000 dollars. Now Griffith had pyramided his profits on Bonura to 27,500 dollars. Zeke finished the season with the Cubs who then sold him to Minneapolis. The Millers didn't get their money's worth out of him either. Two months later he went into the army. Everybody, it seemed, lost money on Bonura except Griffith, who had capitalized, too, on Zeke's box-office appeal.

Zeke was something special. It's still uncertain how he got his nickname, but the accepted version dates back to his undergraduate days at Notre Dame. He went out for football and an assistant coach, noting Bonura's heft, is reported to have commented, "Boy, what a physique!" Zeke became his nickname thereafter.

Bonura's higher education also included a few terms at Loyola University in his native New Orleans, but where he learned his geography is somewhat vague. At the end of his first season in Washington, after putting in several years with the White Sox, Zeke proudly announced on the last day that he was driving his new car to New Orleans.

"This new job can fly," Zeke said. "I'll be in Chicago in thirty hours."

"Chicago?" a newspaperman inquired incredulously, "I thought you were going home to New Orleans."

"That's right," said Zeke, "I'm going to New Orleans, but from Chicago I know every inch of the road."

Injured legs figured in Bonura's travels as much as base hits. In fact, it was an incongruous combination of injured leg and a horsefly which led to his first journey to Washington in the Spring of 1938. In July, 1937, the White Sox were playing the Detroit Tigers, with the score tied 2 to 2 in the last of the ninth inning. Bonura was on third base, with Tommy Bridges pitching for the Tigers. At a time when it was regarded as suicide to attempt a steal on Bridges, Zeke looked at the Chicago bench and suddenly, to the astonishment of everyone—including Bridges—broke for home. He made it safely when the befuddled Bridges threw late to the plate. But in the process Zeke had injured his leg.

As he limped off the field manager Jimmy Dykes fell into step beside him. "Nice work, Zeke," Dykes commented. "That was the first time you stole a base in four years but you picked the right spot to do it."

Bonura scratched his head. "Well, Jimmy," he replied, "you gave me the sign to steal so I did. I saw you wave your scorecard."

Dykes recoiled like a man suffering from a bad dream. "Sign? Steal? Holy smokes, Zeke, I was just waving the scorecard to brush a horsefly off my nose!"

But Bonura, with his injured leg, was temporarily out of the line-up. Dykes was later to learn how Bonura interpreted the word "temporary." Zeke was out for a week, then two weeks. When a month elapsed, Dykes began to get suspicious. One night the manager dropped into a State Street night spot. What he saw made his neck veins bulge with anger. There was Zeke, his first baseman with the ailing leg, negotiating a nifty rumba on the dance floor with his lady fair.

From then on Bonura's days with the White Sox were numbered. Dykes promptly told a Chicago reporter that "Zeke is dogging it." Bonura became incensed, and henceforth he and Dykes exchanged few words. When Griffith, who periodically tries to obtain a slugger for his vast ball park, proposed a Bonura-Kuhel trade the following spring, Dykes snapped it up.

When the announcement of the trade broke in the spring of 1938, the happiest man in Washington was neither Griffith nor manager Bucky Harris. It was Vice President John Nance Garner. Cactus Jack had taken a fancy to Bonura two years earlier and had repeatedly urged Griff to buy, trade, or steal him from the White Sox. When Garner saw the news of the trade in the papers, he promptly turned the Senate over to a member of that body and telephoned Griff his congratulations.

Garner was jubilant. Bonura was his favorite player. Garner never tired of hearing Bonura's yarns. Garner once asked Zeke if it were true his father gave him 100 dollars every time he hit a home run. Bonura replied, "Yeah, it's true. I've been pretty hard on the old man recently."

Bonura's arrival in the 1938 spring training camp of the Nats prompted some caustic comparisons on the fielding ability of Bonura and Kuhel. When a reporter suggested that Bonura didn't originate as many first-to-short-to-first plays as Kuhel, Zeke replied in terms which reflected the mood of Griff and Harris. "Look," he said, "the only thing I'm interested in is originating some runs up there at the plate with my stick."

Admittedly, Zeke was no gazelle around the first base bag, but Griff and Harris were willing to overlook that deficiency as long as Zeke was batting across those runs. Optimism abounded in the 1938 camp as Griff and Harris conjured up beautiful dreams of Bonura driving across one Senator after another.

Bonura's finest hour was the opening game of the 1938 season. Just before the game started he went over to the Vice President's box for a pre-game chat with Garner. Zeke told the Vice President, "I'll hit a special home run for you today."

Sure enough, on his first trip to the plate as a Nat, he slugged the third ball pitched on a direct line into the centerfield bleachers. Zeke ran around the bases at full speed, crossed the plate and rushed directly to Garner's box. The happy Vice President hugged Zeke then and there.

Unfortunately for Bonura and the Nats, Zeke couldn't keep up that pace. On June 15, the 210-pound Bonura was hitting exactly .190. Wasdell was recalled from Indianapolis. Bonura rode the bench, finally finishing out the season with a .289 average, including twenty-two home runs and more than one-hundred runs batted in. Offsetting that tolerable performance, however, was a quite intolerable showing as a fielder. Dykes had often said that Zeke let in three runs for every run he batted in, and at the end of the 1938 season Harris was ruefully inclined to agree.

The league fielding statistics smiled on Bonura but the customers laughed at him. The official figures often listed Bonura as the leading fielder of the league, based on chances and errors. Actually, of course, they did not take into account the extraordinary number of ground balls which he refused to go after and hence could not be charged with errors. Washington fans, accustomed to watching such fancy fielders as Joe Judge and Kuhel, turned sour on Bonura. Even Griffith winced when he watched Bonura take a ground ball, then wave the pitcher away while the runner easily beat him to the bag.

To the fans who were not super-critical of Bonura's play at first base, he was a tremendous hero. Zeke was a ladies' day favorite too. They liked his constant grin, his loud whooping, mitt-pounding, and his excursions into the pitcher's box when a teammate was faltering. There was the day when Zeke failed to field a ball hit to his right, but not very far to his right, on which the batter got a cheap single to right field. It should have been called an error for Bonura. Anyway the batter reached first and started for second, only to think better of it and return to the bag when the right-fielder returned the ball to Zeke at first base.

A woman in Griffith's box applauded loudly. The Nats'

owner was baffled, seeing no reason to applaud anything. "Who are you clapping for?" Griffith asked.

"For Zeke," she replied. "He almost got that man out."

"Holy smoke," said Griffith. "That big bum missed that hit when it went past him. He didn't move out of his tracks for the ball."

"Yes," said the lady, blissfully, "but Zeke got it coming back. He's wonderful."

A chunky, swarthy figure of a man was increasingly in evidence in Griffith's little stucco office at the stadium in these years of the late thirties, and the roster of the Senators was beginning to bear his mark. He was Joe Cambria, taking over as the most active of Griffith's two talent scouts, with Joe Engel occupied chiefly with operating the Chattanooga farm team.

Cambria's baseball background was vague, and still is. Earliest traces of him reveal he was a semi-pro ball player in Massachusetts in his youth. He popped up in Baltimore in 1930 as the owner of a laundry and sponsor of semi-pro clubs. He bought the Albany franchise in the International League cheaply, and the laundry became a sideline. As the Albany owner he did a bit of business with Griffith and luckily for himself made a good friend of the Washington owner.

Cambria's Albany operations often came under the scrutiny of Commissioner Landis, and a half dozen times Landis censured him for irregularities. Cambria had only a vague notion of baseball procedure with respect to player contracts, and when complaints poured into Landis' office the Commissioner threatened to kick him out of baseball. On each occasion, Griffith stepped in to plead for Cambria and temper Landis' wrath. Griffith could do that. Among all the club owners, he had always stood staunchest with Landis and his often irksome rulings.

Cambria's Albany franchise cost him 5,000 dollars, and he sold it to the Giants for transfer to Jersey City for 65,000 dollars. In another year he sold 100,000 dollars worth of ball players. The baseball business took on more appeal for him than the laundry business. To Griffith, with whom he worked closely, he sold cheaply and on a conditional basis. Griffith had the choice of Cambria's players and their relationship burgeoned into a scouting job for Cambria.

In 1937 when Cambria owned the Trenton, New Jersey, club, he sent up a streamlined young outfielder named George Case, a delivery that was to be one of Cambria's greatest triumphs.

Cambria picked up George Case on the rebound. A year before the young man, famed chiefly for his track exploits at Peddie Prep, had sought a tryout with Connie Mack as a pitcher. Mack looked him over and dismissed him with the advice to try outfielding. In his home town of Trenton he joined Cambria's team, batted .338, led the New York-Penn League in stolen bases, and moved up to the Senators.

He was Washington's regular left-fielder for the next nine years and set a new record by leading the league in base stealing for five consecutive years, beginning in 1939. In only one year was he seriously challenged for that honor. Case stole three bases on the last day of the 1943 season to beat out Wally Moses of the White Sox.

Case could run, but he couldn't slide and never learned. As a consequence he came up with leg sprains and wrist sprains that kept him out of action frequently. He wasn't a power hitter, but he closed out his career with a .284 lifetime average. In the outfield he was off with the crack of the bat, and often in the wrong direction. But with his speed he could rectify many of those mistakes.

Until Case came along, Cambria's chief boasts were two wild lefthanders he delivered to Griffith: Ken Chase and Joe Krakauskas in the mid-thirties. Chase was brilliant on occasion and somewhat of a hard luck pitcher, but he never did make good. He was too wild. Krakauskas was even wilder. On a day when he was pitching against Hank Greenberg in Florida and manager Del Baker was tipping off Krakky's delivery to Hank, a high inside pitch almost decapitated Greenberg who was looking for a curve. Greenberg eventually struck out, glad to get away from there, and buttonholed Baker on the way to the bench. "Don't ever try to tip me off again on what that guy is going to throw," said Hank. "You can't possibly know, because he doesn't know himself."

Cambria had an interest in the Salisbury, Maryland, club in the Eastern Shore League, and in that circuit he noted a tall young first baseman named Mickey Vernon. Vernon was just one year out of Villanova and the semi-chattel of the Browns who could have signed him for 800 dollars. They passed him up at that figure. Cambria signed him for the Springfield, Massachusetts club of which he owned a part. After Vernon hit .328 and .343 in two years of minor-league ball, Cambria delivered him to Griffith in 1939 at a price to be named by Griffith if the lad made good. It was a nice arrangement for Griffith. Never did he have to make any great initial outlay where Cambria-owned prospects were concerned. Vernon was Washington's regular first baseman in 1941, won the American League batting title in 1946, and Griffith tossed Cambria a couple of sizable bonuses.

The sand lots and the low minors comprised Cambria's field in those years. Without authority to spend Griffith's money, and with no great trust reposing in his scouting ability, he didn't mingle with the other big-league scouts in the Double A leagues, but stuck to the off-tracks. Pretty soon, Cambria discovered Cuba.

The Washington Club developed a sizable Latin quarter as Cambria filtered his low-cost Cubans into Senator uniforms. In the Havana winter league he found a hefty little third baseman named Bobby Estalella who could hit a long ball when he connected and could play third base as well as any D-Leaguer.

"Poppa Joe" brought Estalella up in 1935, and Harris had him at third base for fifteen games. He batted .314 and fielded about the same. But the ground balls he wasn't grabbing up he was knocking down with his chest, his chin, or any other part of his anatomy that was handiest. He hit a couple of home runs, and the Senators' fans adopted him. They called Griffith Stadium each day to assure themselves that Estalella would be in the line-up. Otherwise they were disinterested in the Senators that day.

Estalella never made it. He was around until 1939, and

208

got another big-league chance with Connie Mack before jumping to the Mexican League.

Cambria wasn't discouraged, though. Out of Cuba he fetched a rotund little left-handed pitcher named Rene Monteagudo in 1938. The Senators encountered him first at Greenville, South Carolina, where Cambria owned another ball club. Monteagudo held them to four hits, but they beat him, 2 to 1, in an exhibition game. Griffith took Monteagudo on. His chief virtue proved to be that he could speak English. He pitched Cuban and was released to Jersey City.

The next year Cambria showed up with his latest Latin. This one was a Venezuelan. Cambria had found him pitching in Havana, however, and signed him one day after luring him to a park bench. He said his name was Alexander. Four days later it was discovered that this was only the Americanized version of his first name. He turned out to be one Alejandro Carrasquel, of Caracas, and it was initially evident that this fellow knew how to pitch.

Cambria said Carrasquel was twenty-eight years old. Carrasquel said he was thirty-two years old. Touring Cubans at Orlando said Carrasquel was thirty-five. He was a forbidding looking fellow, tall, with accentuated facial features, swarthy and pock-marked. With a cutlass in his hand and a knife in his mouth, he could have doubled for any respectable pirate boarding a victim ship.

Carrasquel made it, with the help of Tony Giuliani, the Senators' Spanish-speaking catcher of the era. Alejandro was around for seven years with the Senators, pitching more good ball than bad ball. He won fifty games while losing thirty-nine. He was another Cambria triumph despite his fondness for the rumba and stay-out habits. At the end of the 1944 season, he was sold to the White Sox for 7,500 dollars, refused to report, jumped to the Mexican League, and left a clear cash profit with Griffith who pocketed the White Sox purchase price.

The most heralded Cambria product, though, was one Roberto Ortiz, the biggest Cuban he ever lassoed and brought out of the Pearl of the Antilles. Cambria trekked the canebrakes on hearing word of Ortiz's pitching feats for a hinterland Cuban team, and he threw a net over the massive young man. He introduced him at Orlando as "faster than Johnson and a longer hitter than Jimmy Foxx."

Skeptical Bucky Harris was unconvinced, however. He tried to talk to Ortiz, but the language barrier was too tough. Harris turned to Cambria and said, "You ask this guy whether he's a pitcher or an outfielder. Let's see what he wants to do." Harris was assuming that Cambria had learned some Spanish from his travels in Cuba, but he was overrating Poppa Joe. Not a word of Spanish had Cambria learned yet. His interrogation of Ortiz was fruitless. It consisted of putting to him in English the same questions Harris had asked, with one slight difference. Cambria yelled the questions, in the delusion that Ortiz might understand shouted English.

Ortiz did throw a ball hard. Al Evans and Jake Early, the Senators' catcher, couldn't hold him. He knocked the mitt off Evans' hands a couple of times. He was wild, and the two catchers were understandably timid. Griffith imported Al Lopez from Tampa to give Ortiz a whirl. Lopez caught Ortiz' stuff as easily as picking off daisies, but the pitcher was still wild. They gave him up as a pitcher a year later, and after that gave him up as an outfielder, and after that Ortiz gave up American baseball, taking the well-beaten path to Mexico.

Cambria's Cubans kept coming, though. Gilberto Torres, a scholarly fellow whose father had caught for Washington two decades before, joined the Senators as a shortstop. But he had been playing minor-league ball in the States for most of ten years. It was during the war, though, that Cambria's draft-exempt Cubans were more favorably received. Their draft status at a time when talent was uncertain had an appeal for Griffith. In the 1944 training camp at College Park, Maryland, no fewer than twelve Latins were on the roster. They set up a furious babble in Spanish, but except for Mike Guerra, the little catcher, and Torres, there wasn't a big leaguer among them. At the war's end when Griffith visioned a new flow of American talent he called Cambria off the Cuban beat.

Harris was working on one-year contracts in his second term as manager of the Senators, and Griffith was faithfully renewing their pact at the end of each season. This he did despite six consecutive years in the second division from 1937 to 1942. He was expecting no pennants with the sows' ears he was giving Harris to work with.

Griffith made a 40,000-dollar bid to improve the situation, though, in 1939. He bought Jimmy Pofahl, a shortstop, from the Minneapolis club, and found himself stung badly. Pofahl reported to spring training with a throwing arm more suitable for beanbag than major-league ball, and Griffith screamed to Mike Kelly of Minneapolis that he had been swindled. He tried to call off the deal, but when Pofahl confessed that he'd hurt his arm in a taxicab door accident between seasons, it stuck.

In the Spring of '39, Griffith announced from training camp: "Two players will make or break this club." He was referring to his rookie first baseman, Jimmy Wasdell, and the Cuban Estalella who showed hitting promise. Wasdell didn't last until midseason, and Estalella wound up at Minneapolis. The Senators finished sixth, a notch below their 1938 finish.

If Griffith had one obsession, it was an eternal quest for a right-handed hitting outfielder. Except for the years when Fred Schulte served him well and helped to win the 1933 pennant, all of Griffith's good outfielders had been left-handed, beginning with Milan, and embracing a list with Goose Goslin, Heinie Manush, Sammy West, and his latest, Taft Wright.

In 1940, he thought he envisioned right-handed hitting strength in Gerry Walker, the tempestuous Detroit outfielder who was on the block, and in an ill-guarded moment he grabbed up Walker in a trade for Wright, a fellow who had batted .350 and .309 in consecutive years. It was a bad deal. Wright went to Chicago and hit .337; Walker came to Washington and batted .294.

But in another direction the Senators had been blessed. In 1938 they picked up from Atlanta for the 6,500-dollar draft price, a fattish fellow named Dutch Leonard who was throwing a knuckle ball. The next year Leonard and his butterfly ball performed the feat of winning twenty games for a sixth-place Washington club.

211

But Griffith came up with the prize pitching rookie of the year in 1940, and out of a D league at that. So glowing were the reports of John Ganzel, Griffith's Florida State League operative, about the talents of a tall young fellow named Sid Hudson, that Griffith laid out 5,000 dollars, the biggest price he ever paid for a Class D Leaguer.

Hudson had won twenty-eight games for Sanford in the Florida State League, and in training camp manager Harris went overboard in his enthusiasm for the lad. Harris, Griffith, and Ganzel were disappointed, however, when Hudson was knocked out of the box in his first seven major-league starts. Harris stuck with him though, and at the end of the year Hudson was a sensation with seventeen victories. He helped the Senators to finish seventh.

The consistent Travis was the club's only .300 hitter in 1941. Zeke Bonura tried again and was found wanting again, and Harris installed the drafted George Archie at first base. Later Mickey Vernon took over and finished as the regular with a creditable .299 batting figure. Save for Buddy Lewis who hit .297 after being shifted from third base, there was no punch in the outfield. The veteran Doc Cramer, obtained from Detroit, and George Case, were hitting in the .270's. Leonard and Hudson won thirty-one of the seventy victories that enabled the club to finish in a tie for sixth in 1941.

A young pitcher named Early Wynn came along, though. He had walked into the Sanford, Florida, training camp of the Senators' Chattanooga farm team three years before, wearing jeans, barefooted, with a glove dangling from his belt, and pestered manager Clyde Milan for a chance to pitch. The indulgent Milan said, "Okay, kid," and was so impressed he hustled the boy back to his Hartford, Alabama, home that night for his parents' signatures on a contract.

Harris brought Wynn up from Charlotte where he had won fifteen games, and he, too, was impressed, but only with the fellow's potentialities. He sent him back for more seasoning, but admitted later he was prodded into that act. When Wynn came to bat with two on base and under instructions to sacrifice, he bunted into a triple play!

Newsom was back in '42. He'd been on a gypsy tour of the

league since 1937 when the Senators shipped him to Boston. One-half season of Newsom was enough for Joe Cronin at Boston and he shipped him to the Browns. The pennant-minded Tigers were intrigued with Newsom's twenty wins for the Browns in '38, and landed him in a ten-player deal. He won twenty-one to help pitch Detroit to the 1940 pennant and was boasting he was the highest-paid pitcher in baseball when Walter Briggs paid him 40,000 dollars in salary and bonuses for 1941.

When he flopped with the Tigers in '41, winning only twelve and losing twenty, general manager Jack Zeller chopped his basic pay from 33,000 dollars to 13,000 dollars. Newsom refused to sign and called Zeller a lot of names. "I'll sign that contract only when you grow hair on that bald head of yours," Newsom told Zeller. Griffith stepped into the salary impasse and bought Newsom for 15,000 dollars.

It didn't help. Newsom won eleven and lost seventeen for the Senators and helped only to pitch the club into a seventh-place finish. Harris was taking a dim view of Newsom anyway. He was the bellwether in the first clique ever to be established on a Washington club under Harris. Newsom, pitcher Jack Wilson, and outfielder Roy Cullenbine were giving rookie shortstop Bob Repass a fast time of it. They were a group apart from the rest of the club, dining out and hitting the night spots. Harris asked Griffith to get rid of them all, and one by one that was done.

Wilson, a big right-hander, had come from Boston in a deal that also brought Stan Spence in a swap for pitcher Ken Chase and outfielder Johnny Welaj. Repass, a former Cardinal farmhand, was a draftee from Columbus, and in spring training looked like a composite of Hans Wagner, Marty Marion, and Pewee Reese. But with the start of the season he proved to be just a minor leaguer and couldn't beat the .208-hitting Pofahl for the shortstop job.

Harris unloaded Wilson to Detroit in what was supposed to be a swap for Eric McNair. But McNair wouldn't report, and Griffith settled for a 5,000-dollar payment, less than the waiver price. Wilson was with the Senators in Detroit the day of the deal, and pitched for the Tigers that afternoon.

In Washington, the wives of Wilson and Repass were listening to the radio play-by-play in the same apartment. As a Tiger, the first batter Wilson faced was his pal Repass. On the first pitch, Repass hit his first major-league home run.

Griffith got back all his money for Newsom in September by selling him to the Brooklyn Dodgers for 25,000 dollars. The Yankees bought Cullenbine on the same day—the deadline for World Series eligibility.

Dutch Leonard was almost a total loss in 1942, breaking his leg in April on a rare play by a pitcher, a slide into first base. He was out until September. Harris was operating with perhaps the worst Washington infield in history. Vernon was doing well enough at first base, but at short and second the Senators were reduced to playing a pair of tender rookies from the Southern Association, Johnny Sullivan and Ellis Cleary. Cecil Travis and Buddy Lewis had gone to war, depriving the club of its best punch.

Chapter XIII

THE eight long years came to an end for Harris two days after the '42 season ended. He quit as manager, at least on invitation if not under compulsion. Griffith announced, "A change in managers seems to be in order." He had ascertained there was a spot for Bucky managing Buffalo. It was all very amicable.

Everybody knew that Griffith would continue his custom of naming a manager from his own club. Nobody was surprised when his choice was Ossie Bluege, the only remaining veteran of "the old days." Bluege had been Harris' coach since retiring as an active player. Anyway, a manager was not the most important factor in baseball at this time. The war was in full cry, and there was doubt that baseball would keep operating.

Griffith gave Bluege a revamped ball club, swinging with new vigor into a trading-buying spree. In another attempt to

214

procure that will o' the wisp, a good right-handed hitting out-fielder, he wangled Bob Johnson away from Connie Mack, with whom Johnson was having salary troubles. Estalella was shipped to the A's in the deal. The Senators came up with a new second baseman in Gerry Priddy, a consideration of the 1941 maneuver that had sent Cullenbine and pitcher Bill Zuber to the Yanks. Pitcher Milo Candini also accrued in that swap. Rick Ferrell was traded to St. Louis for outfielder Gene Moore.

Mickey Vernon was now the fixture at first base. The season before, Griffith persuaded the Yankees to sell him Mike Chartak but balked at their price of 14,000 dollars, offering 12,000 dollars. He met the Yankees' argument that the Browns were already offering 14,000 dollars for Chartak by convincing Ed Barrow his sale to Washington would be for the good of the league—that with Chartak the Senators could draw bigger crowds and the Browns weren't drawing anyway. The Yankees' bigger share of the gate receipts would compensate them for taking 2,000 dollars less for Chartak, Griffith argued. The Yankees fell for it. Six weeks later they were furious at Griffith who sold Chartak to the Browns for 14,000 dollars.

Early Wynn became an eighteen-game winner. Little Mickey Haefner, bought from Minneapolis for 20,000 dollars, won eleven and lost five. Lefty Gomez was given an early trial and dismissed. The pitching stood up nicely, without a .300 hitter on the club. Rookie Candini won seven in a row and finished up with eleven and seven. Carrasquel had the same good record.

The Senators moved into the first division in August and then unreeled a winning streak that moved them into second behind the fast-flying Yanks. George Case was having one of his finest years, but third base and shortstop were troubling Bluege. Young Cleary at third was a favorite of the fans, but he was a light hitter and erratic. In a more extreme way, the same could be said for young Johnny Sullivan at shortstop.

Cleary was a pugnacious character. He was the Senators' property in the minors for five years before Griffith brought him up. He admired the fellow's spirit, but doubted his skill. At Charlotte one day he ducked two head-high pitches, dropped his bat, walked to the mound, and calmly flattened his tormentor. In Richmond, where a heckler was taunting the Charlotte players in their parked bus, he got out of his seat, punched the fellow in the nose, and landed in jail.

He wasn't much of a fielder, fighting the ball as well as anything else that challenged him. But he was a tolerable lead-off man. When Spud Chandler blanked the Senators, 1 to 0, on one hit in April, Cleary made that one hit. At Detroit, catcher Birdie Tebbetts prophesied that "Cleary will get hit in the head if he keeps crowding the plate and sticking his neck out like that." That's what happened. Cleary was beaned his first time up. He went down, stayed down for thirty seconds, and then galloped happily to first base unhurt. Asked why he stayed down so long he said, "I wanted to be sure they'd give me first base. In Chattanooga when I was beaned one time, I didn't go down and the umpire claimed the ball had come off my bat and wouldn't give me the base."

Cleary knocked down Charley Gehringer of the Tigers, and that team planned to get even. McCosky later slid into third, spiking Cleary and putting him out of the game. On the bench Johnny Sullivan shook his head and said, "I feel sorry for McCosky." Sullivan was asked why the sympathy for McCosky when it was Cleary who got hurt. "I know," said Sullivan, "but McCosky will get it good from Cleary the next time."

Cleary didn't stick the season out, though. Still seeing a pennant chance for his club, Griffith sent him to the Browns along with 40,000 dollars in cash for third baseman Harlond Clift and pitcher Johnny Niggeling. Niggeling, the old knuckle-baller, was a help, winning four of his six starts, but Clift wasn't. He played only eight games for the Senators before contracting his children's mumps on a visit to his family in St. Louis.

Old faces began to reappear, too. Buck Newsom came back from the Browns in September for his third term with the club and won three in a row. Jake Powell was bought from St. Paul, and it was clear he hadn't changed much. He reported wearing a deeply blackened right eye, a souvenir of a battle with Eric McNair the day he was bought by the Senators.

George Case, in a special exhibition, with official A.A.U. timers, circled the bases in 13.5 seconds to break the world's record of 13.8 set by Hans Lobert in 1910. Case stole fifty-six bases that year, but it didn't help. The Yankees held their big lead safe through September, and the Senators had to be content with second place, ten and one half games behind.

The Senators' second place finish in 1943 was their best in a decade, and left Griffith, Bluege and the eager Washington fans who picked them to win the pennant in '44 quite unprepared for what did happen. Bluege, now hailed as a minor miracle man, found his fame short-lived. The 1944 Senators took one of the biggest drops in their history. They finished last—a galling blow to Clark Griffith who since moving to the capital in 1912 could boast that he never had an eighth-place club.

They had an excuse. Selective service struck hard. Ray Scarborough went into service. The Army's grab of Gerry Priddy wrecked the Washington infield. Vernon was already in the Navy, and Bob Johnson had finished up the previous season at first base. Jake Early and Al Evans, the good catchers, were both in uniform— Uncle Sam's. Clift was on call by his draft board and wouldn't report.

Joe Kuhel was claimed from the White Sox to play first base. Griffith was again patching frantically. He shipped Newsom off again for Roger Wolff of the Athletics. The 4-F's became important assets to all the clubs. Griffith decided to use the Cubans and had a dozen of them in his College Park, Maryland, training camp. Shortstop Gil Torres, catcher Mike Guerra, and outfielder Roberto Ortiz remained.

Weak-hitting, wild-throwing George Myatt, a Giant farm-hand, was at second base, with the slow-moving Torres at third base. Only Stan Spence hit .300. In midseason, with a ruling by Selective Service that Cubans in the United States must register for the draft, Torres, Guerra, and Ortiz hastily left for Havana. At one point, so great was Griffith's desperation, he signed an outfielder named Eddie Boland, of New

York City. Boland at the time was playing for the New York Sanitation Department team. Rene Monteagudo, the little pitcher, was called up from Chattanooga and saw outfield duty.

The Senators never got out of the second division after the early weeks. But paradoxically they were a pennant factor. They crushed the Boston Red Sox in an important series that blighted the Boston hopes. They startled the surprising Browns on an August decline by beating them three out of four while the Browns were contesting Detroit for first place.

Going into the last day of the season, the Tigers and Browns were tied for the lead. The Senators helped deposit the pennant in the Browns' lap by knocking over the Tigers, 4 to 1, as the Browns beat the Yankees. A home run by Stan Spence with a man on was fatal to the Tigers. The blow was coupled with Dutch Leonard's four-hit pitching against Dizzy Trout. Leonard later revealed that on the morning of that game an anonymous telephone caller offered him 10,000 dollars to throw the game, and he dismissed it as crackpot stuff.

The club the Senators wanted least to help was, ironically enough, the Browns. Bad blood existed between them all season. In July a free-for-all was touched off in Washington when Nelson Potter hit Case with a pitched ball, and the pair of them slugged it out. Later when Roger Wolff hit Stephens on the leg with a ball, manager Luke Sewell rushed out to the mound and yelled, "Your lousy eighth-place club is always trying to cause trouble." In St. Louis later in the year the battling flared again. Tom Turner, the Browns' 205-pound, third-string catcher, was heckling the Senators' Cubans with vile names, singling out little Mike Guerra. Guerra told him to shut up. Turner yelled another insult. Big Robert Ortiz tapped Guerra on the shoulder and said, "I fight for you."

Ortiz went to the Browns' dugout armed with a bat and confronted Turner. "You wanna fight?" he said. Turner told him to drop the bat. Ortiz tossed the bat away and with the same motion tossed a right-hand blow into Turner's face. They squared off with players of both clubs making no move to interrupt and battled for five minutes with Ortiz the clear winner, a fact that pleased mo ↙ of the Browns with whom Turner was not popular. Oruz gained the decision plus a broken thumb.

A long-standing friendship came to an end, even before the game. Bluege told his old Senator roommate Sewell, "Lay off my Cubans or you and I are going to fight." Sewell believed Bluege was kidding, but changed his mind when Bluege gave orders to the Senators to take two Browns with them if they were thrown out of any game. One man was enjoying the Senators' and Browns' rivalry immensely. He was Stan Spence who hit eighteen home runs that year, eleven of them against the Browns.

In the major-league meetings in 1944, Clark Griffith was a member of a strident minority of two—the Browns were the other—in demanding more night baseball. He had spent 230,000 dollars putting the lights in his Washington park in 1941, and the added cash the night games fetched was permitting him to go into the market for better ball players.

He was the most vigorous exponent of unlimited night baseball and raised his voice loudly against the attempts to restrict each club to fourteen night games at home. He wangled twenty-one games out of one meeting, and later gained permission to schedule forty-two under the lights.

For Griffith, his stand on night baseball was a complete about-face. When Larry McPhail first installed the lights in Cincinnati, he called it "bush league stuff." It wasn't right, it wasn't good, said Griffith. "Baseball was meant to be played in God's own good sunshine," he sermonized.

But when God didn't strike McPhail down, and the Cincinnati club started profiting handsomely from increased night attendance, Griffith presumed the Almighty really wasn't offended at night baseball.

He pleaded Washington's peculiar employment situation without any factory swing-shifts, and demanded that the majors approve unlimited night ball as a patriotic war-winning measure to bring relaxation to the great number of workers. Motivating him, too, and not quite so unselfishly, was the fact that he now had four knuckle-balling pitchers in Dutch Leonard, Roger Wolff, Johnny Niggeling, and Mickey Haefner, and their effectiveness at night was something special.

All of a sudden in 1945 the American League pennant started fluttering before the eyes of Griffith, Bluege, and their eighth-place Senators of the year before. Their flight from the league's coal hole into top contention within a year was threatening to be capped with the first pennant ever won by a team that had finished last the previous season.

Their steep climb came unheralded. Griffith, who in many a year had painstakingly plotted, revamped, and patched when he believed a club of his had flag possibilities, had not expected much from this 1945 team. And when his Senators lapsed into seventh place on June 12, there was no reason to believe he had a good ball team.

And then things began to happen. His knuckle-balling quartet of Wolff, Leonard, Niggeling, and Haefner began to win sensationally. One month later to the day, the Senators were in second place challenging the Tigers for the lead.

Buddy Lewis' return from war service in midseason was a shot in the arm. Wolff, the ne'er-do-well from the A's, who had won only four games the season before, was on his way to twenty victories. Leonard was headed for seventeen wins and seven defeats. Haefner was in for a sixteen-win season. Little Marino Pieretti from the Coast League was to be a fourteen-game winner.

Stan Spence was still in service, but Lewis and George (Bingo) Binks were taking up the slack with their hitting. George Myatt at second base was having the finest year of his career. Al Evans was out of the Navy, helping Rick Ferrell with the arduous knuckle-ball catching. They won twelve out of fifteen on a Western swing in June and July. When the pressure was on in August, they met the Red Sox and A's in five double-headers in five days and won nine of the ten games.

The Tigers moved into Washington on September 13 with a half-game lead for a crucial five-game series. The capital was in a frenzy. Managers Bluege and Steve O'Neill led with their aces in the first game of a double-header. Dutch Leonard was pitted against Hal Newhouser. In two years New-houser had lost none of his ten starts against the Senators. In the second inning rain held up the game for an hour and six minutes. When play resumed, Newhouser was out with a rheumatism attack and Frank Overmire was pitching for Detroit. At the end of five and one-half innings the Tigers took a 4-to-0 lead, and then the Senators tied it at 4 to 4 in the sixth on hits by Binks, Ferrell, and Torres. A ninth-inning triple by Doc Cramer swung the game to the Tigers, 7 to 4. Dizzy Trout beat the Senators in the second game, 7 to 3, and it was a crusher, almost.

The next day's double-header brought a split with Wolff beating Newhouser, 3 to 2, and Bridges winning the next, 5 to 4. But the Senators had something left. In the fifth game after Walter Masterson let go of a 5-to-0 lead, they came back to blast out a 12-to-5 victory and cut the Tigers' margin to a game and a half.

On September 23 at Philadelphia with the Senators ready to wrest the lead away from the Tigers any day, came the cruelest break of all. Masterson was locked in a 3-to-3 duel with the A's in the twelfth inning after allowing no hits in four innings of relief work. He had two out and nobody on. Then Ernie Kish hit a lazy ball to center field. Binks trotted under it, lost the ball in the sun, and the Senators were beaten on Kell's single to center.

The miscreant Binks was in trouble with his teammates. He had neglected to take his sunglasses into the outfield after the sun came out on what had been a gray day. An inning earlier, outfielder Sam Chapman of the A's had stopped the game to call for his sunglasses, but Binks never took the hint that the sun was now present. There were threats to deprive Binks of his World-Series or second-place share.

With four games of the season left for the Tigers, they had a one-game lead over the Senators. And now the Washington club was sweating it out in a queer sort of finish. They were all through, their season ended. Clark Griffith, never suspect-ing that his club would be a pennant contender, had rented out his Stadium to the Washington Redskins for the last week in September and arranged the baseball schedule to crowd in the Senators' dates earlier. The double-headers had taken their toll of the Washington pitchers too.

In the hope that the Tigers would merely break even with the Browns in the last four-game series and thus send the race into a tie necessitating the play-off, the Senators hung around hopefully. They were at Griffith Stadium with their bags packed, ready to race to Detroit for a play-off, if necessary. And then word came that Hank Greenberg, out of the Army, had hit a home run with the bases full in St. Louis to clinch the pennant for the Tigers by a game-and-a-half margin.

The wartime ball player was finding his level in 1946, and the Senators leveled off to fourth place. They were the jewel of consistency in that respect, attaining fourth early in the campaign and staying there to the finish, beating off a last-week threat of the White Sox to dislodge them from the first division.

What the team did produce though was another American League batting champion—the fourth in the Senators' history. Mickey Vernon joined Delahanty, Goslin, and Myer in that small company of batting leaders. His average was .353, beating Boston's Ted Williams who was supposed to overtake Vernon in the last weeks. But Williams fell farther behind.

Vernon's ascent to the top was not fluky. He was hitting as high as .383 at one point in midseason, and against predictions that he would fold he maintained his hot pace, dropping hits into all fields and legging out many a bunt and infield grounder with his good speed.

With that fourth-place club, Clark Griffith profited handsomely. For the first time in history, the Senators topped the 1,000,000 attendance mark at home.

Cecil Travis and Gerry Priddy came out of the army, but only Priddy bolstered the infield. The popular Travis was a pathetic figure at shortstop and later at third base, hobbled by ailing feet that had been frozen in the Battle of the Bulge. Before the season opened, Griffith traded George Case and his twenty-game winner, Wolff, to Cleveland for the supposedly long-hitting Jeff Heath. Heath neither hit long nor stayed long. They sold him to the Browns after three months in a deal that brought Joe Grace as his successor. Sherry Robertson, Griffith's nephew who was up from the Piedmont League, was in the line-up at second base, shortstop, and finally the outfield.

Gil Coan, the spring training sensation from Chattanooga, for whom the Cubs' 100,000-dollar bid had been rejected by Griffith, stayed around and never made good. Neither did he make good in a special 100-yard race with George Case who, wearing a Cleveland uniform now, beat him by a full stride to dispel the belief that Coan was the fastest man in the league.

Buck Newsom was back again. He talked Connie Mack into giving him his unconditional release, well aware he could talk himself into a job with Griffith. After three pinochle sessions, Griffith signed him, always confident he could win back from Bobo at pinochle whatever he might have overpaid him for pitching. Newsom was overpaid. He won only eleven games.

On December 10, 1946, sadness came to the nation's capital and the country at large. Walter Johnson, after a nine-month illness in Georgetown Hospital, died from the ravages of a brain tumor, wasted in body but still vibrant in the memory of the baseball fans of two generations.

In April they had admitted the Big Train for treatment after he complained of "numbness" in his left arm, at his Germantown, Maryland, farm. The critical state of his illness was soon ascertained. Washington fans were in almost daily pilgrimage to his bedside when they were permitted. Clark Griffith was in close attendance. The day before Johnson's death, Griffith emerged from the hospital room moist-eyed to report that the Big Train was unconscious.

In the ecclesiastic splendor of the Washington Cathedral, the Very Reverend John W. Suter conducted the funeral services with saddened thousands paying tribute in the Great Choir. President Truman had expressed the nation's grief in a message to Johnson's surviving family of two daughters, three sons, and his white-haired mother.

From far-flung sections of the Nation came Johnson's old teammates to pay him their last tributes. The pall bearers, actual and honorary, were the men he knew best: Griffith, Bucky Harris, Muddy Ruel, Joe Judge, Sam Rice, Clyde Milan, Nick Altrock, Tom Zachary, Jim Shaw, Roger Peckinpaugh, Eddie Ainsmith, and Jack Bentley, the pitcher he outlasted in that famed seventh World Series game of 1924.

The Very Reverend Suter omitted the eulogy. But in simple, impressive tones he spoke toward Heaven and gave thanks "for all the goodness and courage which have passed from the life of this, Thy servant, into the lives of others, leaving the world richer for his presence . . . for a life's task faithfully and honorably discharged . . . for gracious affection and kindly generosity, for sadness without surrender and weakness endured without defeat."

At the Rockville Union Cemetery, on a chill, windswept countryside in his beloved Maryland, Walter Johnson was laid to rest.

Chapter XIV

THE Senators had made their second-place finish of 1946 before the other clubs had properly reorganized after the Second World War. The second year of peace was without honor to the Washington club, and save for Early Wynn their fast skid might have carried into the cellar.

Wynn was their only winning pitcher. He turned in seventeen victories and developed a happy habit of beating Hal Newhouser, a tormentor of the Senators ever since he came into the league to throw his left-handed stuff at Washington clubs that were predominantly left-handed. Wynn was the Senators' stopper. He braked an eleven-game losing streak of the Senators, and then brought a halt to another six-game string of losses. In each case he outpitched Newhouser.

The Senators hit seventh-place in May and were never out of it. Masterson shut out the White Sox in 16 innings, 1 to 0, and in consecutive starts blanked the Tigers, 1 to 0, and the Browns, 3 to 0, but at the end of the season he was an in-and-outer. Marino Pieretti, the 1946 winner, proved a one-year wonder.

And Bluege was having trouble with his ball players. He was feuding with Gerry Priddy, the good second baseman, whom he had bawled out in front of the whole bench. Pitchers were squabbling that they were worked out of turn. Bluege, the quiet third baseman of fifteen years, had become the manager with a sharp tongue.

In Cleveland the players blamed him for the long delays in obtaining their hotel rooms in the western cities that occasioned long waits in the lobbies. They drew up a petition asking more consideration. Bluege called them together in a locker room session, asked them to sign a statement denying there was any revolt, and that they bore him no ill will. They signed, with the exception of Gerry Priddy who said, "Let's not kid ourselves, you don't like me and I don't like you."

That finished Priddy. At the year's end he was traded to the Browns for Johnny Berardino. When the latter refused to report, claiming he had a Hollywood offer as an actor, Griffith checked with Berardino who referred him to "my agent." Griffith exploded, said he would do no business with any ball player's agent. The Berardino end of the deal fell through, but Griffith would have no part of Priddy and let the Browns keep him for a cash settlement.

Heaviest blow, though, was the collapse of Mickey Vernon, the league batting champion of the previous season. Now he was labeled as a fluke champ. The hits weren't dropping for him. He was swinging wildly, and his .265 average bore no resemblance to his .353 of the year before. Before the season opened, the Yankees offered third baseman Bill Johnson, outfielder Johnny Lindell, and two pitchers for Vernon, plus cash. Griffith accused Larry MacPhail of trying to disrupt his ball club and would have none of it.

Griffith's ball club was growing old. His outfield players,

225

Joe Grace, Stan Spence, and Buddy Lewis, were in their thirties. Travis, plagued by his frozen feet, announced he was retiring. Now playing shortstop was Mark Christman, relict of the Browns. Rick Ferrell came out of his coaching role to rejoin the catching staff in his fifteenth year as a big leaguer.

At the year's end, Griffith retired Bluege as manager, creating the job of director of the club's farm system for him. Bluege, as a manager, no longer held any charms for Griffith. The old gentleman was disappointed that the team hadn't won a pennant in 1946.

Sure enough, it was to be one of his former ball players who would be Griffith's new manager. He scanned his roster and passed up Rick Ferrell, the only man on the club suspected of being managerial timber. He called the White Sox to ascertain that they would not object if he negotiated with his old first baseman Joe Kuhel, then managing their Hot Springs, Arkansas, farm club. Kuhel got the job.

There were ready quips about Kuhel's task with the 1948 Senators. Well-known was the fact that his hobby was magic, that he was an accredited member of the American Society of Magicians, had been a pupil of the famed cardster, Cardini. He would need all his magic to get the Senators out of the second division.

Kuhel pulled little out of the hat in the way of a ball club. Griffith was on a rebuilding campaign. He acknowledged, "We'll get worse before we get better." In his zest for youth, he traded the veteran Stan Spence to the Red Sox for their good-looking young second baseman who had hit .341 at New Orleans, Al Kozar. At third base, Griffith was committed to young Eddie Yost who had run Travis out of a job the year before. Getting another trial was Gil Coan, the perennial Chattanooga sensation in left field. Griffith's nephew, Sherry Robertson, fast on the bases and owner of a superb throwing arm, was promising to develop as an outfielder. Vernon was a fixture on first, with his slump put down as simply an off year. Johnny Sullivan was getting another shot at shortstop.

But Buddy Lewis, like Cecil Travis, quit. He was tiring

of the baseball business and now had going for himself a profitable auto agency in Gastonia, North Carolina. When Coan failed to hit, Griffith was alarmed and compromised his accent-on-youth campaign. He bought Carden Gillenwater from the Braves and 31-year-old Ed Stewart from the Yankees to buttress his outfield.

Gillenwater didn't hit, but Stewart did and he was giving the club a fine brand of hustle. Kozar justified the Spence trade, but Yost was a good-field, no-hit player. Sullivan flopped at shortstop, and Mark Christman had to take over. Vernon's slump continued into its second year. Not a man hit .280.

After an early flurry, the Senators dropped into the second division, to fifth and sixth. A twelve-game losing streak in the East burgeoned as an eighteen-game losing streak in the West, until it was fractured twice by a double-header win over the White Sox. The Senators escaped the cellar, but there was no escape from seventh place.

Kuhel had the Senators for a two-season whirl. Griffith, completely disenchanted with his old first baseman as a manager, fired him at the end of the 1949 campaign. Kuhel wounded Griffith in his most sensitive area by bringing home a last-place team, the second cellar finish in Griff's thirty-seven-year association with the Senators.

It was a dismal year competitively, but it was not uneventful. The Senators won their opening game and didn't taste another victory until their ninth start. But they came home from their first western trip with an astonishing nine-game winning streak and were hailed as conquering heroes, pennant-bound, despite their current position in a tie for fourth .place. Five thousand fans met them at the station. They were cheered in a motorcade up historic Pennsylvania Avenue. Kuhel was given the keys to the city by the District Commissioners, and the happy fans were parading placards reading "We'll Win the Pennant," "Drink a Toast with Eddie Yost," "We'll Win Plenty With Sam Dente," and generally reacting as if the World Series were the next important piece of business for the Senators. That was on May 9, prompting one skeptic to comment quietly, "First time a town ever won a pennant in May."

Kuhel's was a streaky ball team. It had one skein of seven straight wins, another of eleven. It also encountered a pair of eleven-game losing streaks before Ray Scarborough brought the skid to a halt on each occasion with a well-pitched game. But the team that was going to win the pennant in May, hit the cellar on August 20 and stayed there. The miserable fellows won only sixteen of their last seventy-four games under Kuhel, and their record of a mere fifty wins and one hundred and four defeats was the worst since the Washington team of 1909.

Griffith hadn't given Kuhel much to work with. He was patching again. Paul Calvert, supposed to help with the pitching, lost thirteen in a row. Buddy Lewis came out of a year's voluntary retirement and proved only that he was a year slower. And Griffith did poorly on a trade with Cleveland, made during the winter, when he dealt off first baseman Mickey Vernon and pitcher Early Wynn for first baseman Eddie Robinson and pitchers Joe Haynes and Ed Klieman. There were no stars among that trio, and there was some suspicion that Griffith had traded more with his heart than his head when he demanded the inclusion of Haynes in the deal. Haynes was the husband of his adopted daughter Thelma who had a pronounced preference for living in Washington.

As the season closed, Griffith was a troubled man and with added reason. For the first time since 1920, when he became president of the Senators, his control of the team was being challenged. John J. Jachym of Jamestown, New York, hitherto unknown to Griffith, walked into the Griffith Stadium offices one day in the fall and announced that he had bought forty per cent of the club's stock and was Griffith's new partner. Griffith bristled.

Griffith saw in Jachym an interloper who had designs on moving solidly into the affairs of the Washington team which he alone had bossed for thirty years. He resented the sudden intrusion. Buying forty per cent of the Washington team was, in Griffith's view, an invasion of his private preserves, and

228

he was tempted to reach for the old musket that hung on his wall and blow Jachym to bits, perhaps.

Others found Jachym to be a personable young man with solid recommendations, but from the start Griffith's reaction was one of distrust. Jachym came out of service as a Marine captain who had won the Silver Star for bravery with the First Division on Guadalcanal. A graduate of the Missouri School of Journalism, he had a passion for baseball, had served as a scout for the St. Louis Cardinals, and later bought the Jamestown franchise. He sold it later to the Detroit Tigers at a profit and accepted a post in the Detroit farm system.

Jachym found a financial backer in Hugh Grant, Pennsylvania oil magnate, and for 550,000 dollars bought the forty per cent of the Washington stock held by the heirs of William V. Richardson of Philadelphia, Griffith's original partner in the purchase of the Senators in 1920. Jachym came to Washington confidently expecting to be taken into the firm by Griffith and making plain that he would like to be active in the team's affairs.

Griffith recoiled at the whole prospect of a new and active partner at this stage of the game. For thirty years he had been the only voice that counted in the Senators' affairs. His former partner, Richardson, was content to be inactive to his death and gave Griffith a blank check to vote his shares as Griffith pleased. Nor is there any record that Richardson ever disputed Griffith on any point. Involved in his own export and cement-making business in Philadelphia, Richardson rarely put in an appearance at Griffith Stadium except for the annual stockholders' meeting when he would ply Griffith with compliments on his stewardship of the team. The Richardson heirs similarly were content with a hands-off policy.

Griffith had another reason for alarm. He was wondering if Jachym meant to corral enough additional shares to gain fifty-one per cent control of the team. The Griffith family had made no move to buy additional shares through the years, despite the fact that they owned only forty-four per cent of the stock, and now they could perhaps rue their failure.

When Jachym apprised Griffith of his purchase of the Richardson stock, the eighty-year-old president of the team exploded against the Richardsons for the first time. He said he had their verbal agreement to give him first option to buy, and that such had always been the understanding with Richardson.

Hastily, Griffith set about to garner enough shares to give him voting control. From Wooten Young, Washington businessman and a stockholder in the team, and other friends who held shares, Griffith lined up stockholder support, enough to outvote Jachym. But they wouldn't sell him enough stock to give him actual control.

Armed as he was, however, with proxies, Griffith completely ignored Jachym in the stockholders' meeting that followed in December of 1949. He didn't even vote Jachym a place on the board of directors or any official position with the team. He made it clear that Jachym wouldn't even have desk space at Griffith Stadium despite his forty per cent holdings. Jachym protested that he had no designs on Griffith's authority, but he got not so much as a season's pass from the old gentleman.

It all served to alert Griffith anew, however, to his responsibilities as president of the Senators. The fans were beginning to grumble at teams which had finished seventh and eighth in the last two seasons. Favorable talk about Jachym was being heard on the streets, and Griffith girded for some sort of action that would justify himself and put the young whippersnapper in his place.

In his dilemma, sharpened by the Jachym threat to move in on him, Griffith turned again to an old friend of happier times. Rid of Kuhel, eager to combat Jachym, but as yet without a manager for his team, Griffith reached out once more to bring back Bucky Harris to the Washington scene. Harris, recently fired by the Yankees, had won a pennant with them in 1947 and also a World Series, and had barely missed the 1948 pennant. Harris in 1949 was managing San Diego in the Coast League. Griffith was weary of rookie managers like Kuhel. He wanted a proven baseball man this time. He needed to solidify himself with Washington. Harris was more

230

than acceptable to the fans in the capital. Hiring him would take the pressure from Griffith, the latter rightly reasoned.

So Harris got the job again. But this time it was not with hat in hand. Bucky had virtually been promised the Cleveland managerial job and could make demands on Griffith. He got a two-year contract at a weighty figure. Griffith had demonstrated back in September how heavily he leaned on Harris when he bought outfielder Irv Noren from the Hollywood Coast League team. It was a 65,000-dollar deal, mostly cash, and Griffith wouldn't make it on the reports of his own scouts. He asked Harris for an opinion, and when Bucky gave him the nod, and not until, did Griffith buy the player.

Harris did make things easier for Griffith with a fifth-place finish that was a refreshing switch from the cellar team of the year before. Virtually the same cast that floundered under Kuhel was making a strong first-division bid under Harris, and the difference in managers was apparent. Harris bludgeoned Griffith into parting with Ray Scarborough, infielder Al Kozar, and first baseman Eddie Robinson in a swap with the White Sox for second baseman Cass Michaels, pitcher Bob Kuzava, and outfielder John Ostrow. To fill the vacancy at first base, he swapped Cleveland rookie pitcher Dick Weik to get Mickey Vernon back.

If Jachym was counting on any discontent among the Washington fans or stockholders to help make a place for him in the Senators' organization, he was disappointed. With Harris' team looking like first-division stuff and the fans applauding, Jachym saw little future for himself in Washington. He waited until the six-month capital gain period arrived early in the summer and then sold out his forty per cent share to H. Gabriel Murphy, Washington insurance man, at a neat profit of 85,000 dollars on the deal.

Griffith welcomed his new partner, Murphy, whom he had known for many years, beginning when Murphy was graduate manager of athletics at Georgetown University in the late twenties. For years Murphy had negotiated the rental of Griffith Stadium for Georgetown football games.

The new partnership quickly took a sharp turn in Griffith's favor. Murphy demonstrated his will to cooperate by immediately selling Griffith three hundred shares of stock that gave the team president actual fifty-two per cent control. In return, Griffith assigned to Murphy an option to buy the Griffith stock if he or his heirs chose to sell. From Murphy, Griffith took a cross option on the Murphy stock.

With Jachym out of the picture, even a seventh-place finish by the Senators in '51 couldn't dislodge Harris, who achieved little in the pennant race but made a notable trade that was to stand the Senators in good stead in the future. He dealt off Bob Kuzava to the Yankees in midsummer for Bob Porterfield, Tom Ferrick, and Fred Sanford, all pitchers. Porterfield was to be the biggest prize in years on the trading mart.

Harris' teams of the early '50s were beginning to take on some character and some characters. One of these was Señor Conrado Marrero who resisted the English language, liked to pull on fat Havana cigars, was shaped like a kewpie doll, and pitched sometimes like a composite of all the greats in history.

Marrero's appearance in the Senators' Orlando, Florida, training camp in the spring of 1950, initially brought only mutterings from Harris who was surfeited with scout Joe Cambria's shiploads of incompetent Cubans. He mumbled something about "another one of Cambria's bums" when he first glimpsed Marrero pitching baseballs with a motion that was a cross between a machete-swinger's delivery and a fencing master's prod.

Even when Marrero was getting the hitters out in the exhibition games, Harris was only guardedly impressed. "He's been playing winter ball, and he's ahead of them," said Bucky. "But I must say he seems to know how to pitch." In addition, Harris wasn't delirious about Marrero's future value. The Señor was saying that he was thirty-four years old, but former big leaguers were sure they had batted against him in Cuba twenty years ago.

Unable to be choosy, Harris found work for Marrero as a relief man after the season started. He began to take a liking to the Cuban when, in eighteen innings of relief work, he gave up only one run and was showing control of his knuckle ball. By midseason of 1950, Marrero not only had done well, but he was a popular fellow on the club and did more than any other Cuban to break down the unadmitted but ever-present caste system on the Washington teams. "Conrado showed us that the Cubans were nice fellows, that they didn't have horns, and weren't taking bread and butter out of the other players' mouths," said Bucky.

Marrero, in addition to his good knuckle ball, also showed a determination not to learn the English language. But his pitching was so valuable, Harris was content to carry outfielder Roberto Ortiz merely as an interpreter for Conrado. It was Ortiz who helped provide background on Marrero by patient questioning. It was learned that Conrado was a respected cattle rancher in Cuba during the off season and that he was a family man. "Ask him how many children he has?" Harris told Ortiz. After a spate of Spanish with Marrero, Ortiz reported to Harris. "He say he have one wife, two leetle shortstop, one leetle pitcher."

When baseball writers attempted to wheedle from Marrero his exact age, he merely grinned and pointed awkwardly to the number on his baseball shirt which read "22." When Dizzy Dean, in an interview, opined that the only way to beat Marrero was to wait him out, Ortiz got the little Señor's reaction in Spanish. "He say tell Dean," said Ortiz, "that Marrero got plenty time."

Marrero came up to the Senators from the Class B Havana club of the Florida International League where in 1949 he was a standout with twenty-five wins and eight defeats. He won only six in his first year with the Senators, but he was never to have another losing year. His infrequent starts kept him out of the big-winner circle, but he was a tremendous spot pitcher and his earned-run averages were yearly among the best.

Ted Williams, one of Marrero's favorite victims and one of the fellow's fondest admirers, summed up Conrado's baffling pitching motion one day with the observation, "He throws you everything but the ball. You see him out there warming up and you want to grab a bat quick and hit against him. When you get there, he has you groping for that knuckle

233

ball. You got to swing at his first pitch. You let him get ahead of you on the count and you're dead."

He was due to pitch against the Red Sox in Boston one day when Harris pointed out that Fenway Park was packed. "Big crowd," said Harris. "Mucho crowd, mucho peetch," grinned Conrado. He was in trouble in the first inning but fanned Williams with the bases full and walked jauntily back to the bench. After throwing his glove in Harris' lap and sticking out his chest, he pointed to himself and said grandly, "More money now."

There were vigorous efforts by Harris and Griffith to elevate the Senators, but the best they could give Washington fans was a fifth-place ball team in 1952 and again in 1953. However, they could not be accused of a dull operation. They enlivened the scene with a series of player deals that almost amounted to a trading binge, and in no instance did they come off second best. They weren't good Washington teams, but neither were they poor ones.

Their deals were mostly with the Yankees, and for good reason. The Yankees had the ball players. Harris, after three seasons with the Yanks was painfully aware of the inadequacy of the Senators' farm system and yearned for some of the talent he knew with the Yankees. "Let's not kid ourselves," he told Griffith. "The Yankees have the best scouts and they come up with the best players. Let's go after some."

When the Yankees ran into a pitching shortage in June of 1951 and began to covet Kuzava, the Senators' southpaw, Harris was willing to talk trade. He was in a position to make demands with the Yanks shooting for no less than the pennant. When the Yanks offered him a pair of so-so veterans, pitchers Tom Ferrick and Fred Sanford, plus 50,000 dollars in cash "and perhaps another player out of our farm system," Harris evinced an interest.

"Toss Bob Porterfield into the deal and I think it can be made," said Harris. When the Yankees agreed, Harris told George Weiss he would have Griffith's decision on the trade before the day was over.

The Yankees were ready to include Porterfield with no

234

great sense of loss. He was down on their Kansas City farm team where he had a mere 2-to-2 record and a reputation as a sore-arm pitcher who had flopped in two previous tries with the Yanks.

Before taking the deal to Griffith, Harris took the precaution of calling Porterfield by telephone at his Kansas City home. He asked the pitcher a two-part question: "Do you want to pitch for me in Washington, and how's your arm, Bob?" Porterfield fairly shouted into the phone "My arm is all right Bucky, and I'll pitch my head off for you if you can get me." The trade was made.

Porterfield, the Yankee reject, pitched good ball for Harris in 1951 and 1952, but it was in 1953 that the handsome right-hander came up with his best performance and emerged as the pitcher with most wins in the American League. His twenty-two victories and only ten defeats were embellished, too, by nine shutouts, another league-leading statistic. Never was a manager's confidence in a formerly discredited pitcher more justified.

Big Bob's brilliant return to the majors was a reclamation project warmly satisfying to Harris who could enjoy the Yankees' discomfiture at having lost so valuable a player. It was L'Affair Porterfield which back in 1948 played a big part in Harris being fired as manager by the Yankees, although his major sin was his failure to win a second straight pennant by a game-and-a-half margin.

When Harris' '48 Yankees were skidding for lack of pitching, Harris suggested to general manager Weiss that Porterfield, the winning right-hander on their Newark farm team, be brought up to bolster the staff. Weiss refused to raid the Newark team. New York baseball writers pointed out that Porterfield, with his 15-to-6 record at Newark was ready for the majors and took up with the top brass the cause of Harris, a bit to his embarrassment. Weiss blamed Harris for inspiring the stories. Porterfield was brought up to the Yanks late in the season, but too late. He won five and lost three, but the Yanks were nosed out. Harris was fired at the season's end.

Bucky may have been *persona non grata* with the Yankee officials, but he left behind many a friend among the Yankee ball players. That fact paid off for him in May of 1952. With the Yankees pennant-minded as usual and eager to buttress every position, he suddenly got an offer for Irv Noren, the Senators' talented center fielder.

The Yankees wanted Noren as insurance against the knee condition of Mickey Mantle who had broken down in the 1951 World Series and undergone an operation. They offered Griffith and Harris two outfielders, Jackie Jensen and Archie Wilson, and infielder Gerry Snyder. Harris wanted Jensen, the Yankees' 75,000-dollar bonus-baby outfielder with right-handed batting power and a deadly arm plus speed. But Griffith as usual was demanding "something extra" before closing a deal. The Yanks indicated the Senators could also have one of their second-line pitchers.

The Senators were playing in Yankee Stadium when the deal was broached. Rumors of it reached the Yankee bench, and Yogi Berra intercepted Harris under the stands before the game.

"How close are you to a deal, Bucky?" Berra asked.

Harris explained that it might be closed if the Yanks tossed in an acceptable pitcher.

"Bucky, you're one of the guys I like, you know that," said Berra. "Get 'em to throw in Frank Shea. They ain't letting him pitch here. I been warming him up. He's got the most stuff on this ball club. Take my advice and take him."

The Yanks were not averse to tossing Shea into the trade, and at the end of the season they had to be confounded. With the fifth-place Senators, Shea had an 11-to-7 record in 1952, and a sparkling 2.35 earned-run average. He was a winning pitcher again in '53 with a 12-to-7 record, and Harris was adding to his laurels as a trader.

As with Porterfield, Harris was renewing an old association with Shea who had been a big winner for him in the Yanks' pennant-winning year of 1947. When he first met Shea, the pitcher was a brash rookie from the Coast League in the Yanks' St. Petersburg, Florida, training camp in the spring of '47. One day Shea approached him in the dugout at St. Pete waving a fistful of clippings and demanding "What's going on here, Bucky?" He was displaying the rave notices

236

Harris had been giving the New York papers concerning rookie pitcher Don Johnson, a willowy right-hander up from Kansas City who had been showing a blazing fast ball in the exhibition games. Shea was Johnson's roommate in room 323 at the Soreno Hotel, Yankee headquarters. But there had been no mention of Shea in the dispatches. "Listen here, Bucky," said Shea assuming an expression of mock-hurt. "You've got the right room but the wrong roommate. Frank Shea, not Don Johnson, is going to be your great pitcher."

Harris knew Shea as a lockerroom cutup with the Yanks, but also as a reliable pitcher who later came through with two World Series victories in 1947. Off the field, Shea was crazy enough to be a left-hander. He liked to describe himself as "a right-hander with a southpaw psychosis." He liked, too, to imitate the radio announcers with his own lockerroom spiel as he slapped an empty cup over the end of a bat to simulate a microphone. "And now folks, it's Frank Shea, whatta pitcher, who is on the mound ... the great Frank Shea from Naugatuck, Connecticut, folks. With his whistling speed and scrumptious curve.... Ladies and gentlemen, the major leagues have never seen the equal of this Shea ... and now believe it or not, we give you Frank Shea, himself...."

Griffith and Harris gave their 1952 roster a double shuffle the day they announced the Noren deal with the Yanks. A few hours later, they traded outfielder Sam Mele to the White Sox for outfielder Jim Busby and infielder Mel Hoderlein. It took a year for the Senators to realize full value on that one, but it paid off handsomely in 1953 when Busby became the fifth-leading hitter in the league with his .312 average and earned Harris' description as "the finest center fielder in the league."

The Senators got one good year out of Jensen, his first one in Washington when he hit .280, batted in eighty-two runs, and gave them tremendous protection in right field, besides adding to the club's speed. The former Golden Boy, an All-American fullback at the University of California, responded to the chance to play regularly by making good. He moaned his failure to get a chance to play steadily for the Yanks, declaring Casey Stengel "jerked you out of the line-up if you went hitless and you weren't under that kind of pressure in Washington. When I was traded to Washington, Bucky Harris told me 'you're our right fielder and you're batting third.' It was wonderful to know when you got up in the morning you were going to be in the line-up that day. With the Yankees, you couldn't be sure."

But baseball being what it is, Jensen couldn't be sure of being with the Senators for long either. When he slumped to a .266 average in 1953, he was traded off at the end of the season to the Red Sox for pitcher Mickey McDermott, an eighteen-game winner, and outfielder Tom Umphlett. The results of that trade are for the future to decide, but the consensus of feeling when it was made was that Harris had held a gun on the Red Sox management to bring it off.

Griffith, who approved the Jensen deal heartily, admitted that he might be sacrificing batting power for more pitching, but declared, "McDermott ought to round out a great pitching staff for us. I know we don't have a hard hitting team, but I always did say it's easier to get three runs for a good pitcher and win than six runs for a bad pitcher."

The Senators were the envy of the league at two positions, first base and third base, despite their static position in fifth place as the 1953 season closed. Joe Cambria, the sometimes laughed-at scout, saw two of his products rise to eminence in the American League, first baseman Mickey Vernon as the batting champion and third baseman Eddie Yost as the unchallenged master of his position.

Cambria uncovered Yost on the rebound from the Red Sox. They gave the sixteen-year-old kid from the Long Island sand lots a tryout and decided against him. When the disconsolate boy returned to his home, Cambria was camping on the Yost doorstep and signed him to a Washington contract.

Under manager Ossie Bluege, Yost played seven games for the Senators as a seventeen-year-old third baseman-shortstop in 1944, and then he joined the Coast Guard. Discharged late in 1946, he played eight more games and reported to the Senators' Florida camp the next spring prepared to be farmed out. He wasn't. He couldn't be. Commissioner Happy Chandler, strictly interpreting the GI Bill of Rights passed by Congress, refused to permit the Senators to send Yost to the minors. Every returning GI, Chandler declared, was entitled to go back for at least a year to the job he held before going into the service.

Even a personal appeal by Yost in a letter to Chandler, asking a chance to get some needed experience in minor-league ball, failed to sway the Commissioner. The Senators were forced to keep him; compelled to issue a uniform to the kid who, as the past season ended, had a streak of six hundred and thirty consecutive games going for him in the majors. He is now considered to be the league's finest defensive third baseman as well as one of it's most valuable lead-off men. In the last five seasons he has drawn more walks than any other player and has hit as high as .295 and .283.

Mickey Vernon's struggle for the American League batting crown was the highlight of the closing days of the Senators' 1953 campaign. At thirty-five, he was making a bid to regain the title he had won six years before when he beat Ted Williams. Going into the final day of the season, he had a three-point lead over Cleveland's Al Rosen but not until the final out of the year was it established that Vernon had won with a .337 figure to Rosen's .336.

Vernon made two hits in four times at bat in the final game, and he needed them to stave off the rush of Rosen who out in Cleveland was making three hits. There were whispered charges of collusion by his Washington teammates as Vernon won by his one-point margin. His buddies on the Senators ignored all of the accusations, but couldn't hide some strange sequences on the bases that played a part in protecting Vernon's average.

When word was flashed from the press box to the Washington players late in the game that Rosen had made three hits in Cleveland and had virtually closed the gap between them, the Senators went into a quick huddle and took action to guard against a fifth turn at bat which could cost Vernon the crown if he went hitless.

The Senators' game with the Athletics was already safely won, and it was important to Vernon's average that he not be exposed to another time at bat. If no more than six Senators batted in the last two innings, he wouldn't have to go up. In the eighth, only three Senators batted because Mickey Grasso, who doubled, wandered so far off second base the A's pitcher couldn't resist picking him off. In the ninth, Keith Thomas singled as a pinch hitter and absurdly tried to stretch it to a double: one out. Yost, the man with the best eye for pitching in the league, struck out on a pitch over his head: two out. Pete Runnels struck out, gladly perhaps, and the title belonged to Vernon.

There was a new lilt to the Senators as the 1954 season offered its challenge. It was the high promise that seven long years in the second division were coming to an end. That prospect stemmed from new pitching strength and the comforting memory of spectacular performances late in the 1953 season by players who previously had lagged.

Solid pitching, always a more vital necessity on traditionally power-short Washington teams than on any others in the league, at last has been acquired by Bucky Harris. He could use a bit more depth, but the competence of his starters could evoke the envy of other clubs. To such worthies as Bob Porterfield, Frank Shea, Chuck Stobbs, and Conrado Marrero, all with winning records in 1953, Harris added Mickey McDermott, the eighteen-game winner of the Red Sox.

That the Senators had reason to expect a sparkling brand of pitching in 1954 could be easily acknowledged. Contained in the 22-to-10 record of Porterfield the previous season were nine shutouts, tops in the league. He finished the season winning twelve of his last thirteen starts. Southpaw Stobbs won nine of his last twelve starts. With Boston, Mickey McDermott won ten of his last eleven. Quick arithmetic demonstrates that trio won thirty-one of its last thirty-six games, a superlative record.

The Senators' pitching weakness could be a lack of relief men, plus the infrequent starting assignments of the veterans Marrero and Shea who in these times are once-a-week performers. The retirement of Walter Masterson, valuable in

240

1953 as a spot pitcher, was a bit of a blow but McDermott promised to take up all the slack and more.

McDermott could make it a more abundant life for the Senators but if not, he promises to create a more exciting one. The ex-Red Sox glamour boy should provide welcome relief for those who have complained of the dead-fish character of some Washington teams. The garrulous left-hander, a night-club crooner in the off-season, was rejected by Army doctors a few years back for a punctured eardrum, but if they had examined his ego, their verdict might well have been "unpunctured." He calls himself a triple-threat ball player. "I can pitch, hit, and sing," he says. The quality of his singing may be a subject for debate, but his other talents are officially recorded. He was sixth in the league among the pitchers on an earned-run basis in 1953, and his .301 batting average topped all the pitchers. To the Senators, he represented pinch-hitting talent, long recognized and utilized by his managers at Boston.

Before the start of the 1954 season, McDermott indirectly claimed credit for winning the league batting title for Mickey Vernon the previous year. "It was this way," explained Mc-Dermott. "Vernon beat out Al Rosen of Cleveland by one point, right? Well, Rosen will admit I won that title for Vernon, because Al got only two hits off me in forty-three times at bat."

The Senators were a good ball club in the last six weeks of 1953 after sagging twenty-three and one-half games behind the league-leading Yankees. They lost no more ground to the Yankees after August 23. Not only were Porterfield and Stobbs reeling off a slew of pitching victories, but Eddie Yost unshackled himself from his batting slump and improved his .241 average of August 16 by thirty-one points at the season's finish. Jim Busby, who had sagged to .280, finished grandly with .312. The resurgence of that pair gave Senator fans winter-long comfort.

The mystery man of the Senators as the new season opened was Pete Runnels, the wonder-boy shortstop of 1952, who was a sophomore flop in 1953. His hitting slumped from .285 to .251 and his fielding was equally disappointing. He posed the team's biggest question mark. A return to his rookie-year competence by Runnels would give the Senators their biggest single lift.

First base was not one of the Senators' problems since Mickey Vernon, the league's batting champion, showed little sign of slowing, despite his thirty-six years. Harris would have welcomed more batting power than Wayne Terwilliger's at second base, but his fielding drew no complaints. From Eddie Yost, the Senators again could anticipate the finest third base protection in the league plus the asset of his ability to get on base more than any other lead-off man. But only Vernon, among Harris' infielders, boasted the special charm of hitting a consistent long ball. Otherwise the power factor was missing.

The Senators' 1954 catching was uniform with most of the other positions completely adequate defensively, but unterrifying to enemy pitching. Ed Fitzgerald, bought from the Pirates on waivers the year before, crowded .201-hitting Mickey Grasso out of the first-string catching job.

To offset the Senators' lack of power, Griffith and Harris patiently set about assembling a team otherwise calculated to make the most of the natural advantages of playing in Griffith Stadium, home of the league's most distant outfield fences. The deal that brought outfielder Tom Umphlett from the Red Sox with McDermott in exchange for Jackie Jensen was dictated partly by the Senators' fondness for the Umphlett type of outfielder. He batted .286 at Boston, but was no fence-buster. His spray-type hitting is more suited to Griffith Stadium's vast expanses. So has been Busby's.

The acquisition of Umphlett was smartly deliberate for another reason, his speed in the outfield. Umphlett was such a sensation in his first year in the American League that Ted Williams, landing in California on his return from Korea in July, was prompted to ask curiously, "Who is this guy Umphlett with the Red Sox? I see where he chased Dom Di Maggio into retirement and crowded Jim Piersall out of center field. He must be the world's greatest ball player."

Busby in center field and Umphlett in left assured the Senators superb protection in two of the outfield posts. Harris sought protection in right field by acquiring Roy Sievers from

242

Baltimore in a swap for Coan. He preferred to gamble on Sievers' throwing arm rather than on Coan's slumping bat.

The Senators, down through the Griffith years which began in 1912 in Washington, could probably best be labeled as the country store of major-league baseball. At eighty-four, Clark Griffith still presides, figuratively in shirt sleeves and eye shade, scorning any need for a general manager in the fashion of every other big-league club, and still dedicated to over-the-counter bargaining for talent with which to stock his team.

His has been the snuggest operation in the majors, and a successful one. His Senators are one of the two debt-free teams in the American League. He has been a master at cutting the overhead. Until recent seasons, he shouldered the manifold duties of club president, farm system operator, chief scout, and public relations man. For those with business with the Washington team, going through channels meant, and still does to great extent, walking into Griffith's office.

If the pennants have been infrequent, only three in Griffith's thirty-two years in the capital, so have the last-place finishes. There were only three. If the Senators have not always been pennant threats, neither have they been push-overs. Against the game's invasion by rich men, Griffith has had to call on resources other than wealth to keep pace. In his hands, the Washington franchise has become one of the most desirable and most valuable in the league.

Griffith talks of another pennant, but not "just one more pennant." To him that sounds too final. "I'm seven years younger than Connie Mack," he likes to say.

On that day when Griffith does yield the reins of the Washington Senators, the game will have lost one of its notable figures and certainly one of the most quotable. His idiom has been one of the delights of persons close to him. Remembered here is the time he took personal affront at a biographical article by a Washington baseball writer for a national magazine.

"I don't like it," said Griffith. "You said some bad things about me. I thought you were a friend of mine."

When the writer pointed out that ninety-eight per cent of the article was favorable to Griffith, it was still useless. "It's the bad two per cent that counts," said Griffith. "That poisoned me. I don't care about the nice things you wrote. You can't poison a man and then pump his stomach out and still call yourself his friend."

A few months ago Griffith made clear the future policy of the Washington operation perhaps. He elevated his nephew, forty-one-year-old Calvin Griffith, to the post of executive vice president of the Senators, announcing young Griffith "would have wider authority."

It means no deviation, necessarily, from Clark Griffith policy even in the distant future. Calvin Griffith learned baseball at the knee of his uncle, as bat boy, bullpen catcher, business manager at Chattanooga, farm team manager at Charlotte, North Carolina, and vice president of the Senators in charge of player salaries and radio-television contracts.

Clark Griffith has scorned the elaborate and expensive farm systems of other teams choosing to barter for his ball players, but in the important detail of nominating his own successor as top boss of the Senators he prefers to breed and groom one, in his own image he hopes. For the Senators, if past is prologue, the shape of things to come may already be familiar.

Appendix

Baseball in the Good Old Days — The Senators' Financial
Status in 1902

Statement — Season 1902

MONEY RECEIVED

Gate receipts:

Received at home		$45,629.88	
Received abroad		28,407.44	
Privileges		2,000.00	$76,037.32

MONEY PAID OUT

Sundry expense		$ 3,656.55	
Insurance		334.35	
Park account		3,073.39	

Salary account:

T. F. Loftus	$3,000.00	
Delahanty	4,000.00	
Ryan	2,400.00	
Kiester	2,000.00	
Wolverton	2,343.64	
Ely	2,800.00	
Coughlin	1,800.00	
Carey	1,800.00	
Donohue	620.18	
Clark	2,123.39	
Orth	3,500.00	
Townsend	2,100.00	
Carrick	2,600.00	
Lee	1,800.00	
Patten	2,200.00	
Doyle	1,516.50	
Drill	2,000.00	
Potter	600.00	$39,203.71

Advertising	$ 768.22	
O'Brien ground keeper	205.71	
10% fund	3,193.04	
Railway fare	2,571.41	
Hotel account	2,400.25	
Paid visiting clubs	19,277.15	$75,023.78

Cash in bank $ 1,013.54

Resources

Cash in bank	$ 1,013.54	
Season books	150.00	
Harry Wolverton ck.	564.92	
Due from Philadelphia	300.00	
Collected on tickets	168.00	
Frank Smith Ry. ticket	21.05	$ 2,217.51

Liabilities

Tappan & Co.	22.50	
Score keepers	200.00	
10% fund	150.63	373.13
		$ 1,844.38

Index

Compiled by Bonnie Hanks

247